# Cognition, Truth and Reality

# Cognition, Truth and Reality

*Insights from Indian Philosophical Texts*

Srilekha Datta

Suryodaya Books

Cataloging in Publication Data — DK

[Courtesy: D.K. Agencies (P) Ltd. <docinfo@dkagencies.com>]

**Datta, Srilekha, author.**

Cognition, truth and reality : insights from Indian philosophical texts / Srilekha Datta.

pages cm

Includes bibliographical references.

ISBN 9789392443077

1. Nyaya. 2. Vaiśeṣika. 3. Philosophy, Indic. 4. Knowledge, Theory of – India. 5. Metaphysics. 6. Cognition. I. Title.

LCC B132.N8D38 2024 | DDC 181.43 23

ISBN: 978-93-92443-07-7

First Published in India 2024



*Printed and published by:*

Suryodaya Books

"Suryodaya", D-36A/1, Mohan Garden

Najafgarh Road, New Delhi - 110059

Mob.: 9871394811

*Distributed by:*

D.K. Printworld (P) Ltd.

Regd. Office : Vedaśrī, F-395, Sudarshan Park

ESI Hospital Metro Station, New Delhi - 110015

Phones : (011) 4172 2626, 98713 94815

e-mail : indology@dkprintworld.com

Web : www.dkprintworld.com

*To the memory of*

*my parents*

*Late* ***Manmatha Chandra Chaudhuri***

*and*

*Late* ***Padmalaya Chaudhuri***

# Preface

INDIA has a rich heritage of philosophical thoughts and it is highly desirable that Indian students of philosophy should have a considerable knowledge of the philosophy which originated in India. For realization of this goal, classical Indian philosophy was included in the curriculum at Jadavpur University since its inception. For the study of Indian philosophy many original philosophical texts in Sanskrit language are recommended and followed. But most of the students being deficient in Sanskrit, feel the need of some books which are based on original texts but are written in vernacular or in English. During my long teaching career at Jadavpur University, I was aware of the difficulty faced by the students, and cherished a plan to write for them. Finally, long after my retirement, I took the initiative, better late than never. I decided to prepare this volume containing a number of essays on various fundamental topics of Indian philosophy. Discussions in these essays are text based; but in most of them I have put in some of my ideas and interpretations in addition to the exposition of different philosophical positions. Nine essays in this volume were previously published in some anthologies and journals brought out by Jadavpur University and Rabindra Bharati University, details of which are given here. If the students and researchers find this book helpful in understanding some basic topics of Indian philosophy, that would be my reward.

I would like to express my gratitude to many persons who helped me in this effort. Being at a quite advanced age, I was somewhat hesitant to undertake this project, but I got inspiration from my former senior colleague at Jadavpur University, Dr Krishna Roy who is academically active even at the age of eighty. I thank her for the encouragement I received from her. I extend my heartfelt thanks to my former colleague Dr. Ratna Dutta Sharma. She was most enthusiastic about my plan for this book. She was the first reader of almost all the essays in this volume. Her constant encouragement was my inspiration. I am immensely indebted to Dr. Indrani Sanyal, who was also a former colleague of mine. She helped me in many ways, to mention specially, I received her valuable suggestions regarding the matter of publication. She introduced me to Shri Susheel Mittal of Suryodaya Books, in whose able hands I could confidently consign the task of publication of my work. I sincerely thank Dr. Gopa Gupta, retired Professor of Bethune College, Kolkata for her help in correcting the typescript. My lack of knowledge of digital technology was a hurdle for me in executing this project. I am indebted to some younger persons for their help in this matter. They are: Dr. Shreyasee Majumdar, Assistant Professor of Hooghly Mahasin College, West Bengal, Dr. Suvankar Ghosh Roy Chowdhury, Assistant Professor of English at Raidighi College, West Bengal and the last but not the least, my granddaughter Smt. Adwitiya Pal, a student of class X. My appreciation and blessings are for all of them. Dr. Gopinath Mondal, Assistant Professor at Jadavpur University and Shri Saheb Samanta, a Research Fellow at Jadavpur University helped me by procuring necessary books from libraries. My sincere thanks to them. I thank Sri Satyajit Das and Sri Subrata Mukherjee who prepared the typescript of this volume. Before concluding, I must also mention that my daughter Smt. Shreyasi and my son-in-law Shri Koushik Pal gave me constant support and helped in whatever way they could to make my effort successful. I bless them and wish for their well-being.

*6 March 2023*
*Kolkata*

**Srilekha Datta**

# Acknowledgements


THE following essays in the present collection were published earlier:

- "On The Nature of Koṭi of Saṁsaya", *Jadavpur Journal of Philosophy*, 3(2), 1991.
- "An Analysis of The Concept of Pramā and Pramāṇa in Nyāya", in *Essays in Indian Philosophy*, ed. Sukharanjan Saha, New Delhi: Jadavpur University and Allied Publishers, 1997.
- "Validity Is Not Enough", in *Logic, Identity and Consistency*, ed. Pranab Kumar Sen, New Delhi: Jadavpur University and Allied Publishers, 1998.
- "Types of Inference in Indian Logic", in *Foundations of Logic and Language*, ed. Srilekha Datta and Amita Chatterjee, New Delhi: Jadavpur University and Allied Publishers, 2003.
- "The Self and Self-Knowledge in Indian Tradition", *Rabindra Bharati Journal of Philosophy*, X, 2004, published by Rabindra Bharati University, Kolkata.
- "Udayana's Doctrine of Jātibādhaka: A Defence", *Jadavpur Journal of Philosophy*, 1(1), 1989, Jadavpur University, Kolkata.
- "Concept of Sattā in the Nyāya-Vaiśeṣika System", *Jadavpur Journal of Philosophy*, 19(1), 2009, Jadavpur University, Kolkata.
- "Dr̥ṣṭisr̥ṣṭivāda: The Culmination of Advaita Idealism", in *Perspectives on Radhakrishnan*, ed. Nirmalya Narayan Chakraborty, Kolkata: Rabindra Bharati University, 2007.
- "Meaning and Truth of a Sentence: An Indian Point of

View", in *Contemporary Philosophy and Prof. J.L. Shaw*, ed. Purushottama Bilimoria, Kolkata: Punthi Pustak, 2006.

I express my gratitude to the following institutions and persons for granting me permission to reprint my articles mentioned above, in the present volume; the Registrar, Rabindra Bharati University and editors of the respective books and journals published by the Department of Philosophy, Rabindra Bharati University; Department of Philosophy, Jadavpur University and editors of respective books and journals published by them. I put on record my sincere thanks to all of them. I take this opportunity to express my gratitude and thankfulness to Professor J.L. Shaw and Professor Purushottama Bilimoria, the editor of the book *Contemporary Philosophy and J.L. Shaw* who first published my article titled "Meaning and Truth of a Sentence" in their book.

# Contents

# Introduction

THIS book is a collection of essays on some basic concepts and issues discussed in Indian epistemology and metaphysics. First eleven essays deal with various epistemological topics. Chapter 1 is on *saṁśaya* (doubtful cognition). Doubt has an important position in philosophical enquiry. Specially the Nyāya school of philosophy, which is well known for its theory of logical debate (*vicāra*), holds that logical debate starts with *saṁśaya* (doubt). So, in Nyāya texts, we find a detailed account of *saṁśaya*. This essay represents a comprehensive study of the Nyāya-Vaiśeṣika position regarding *saṁśaya*. Definitions, causes and types of *saṁśaya* – all have been discussed here. It contains also a critical analysis of some important issues relating to *saṁśaya* and suggests some plausible answers to some relevant questions.

The second chapter is on the same topic, *saṁśaya*, but it concentrates on one single issue. It is about the nature of the *koṭis* of *saṁśaya*. In a doubtful cognition, there is no uncertainty regarding the subject (*dharmī*) itself, doubt pertains only to the predicate part (*dharma* or *koṭi*), where alternative properties appear as possible predicates to the subject. There is difference of opinion between the old and new schools of Nyāya regarding the nature of the *koṭis*, as to whether there can be more than two *koṭis* and whether all *koṭis* can be positive or whether should there be two *koṭis* only, one of which must be positive and the other negative. These points are discussed in the essay, and the position held by the old school of Nyāya has been defended. According to it, there can be all positive *koṭis* in a *saṁśaya*, therefore, it is not necessary that there should be a positive and a negative *koṭi* in all cases of doubt as maintained by the Navya-Naiyāyikas.

The next chapter deals with two basic concepts of Indian epistemology, viz. *pramā* and *pramāṇa*. Besides clarifying these concepts from the Nyāya point of view, another problem has been addressed. The Naiyāyikas face a dilemma as to whether the status of *pramā* can be given to certain pieces of cognition which are true (*yathārtha*) only by accident but are not derived through *pramāṇa* (proper means). In Nyāya texts, some problematic cases are considered where the cognition, though not caused by *pramāṇa*, turns out to be true (*yathārtha*).

The fourth chapter is about the Nyāya theory of ascertaining the truth of a cognition, which is called *parataḥ-prāmāṇyavāda-jñāpti pakṣa*. Regarding the truth of a cognition two questions are asked:

i. how does a piece of cognition becomes true? and

ii. how is a cognition known to be true?

The second question relates to *prāmāṇya-jñāpti* and the first question relates to *prāmāṇya-utpatti*. The previous paper contains a brief account of the Nyāya theory of *parataḥ-prāmāṇya-utpatti-pakṣa*. The present essay is about the Nyāya theory of *parataḥ-prāmāṇya-jñāpti* vis-à-vis the theory of *svataḥprāmāṇya-jñāpti* as held by other philosophical schools like Advaita Vedānta and Mīmāṁsā. An account of the Nyāya theory along with its criticism by the *Svataḥprāmāṇyavādins* and the way the Naiyāyikas established their position is given in this essay. According to the Naiyāyikas, truth or falsehood of a cognition can be ascertained by means of inference (*anumāna*). The *Svataḥprāmāṇyavādins*' objection to this position is that this way of establishing the truth of a cognition would lead to infinite regress (*anavasthā*). How the Naiyāyikas overcome the charge of infinite regress has also been discussed in this essay.

Chapter five is on *smṛti* (memory). *Smṛti* and *anubhava* are two basic types of cognition accepted by Indian philosophers. *Smṛti* is recollective awareness, which is caused by the previous experience of its object, through impression (*saṁskāra*). According to the Nyāya-Vaiśeṣika philosophers, *smṛti* cannot be regarded as *pramā* (true cognition). This part of the topic has been discussed in the third essay of this collection. The present essay concentrates on two other questions. First, in the Nyāya epistemology *smṛti* (recollective cognition) is considered to play a role in causing different types of cognition like *pratyakṣa, anumiti, upamiti* and *śābda-jñāna*; but if *smṛti* is not *pramā* (true), then how can the cognitions which are causally dependent on it be true? Second question is: what exactly is the object of *smṛti*? Is it only a thing which was previously experienced? Or, does the thing along with the previous experience as well as the experiencer become the object of *smṛti* (recollective awareness)? These questions and their answers from the Nyāya point of view have been elaborated in this chapter.

The sixth chapter deals with the question how or in what sense a perceptual cognition (*pratyakṣa-jñāna*) can be regarded as direct awareness as in *sākṣāt-jñāna*. This question arises because, excepting *nirvikalpaka pratyakṣa* (indeterminate perception), all other types of perceptual cognition is meditated by some cognition or other. This essay contains an account of the problem and considers different possible interpretations of the concept of *sākṣāttva* as the characteristics of perceptual cognition. The critical assessment of the Nyāya-Vaiśeṣika concept of *pratyakṣa* as done by Śrīharṣa, a renowned Advaita Vedānta philosopher in his book *Khaṇḍanakhaṇḍakhādya*, has also been discussed.

The Nyāya theory of object-perception is discussed in the seventh chapter. The objects, which are perceptible according to the Nyāya theory, have been enumerated there. The causal conditions for perception of different kinds of object have also been mentioned. In the later part, some problematic cases of object perception have been considered and, in particular, the Nyāya-Buddhist controversy over the possibility of perception of substance has been dealt with. Special problems regarding visual perception (*cākṣuṣa pratyakṣa*) of substances and auditory perception (*śrāvaṇa pratyakṣa*) have also been discussed.

The eighth chapter titled "Validity Is Not Enough" is about the Nyāya theory of inference (*anumāna*). *Anumāna* has been accepted by most of the Indian philosophical systems as a *pramāṇa*, i.e. a source of knowledge. According to the Indian philosophers, *anumāna* as a way of knowing must not only be formally valid but must also yield a true conclusion. Indian theories of inference lay down conditions for correctness or validity of the inferential process in such a way that fulfilment of those conditions ensures the truth of both the premises and the conclusion. Thus, on their theory, in case of every valid inference a true conclusion follows from premises which are also true. The Nyāya theory of inference has been discussed here to show that it realizes the ideal of validity united with the truth of an inference. The Nyāya provides a theory of inference which establishes valid inference to be, invariably, a source of knowledge.

The chapter ninth is about the types of inference in Indian logic. *Anumāna* is classified into different types under different schemes of classification. Each of these schemes uses some particular characteristics or other as the basis of classification; for example, some classification is based on the nature of *sādhya*, some on the types of *vyāpti* and some on some other characteristics. In this essay a survey is done on various classifications found in different systems of philosophy and an attempt has been made to find out whether any of these schemes can be regarded as the basic one.

Chapter ten deals with *upamāna pramāṇa*. Some philosophical schools accept similarity (*sādṛśya*) or, to be precise, knowledge of similarity as a source of knowledge. The Nyāya, Vaiśeṣika, Mīmāṁsā and Advaita Vedānta schools admit *upamāna* to be a *pramāṇa*. But there is a disagreement among these schools as to whether it is a separate *pramāṇa* in addition to *pratyakṣa*, *anumāna* and *śābda-pramāṇa*, or, it can be subsumed under some and other of these *pramāṇas*. There is also difference of opinion regarding the object which is knowable through *upamāna pramāṇa*. These issues along with opponing positions have been discussed in this essay.

The eleventh chapter deals with a controversial issue of meaningfulness and truth of a sentence from Indian point of view. Taking the examples of some sentences like "The bachelor's wife is beautiful" and "the present king of France is wise", a question has been raised as to whether all these sentences are meaningless or false. There is a position that maintains that both the sentences mentioned above are meaningful but false. This position can be supported from the point of view of the Grammarian (Vaiyākaraṇa) school of philosophy. But this position is contested in this essay from the viewpoint of the Nyāya school. According to the Nyāya theory of meaning and truth, a sentence containing factually incorrect content can be regarded as meaningful but false, as the second sentence mentioned above. But sentences containing contradictory words or phrases like the first sentence would be considered meaningless and hence cannot be called false. This position of the Nyāya has been explained and argued for in this essay. That the concept of *yogyatā* (semantic fitness) plays a key role in deciding on the meaningfulness of a sentence has been emphasized here.

Twelfth to eighteenth chapters are about some metaphysical concepts and issues in Indian philosophy. The twelfth chapter deals with the concept of the self, i.e. *ātman* and self-knowledge (*ātma-jñāna*). The self (*ātman*) is the most fundamental concept in Indian philosophy and self-knowledge is regarded as the means to the attainment of *mokṣa* (freedom from suffering), which is considered as the goal of philosophy. Every Indian philosophical system accepts the existence of something corresponding to the notion of "I" (*aham*). Every individual has I-consciousness. Something which is the referent of the pronoun word *aham* (I) is called *ātman*. But, there are different opinions among the philosophical schools as to what entity the self is. Two conceptions about the self are found in Indian philosophy:

i. the self is a substance endowed with consciousness (*caitanya* or *jñāna*), and

ii. the self is *caitanya* (consciousness) itself.

A brief account of the conception of the self as maintained by different orthodox philosophical systems is given here. Along with the nature of the self, the nature of self-knowledge is also discussed. In this part of the essay, the questions like what is meant by self-knowledge or what are the types of self-knowledge, and how one can have self-knowledge of different types have been discussed.

The next chapter is on *caitanya*. In the previous essay, it was mentioned that in Indian metaphysical systems, *ātman* is considered either as identical with consciousness (*caitanya*) or as the owner of consciousness. The Nyāya–Vaiśeṣika systems uphold the latter conception of the self. According to them, the self is a substance that possesses *caitanya*. They equate *caitanya* with *jñāna*. In this chapter an objection is raised against identifying these two. It has been argued that in view of some of the metaphysical and epistemological tenets of the Nyāya–Vaiśeṣika systems, it is difficult to justify this equivalence. So there is a need to modify the Nyāya–Vaiśeṣika position regarding *caitanya*. A modified interpretation of *caitanya* is explored and presented with some justification and it is shown to be in compliance with the metaphysical and epistemological positions of the Nyāya–Vaiśeṣika systems. This interpretation needs to be considered by scholars.

The fourteenth chapter deals with the concept of *manas* (mind). In Indian philosophy, *manas* is not identified with *ātman*, but is regarded as a separate metaphysical entity that functions as an inner organ. In the Nyāya–Vaiśeṣika systems *manas* is considered to play a very important role in the entire cognitive life of an individual self. But they admit that *manas* is an imperceptible entity; hence its existence is to be proved by means of *anumāna*. They have put forward a number of inferences by means of which they proved the existence of *manas* and deduced all the characteristic properties of *manas*. A critical assessment of the Nyāya–Vaiśeṣika position regarding *manas* can be found in this essay.

Chapter fifteen is about the Nyāya–Vaiśeṣika doctrine of *jāti-bādhaka* propounded by Udayanācārya. By *jāti-bādhaka* is meant some preventing conditions which either disallows a property from being accepted as a *jāti* (universal) or prevents a thing from being the locus of a *jāti* (universal). Udayanācārya enumerated six *jāti-bādhakas*, but some later Nyāya–Vaiśeṣika philosophers held that the number of *jāti-bādhakas* could be reduced. In this essay the general concept of *jāti-bādhaka*, the purpose for admitting *jāti-bādhaka*, the way each of the *jāti-bādhakas* functions, and the controversy over the number of *jāti-bādhakas* have all been dealt with. Finally, Udayana's position regarding the number of *jāti-bādhakas* is supported with justification.

The sixteenth chapter is on the concept of *sattā*. It is an important metaphysical concept which is used by many Indian philosophical schools, though in different senses. Some philosophers mean by *sattā* the property of being real (*vastutva*); some other mean by it the property of being a positive entity (*bhāvatva*), and according to some others it is a *jāti* which is the most extensive (*parā*). This third conception is held by the Nyāya–Vaiśeṣika philosophers. But this position seems to be weak and problematic and was strongly criticized by other schools. This essay concentrates on the Nyāya–Vaiśeṣika position regarding *sattā* and analyses some of the problems which arise as a consequence of that position and also evaluates the solutions that were offered by those philosophers.

The topic of the next chapter is a doctrine of Advaita Vedānta school, known as Dṛṣṭisṛṣṭivāda, which means, the individual *jīva* creates the world when it experiences it. It is an extreme form of idealism developed by some Advaita philosophers of post-Śaṅkara period. It denies objective reality or the unknown existence of the empirical world and also denies creation in the primary sense of the term. In this essay an account of this position along with some analysis, has been presented. Some historical survey regarding the development of this doctrine has also been done here. In conclusion, it has been observed that this extreme version of idealism developed naturally and consistently from Advaita philosophy. The Advaita concept of *adhyāsa* (superimposition) in two forms – *jñānādhyāsa* and *arthādhyāsa* – can be shown to support Dṛṣṭisṛṣṭivāda. However, this conclusion awaits the opinion of scholars.

The last chapter is about the relation between emotion and morality investigated from the Indian standpoint. According to the Western conception, this is a topic of moral philosophy, but since in Indian philosophy such a division is not done, this topic can be said to be included in metaphysics, emotion or feeling and action, both being metaphysical entities.

This chapter addresses the questions regarding the relation between emotions like compassion, love, fear, malice, etc. on the one hand and moral or immoral actions on the other. It is asked whether an emotion can influence an agent to perform a moral or immoral act; and whether it can prevent an agent from performing a duty. And also the question of whether the performance of a moral act can evoke some emotion in the agent after its performance. Taking some instances from the *Mahābhārata* and Purāṇas, answers to these questions from the Vaidika point of view were explored. The answer is positive and can be justified with reference to Vaidika philosophers' account of Arthavāda *vākyas* and their utility in respect of the injunctive power of imperatives or *vidhi-vākya*.

The last two chapters are somewhat different from the others. In the seventeenth chapter, a purely idealistic position of Advaita Vedānta school is considered. And in the last chapter, a traditional moral point of view of Indian philosophers is constructed and presented for the consideration of scholars.

Previous sixteen chapters follow the realistic trend of Indian philosophy, while treating different issues. Mainly the epistemological and metaphysical position of the realist schools of the Nyāya-Vaiśeṣika has been presented in these essays.

1

# The Nyāya-Vaiśeṣika Theory of Saṁśaya

SAṀŚAYA (doubt) is a cognitive state of mind that everyone experiences at different times. As a cognitive state, it has been the topic of discussion in every philosophical system of India. But it occupies a special position in the Nyāya system. Doubt has been mentioned among the sixteen topics which constitute the subject matter of the Nyāya philosophy.[1] This system of philosophy is also known as Ānvīkṣikī, which means the study of philosophical reasoning. Establishing a position with the help of arguments based on *pramāṇa* (evidence/justification) is called *anvīkṣā* (philosophical reasoning). The Nyāya system, which deals especially with philosophical reasoning, includes some special topics which are particularly relevant to philosophical reasoning and doubt is one such topic. Doubt has been considered a precondition (*pūrvāṅga*) for application of philosophical reasoning. In a philosophical debate (*vicāra*), the debating parties employ philosophical arguments in favour of their respective positions. Philosophical arguments are required because awareness of two conflicting positions regarding some object presented by two opposing parties gives rise to doubt in the mind of the hearer as to which of the positions is true. And the truth of a position can be proved by using philosophical reasoning.

---

1 Vātsyāyana, 1985, *Bhāṣya*, preceding *Nyāyasūtra* 1.1.1 in *Nyāyadarśanam*, ed. Tārānātha Nyāyatarkatīrtha and Amarendramohan Tarkatirtha, New Delhi: Munshiram Monoharlal.

Thus, doubt leads to a desire to know the truth (*tattva-jijñāsā*) about an object and argumentation which follows leads to knowledge of truth (*tattva-nirṇaya*). So, in the Nyāya method of establishing truth, the role of doubt is recognized. Hence, the Nyāya epistemology contains a thorough discussion on the topic of *saṁśaya*.

### Doubt (Saṁśaya) and Certainty (Niścaya)

A cognition can be either of the nature of certainty or of the nature of doubt. One has a cognition of the nature of certainty when one cognizes a thing as qualified by a particular property, without, at the same time, being aware of the possibility of its being qualified by the absence of that property.[2] For example, when I cognize something as a table without entertaining the possibility of its not being a table, it is a case of certainty. A cognition having certainty is expressed in a declarative sentence of the form "This is *x*" or "This is *y*" which is a categorical assertion. It should however be kept in mind that certainty is not equivalent to veridicality. One can very well have a certain but false cognition.

A cognition is of the nature of doubt when one is aware of two incompatible properties as possible qualifiers of a given thing but is not in a position to assert any one of them in particular. So the cognizer is in an oscillating state of mind.[3] Such a cognition is expressed in an interrogative sentence of the form "Is that *x* or *y*?" it expresses indecision regarding the assertion of one of the two mutually exclusive alternatives.

To further explain the nature of doubt, it must be said that it is a form of qualificative cognition (*viśiṣta buddhi*) having as its content

---

[2] Viśvanātha Nyāya Pañcānana, 1988, *Kārikāvalī-Muktāvalī*, ed. Śrī Śaṅkararām Sastri, *kārikā* 129, Delhi: Chowkhamba Sanskrit Pratisthan.

[3] Śrīdhara Bhaṭṭa, 1963, *Nyāyakandalī: A Commentary on Praśastapādabhāṣya*, ed. Durgadhar Jha, pp. 413-14, Varanasi: Varanaseya Sanskrit Viswavidyalaya.

qualificand and more than one qualifiers which are incompatible with one another. These qualifiers appear only as possible alternatives, one of which can be ascribed to the qualificand. But the cognitive state of doubt falls short of asserting any alternative in particular, nor does it assert both, since they are incompatible. These alternative qualifiers are called *koṭis* in Sanskrit language. And it can be said that doubt pertains to the *koṭis* (alternative qualifiers), but there is no doubt that there is a thing that figures as the qualificand in that cognition. For example, when we have a doubt like "Is that a mass of smoke or a mass of dust?", there is no doubt there is a mass, but what is doubted is whether it is smoke or dust.

A state of doubt is regarded as a case of non-veridical cognition (*apramā*).[4] In Vaiśeṣika terminology, it is *avidyā*. A non-veridical cognition is defined by the Naiyāyikas as a cognition that reveals a thing as characterized by a particular property that the thing does not possess. That means, to cognize a thing *A* as *x* would be non-veridical if *A* is not *x*. On the contrary, to cognize a thing as characterized by a property that it possesses would be a case of veridical cognition (*pramā*). But does the definition of non-veridical cognition apply to doubt? It seems that it does not apply. We have seen that in doubt, alternative properties are presented as possible qualifiers of a thing, but none of them is actually asserted to qualify the thing. So, it cannot be said that in a doubt a thing is cognized as qualified by a property that it does not have. If in doubt of the form "Is that thing *x* or *y*?", *x* had been asserted of the thing which is *y*, or vice versa, then the definition of non-veridical cognition would have applied to doubt. Since neither *x* nor *y* has been actually asserted of the thing, doubt cannot be said to satisfy the definition of *apramā*.

Is doubt then a case of *pramā*? One may claim that doubt satisfies the definition of veridical cognition as in case of doubt one of the

---

[4] Śrīdhara Bhaṭṭa, 1963, *Nyāyakandalī*, pp. 411, 414.

two possible but incompatible properties actually qualifies the qualificand. So the cognition is the cognition of a thing as what it really is. For example, when we doubt whether a mass seen at a distance is a mass of smoke or of dust, the mass must be either of them, in any case, it would be true cognition. If it is smoke, then the cognition amounts to cognition of smoke as smoke; and in case it is dust then also it is the cognition of dust as dust, so under both the conditions doubt turns out to be a true cognition by satisfying the definition of veridical cognition.

Against this position two things can be said. First, the reason why a doubt cannot satisfy the definition of non-veridical cognition is also the reason why it cannot even satisfy the definition of veridical cognition. In case of a doubt no qualifier is actually asserted of the qualificand and so there is no question of its being right or wrong assertion. Neither does a doubt assert a thing to be that which it is not, nor does it assert a thing to be what it really is.

The second point is that the assumption, that one of the alternative qualifiers must be true of the qualificand because they are incompatible, can be made only if the qualifiers are contradictory to each other. But being incompatible does not always mean being contradictory; contraries are also incompatible. Now contraries can both be false. So if we doubt whether the thing standing at a distance is a human being or not?, then the thing must be either of two, e.g. human or non-human. But if the doubt is of the form "Is that a man or a tree-trunk?", it may not be either, it may turn out to be a pillar. If doubt always occurs in the former form then one can say that doubt amounts to true cognition as one of the alternative qualifiers must belong to the qualificand. But, though the Naiyāyikas of the modern (*navya*) school hold that in doubt alternative qualifiers are always contradictory, the Naiyāyikas of the old (*prācīna*) school hold that doubts with contrary properties as alternative qualifiers also occur. In the latter cases of doubt, it cannot be claimed that doubt amounts to true cognition.

Besides the above-mentioned difficulties, it would also be counter-intuitive to admit a case of doubt to be a case of *pramā*. If we doubt the nature of a thing, can we claim to have known it? We are merely aware of the thing along with its possible characterizing properties without being able to assert which property actually characterizes the thing. No one would like to consider this to be a case of knowledge (*pramā*).

But the question is how to justify the denial of the status of *pramā* to doubt? The philosophers of the old school of Nyāya justified it in two ways. Vātsyāyana, explains in his *bhāṣya* (commentary) on Gautama's *Nyāyasūtra* 1.1.4 that in case of veridical cognition it must be of the nature of certainty as indicated by the word *vyavasāyātmaka* (determinate) occurring in that *sūtra* (aphorism). But, in doubt, there is a lack of decision, so the cognition is not determinate in character; for this reason, a doubt cannot be a veridical cognition.

Vācaspati Miśra, another philosopher in the lineage of the Nyāya school, commented in his *Tātparyaṭīkā* (explanatory notes on Uddyotakara's *vārttika*, which is a commentary on *Nyāyabhāṣya*) that doubt fails to lead to successful activities and therefore lacks an essential feature of veridical cognition.[5] To explain the point, let us take the case of an action, say, fetching water from a pool. If we are in need of water and see a water pool somewhere, we proceed to fetch water from the pool. Now, if our cognition of a water pool was veridical, then there would really be a water pool there and we would successfully fetch water from the pool. But in some cases, for example, in a desert, the cognition of a water pool could be non-veridical because we may mistake a mirage for a water pool. In that case, our action of fetching water from the pool could not be performed successfully. Vācaspati Miśra explains that in case

---

5 Vacaspati Miśra, 1985, *Tātparyaṭīkā* on 1.1.4, p. 114 in *Nyāyadarśanam* (ed.) Tārānātha Nyāyatarkatīrtha and Amarendramohon Tarkatīrtha, New Delhi: Munshiram Manoharlal.

of a doubt, a thing appears alternately as having incompatible characters. Such a cognition that lacks determinateness about the nature of the object is less likely to be followed by an activity, and even if the action takes place it cannot be successful because a thing having alternate characters cannot actually be there.

It may be argued that when we doubt whether there is a water pool or a mirage, we may still engage ourselves in the act of fetching water, assuming that there is really a water pool and there is also the possibility of the action being successful. But in that case, an alternative (*koṭi*) of doubt is left aside for the time being, and the doubt is treated as a determinate cognition, though lacking in certainty. This type of doubt is called *sambhāvanā* (cognition of probability), where one alternative is suppressed and the other is prominent because the doubter thinks it to be probable.[6] We may try to explain it further. After a doubt of the form "Is that *x* or *y*", the doubter may feel for some reason that *y* may be the case and has the cognition called *sambhāvanā* to the effect "Perhaps that is *y*". This cognition is still a doubt because the cognizer is not in a position to assert categorically that it is *y*.

Now if *sambhāvanā* is a form of doubt and if it can lead to successful action, then the possibility of doubt being veridical cannot be denied. Perhaps for this reason Vācaspati's predecessors in the Nyāya school held that cognition to be veridical must also be of the nature of certainty *vyavasāyātmaka* (*niścayātmaka*).

## Definition of Doubt

In accordance with the method of discussion in classical Indian philosophy, a topic of discussion, after being introduced, must be defined. In case of doubt also Indian philosophers took up the question of definition. They have suggested several definitions,

---

6 Gadādhara, 1970, *Gādādharī*, a commentary on *Dīdhiti* by Raghunātha on *Tattvacintāmaṇi*, ed. Dvivedi et al., p. 1810, Varanasi: Chowkhamba Sanskrit Series Office.

considered them, rejected some of them, and then arrived at a universally acceptable definition of doubt.

The Naiyāyikas describe doubt as *anavadhāraṇam jñānam* (*anavadhāraṇa* means *na* (not) *avadhāraṇa* (certain), which means a cognition that is not of the nature of certainty. One may tend to accept this as the definition of *saṁśaya* because doubt and certainty are considered opposites and any cognition, other than doubt, is *niścaya*. So, if doubt is defined negatively as a cognition other than a cognition which is certain, then it is differentiated from all other kinds of cognition. Thus, it serves the purpose of a definition, viz. differentiation (*vyāvṛtti*) of the definiendum from the rest of the things.

But there is a problem. According to the Naiyāyikas a doubt contains an element of certainty. As we have already seen that doubt is a qualificative cognition (*viśiṣṭa buddhi*), the content of which can be analysed into two parts: qualificand (subject) part and qualifier (predicate) part. Now, there is no doubt regarding the qualificand, as in the example "is that a mass of smoke or dust?" the doubter is certain about the existence of a mass at a distance, but the doubt pertains to the qualifier part, as to its being smoke or being dust. Thus, a doubt containing an element of certainty in one part of it cannot be properly characterized as a cognition that is not of the nature of certainty.[7]

Another characteristic feature of doubt is that it leads to a desire to know (*jijñāsā*). When we doubt the nature of a thing, for example, whether the thing is a human being or a tree trunk, we want to remove this doubt by knowing for certain the truth of one of the alternatives. So a desire to know follows the doubt and doubt can be described as a cognition that caused a desire to know (*jijñāsājanakam jñānam saṁśaya*).[8] But can this be treated

[7] Uddyotakara, 1985, *Nyāyavārttika* in *Nyāyadarśanam*, pp. 234-35. Śrīdhara Bhaṭṭa, 1963, *Nyāyakandalī*, p. 420.

[8] Śaṅkara Miśra, 1969, *Vaiśeṣika Sūtropaskāra: A Commentary on* →

as a definition of doubt? The answer would be negative, because there may be cases of doubt which do not cause a desire to know. We must admit that our desires are influenced by our needs. Our desire to know is also influenced by our need or interest, either practical or theoretical. Objects of our cognitions are classifiable under three heads:

i. pleasant (*iṣṭa*)

ii. unpleasant (*aniṣṭa*), and

iii. indifferent (*upekṣaṇīya*).

A subject or knower has an interest in the first and the second kind of object but does not have any interest in the third kind. For example, while moving through a forest we may take interest in fruits hanging from trees and also in the wild animal present there, but we tend to ignore weeds in the path. We take interest in fruits because we can consume them, they are good for us; we are interested in wild animals because we have to take care to protect ourselves from them, but towards weeds, we are just indifferent. Now if in a situation a person has a doubt where possible alternatives lie beyond his interest, that means if the alternatives in the doubt are indifferent (*upekṣaṇīya*), then a desire to know does not follow. So every doubt is not a cognition that causes a desire to know.

There is another reason why the above-mentioned characteristic cannot be regarded as the defining characteristic of doubt. In the Vaiśeṣika system, which is the sister system of the Nyāya, a kind of non-veridical cognition called *anadhyavasāya* is admitted.[9] They

---

← *Vaiśeṣikasūtra*, ed. Nārāyaṇ Miśra, *sūtra* 2.2.17, pp. 172-76, Varanasi: Chowkhamba Sanskrit Series Office.

Śaṅkara Miśra, *Kaṇādarahasya*, in *Praśastapādabhāṣyaṭīkāsaṁgrahaḥ*, ed. Vindhyeswari Prasad Dvivedi, pp. 115-16, Benares: Chowkhamba Sanskrit Series.

9 Śaṅkara Miśra, *Kaṇādarahasyam* (*Praśastapādabhāṣya*), p. 121.

say that when a person sees a new thing, say, an animal, which he has not seen previously, he wonders "what animal is this?". That means, he does not know what this animal is called. So, though he sees the animal with all its visible characteristics, he cannot identify the animal and therefore cannot assert that "this animal is so-and-so". From this kind of cognition, which the Vaiśeṣika holds to be different from doubt, a desire to know the name of the thing arises. Therefore, if doubt is defined as a cognition which leads to a desire to know, the definition would extend over to *anadhyavasāya* and it would be a faulty definition.

It was a common practice with the Nyāya philosophers to define a thing in terms of *jāti* or universal if possible. A universal is a simple, unanalysable property. Universals are the basis of classification. So a universal property can serve the purpose of a definition properly by differentiating a class of enity from entities of other classes and hence can be accepted as a definition. But such universals are not available in all the cases. Thus, if in the case of a definiendum such a universal is not available, definition in terms of universal would not be possible. Now, if there is a universal of *saṁśayatva* (being a doubt) then doubt could be defined as a cognition which possesses the universal called *saṁśayatva*. But the property of being a doubt (*saṁśayatva*) is not regarded as a universal (*jāti*) by the Naiyāyikas, first because, this property does not characterize a doubt as a whole, but only partially (*āṁśika*). As we have already seen that there is no uncertainty regarding the qualificand or the subject part of a doubt, uncertainty pertains to the qualifier or predicate part. But it is obvious that a universal, being a class-character, must be present in a particular as a whole. The property of being a doubt fails to fulfil this condition and hence cannot be regarded as a universal.

There is a second reason why the Naiyāyikas deny universalhood to the property of being a doubt. On their theory of universal there are certain conditions that prevent a putative universal from being regarded as a universal. There are six such preventing conditions (*jāti-bādhaka*) and a putative universal must be free from these preventing conditions for being recognized as a universal. One such preventing condition is called *sāṅkarya* (mutual overlapping with another property) and the property of being a doubt is vitiated by this condition. According to the standard Nyāya view, doubts are cases of perceptual cognition (*pratyakṣa-jñāna*). As perceptions are caused by various sense organs, there are varieties of perception like visual, tactual and auditory etc. Now, in the case of a visual doubt, the property of being a doubt is present along with the property of being a visual perception; but in an auditory doubt where the property being a visual perception is absent, the property of being a doubt is present; again in a visual perception which is of the nature of certainty, the property of being a doubt is absent though the property of being a visual perception is present. Thus, the property of being a doubt has partial co-location with the property of being a visual perception. This disqualifies the claim to the universalhood of property. So, it is not possible to define a doubt in terms of a universal.[10]

In *Nyāyasūtra* 1.1.23, Gautama uses the expression *vimarśa*, which is said to contain the definition of doubt according to the commentator (*bhāṣyakāra*) Vātsyāyana. He and his successors in the tradition explain how an analysis of the expression renders a full definition of doubt. The word *vimarśa* has two parts: *vi*, which is a prefix, and *marśa*, which is a verbal compound; *vi* signifies incompatibility in this case and *marśa* cognition. So *vimarśa* means cognition of incompatible (things). Some further analysis explicates the definition of doubt from this word. Incompatibility generally means incapability of coexistence at the same place and/or at the same time. So incompatibility between things cannot hold without reference to the sameness of the locus. Hence, cognition of incompatible things would mean cognition of incompatible properties concerning same entity, or, in other words, cognition

---

10 Śaṅkara Miśra, *Kaṇādarahasyam* (*Praśastapādabhāṣya*), p. 116 and *Upaskāra*, p. 176.

of a thing as qualified by incompatible properties. But since the cognizer is aware of the incompatibility, he cannot cognize the thing as qualified by both the properties, so the cognition is of the nature of doubt as to which of the suggested qualifiers actually qualifies the thing. So doubt is defined as a cognition where the qualificand is one and that appears to be qualified by mutually exclusive properties. This definition differentiates a doubt from a cognition with one qualificand and one qualifier, e.g. "the table is brown"; it differentiates a doubt from a cognition with one qualificand and two qualifiers which are compatible, like "the table is square and brown"; and again it differentiates a doubt from a conjunctive cognition where qualifiers are many as well as incompatible, but they qualify different qualificands, like "this is a cow and that is a horse". In none of these cases, there is indecision or doubt.

Hence, a question regarding the nature of incompatibility (*virodha*) that holds between the qualifiers (*koṭi*) in doubt may be raised. Different types of incompatibility or opposition can be there. Contradiction and contrariety are two main types of opposition recognized in Western logic. If the relation between two propositions, *x* and *y* is such, the truth of one entails the falsity of the other and the falsity of one entails the truth of the other, then they are contradictory to each other. And if the truth of one entails the falsity of the other, but the falsity of one does not entail the truth of the other, then those propositions are contrary to each other. The Naiyāyikas too talk about two types of opposition which are similar to contradiction and contrariety respectively. They say that *virodha* can be either *svarūpataḥ virodha* (obvious opposition) or *tadabhāvavyāpyavattvārūpa virodha* (implied opposition).[11] The first kind of opposition holds between a thing and its absence, it

---

[11] Gaṅgeśa, 1970, *Tattvacintāmaṇi*, Anumāna Khaṇḍa, ed. with *Dīdhiti* and *Gādādharī* by Vindhyeswari Prasad Dvivedi, pp. 1804-05, Varanasi: Chowkhamba.

Raghunātha, *Dīdhiti*, *Satpratipakṣa Prakaraṇam* in *Gādādharī*, pp. 1804-05.

is palpable that where a thing is, its absence cannot be there and where its absence is, the thing cannot be there and also that at any place either the thing or its absence must be there. Take the colours red and non-red as examples; if a thing is red, then it cannot be non-red and if a thing is non-red, it cannot be red, but in no case, a thing can be neither red nor non-red. So the Nyāya concept of *svarūpataḥ virodha* (obvious incompatibility) can be equated with contradiction in Western logic.

On the other hand, implied opposition (*tadabhāvavyāpyavattvā-rūpa virodha*) holds between two things when each coexists with the absence of the other, though the absence of both is possible in some loci. For example, take the colours red and blue. Red exists in the absence of blue and blue exists in the absence of red. That means, where red colour is present, blue colour is absent; and where blue colour is present, red colour is absent; but there are things where both red and blue colours are absent, as in things with green or white or yellow or some other colours. Now the opposition between red and blue colour is said to be implied by the fact that blue comes under non-red colours and red comes under non-blue colours and that there is direct opposition between red and non-red on the one hand, and blue and non-blue on the other.

The question regarding the nature of incompatibility is important in the context of the doubt for two reasons. First, there is a difference of opinion between the old and the new school of the Nyāya regarding the nature of the *koṭi* (alternative qualifiers) in a doubt and the difference is based on their stand regarding the nature of the opposition between the *koṭis*. According to the new school, there are two alternative qualifiers, one of which is a positive (*bhāva*) property and the other is its negation (*abhāva*).[12] For example, man and non-man. From this, it is clear that they maintain that the nature of incompatibility between alternative qualifiers is that of contradiction (*svarūpataḥ virodha*). On the

12 Viśvanātha, 1988, *Kārikāvalī-Muktāvalī*, *kārikā* 130.

other hand, the old school of Nyāya holds that the alternatives may be all positive and may also be one positive and the other its negative, there is no hard and fast rule in this regard. It may be, for example, man and non-man; or, it may be man or tree trunk. This shows that the old school holds that incompatibility between alternatives may be either contradiction (*svarūpataḥ virodha*) or contrariety (*tadabhāvavyāpyavattārūpa virodha*).

Second, an answer to the question as to whether one of the alternative qualifiers in a doubt must be true of the qualificand, depends on the nature of incompatibility holding between the alternatives. If the alternatives are contradictory to each other, then one must hold good. If on the other hand, alternatives are contrary to each other, then none of them may be true unless all the suggested alternatives are exhaustive. For example, in a doubt where man and tree trunk are suggested alternatives, the thing or the qualificand may turn out to be neither a man nor a tree trunk but a post. But if the doubt is: "is that a man or not?", then it is sure to be either a man or a non-man.

The nature of opposition between *koṭis* determines the number of alternatives also. It is clear that if the nature the opposition is one of contradiction, then the number of alternatives would be two only. But if the opposition is that of contrariety, then the alternatives may be more than two. So the nature of the opposition between *koṭis* (alternatives) has an important bearing on the Nyāya theory of doubt.

### Causes of Doubt

A cognition, according to the Nyāya school, arises in an individual due to certain causal conditions. An explanation of causation of every type of cognition is given in Nyāya philosophy. So they have also explained how and from which causes doubt arises.

If we begin with a description of the process of causation of a doubt, it would be easier to identify its causes. But before doing that it should be mentioned that on the standard Nyāya view a doubt is always perceptual, either it is a case of external perception or internal perception. An examination of this position will be taken up later, but the causal analysis of doubt is done on the assumption of this position.

The causal process of doubting starts with the perception of the subject (*dharmī*) of a doubt, as characterized by some such property that brings to the mind of the perceiver some possible alternative predicates. But not being in a condition suitable for clear perception the perceiver does not perceive the presence of any of these predicates in the subject, nor does he perceive any other property which implies the presence of any of the alternatives; but at the same time the perceiver is aware of the incompatibility of the suggested predicates so that they cannot both be true of the subject; as a result, there arises a doubt in the mind of the perceiver as to which of the possible alternatives is true of the subject. For example, I see a thing with a particular dimension standing at a distance. The perceived dimension of the thing reminds me of two possible properties, being a man and being a tree trunk. As I am aware that being a man and being a tree trunk are incompatible properties that cannot belong to one and the same thing, I land in a state of doubt: "is that a man or a tree trunk"?[13]

From the causal process of doubt described above, we can gather five causal conditions which jointly lead to the state of doubting. These are:

i. Perception of the subject (*dharmī*) as characterized by some neutral property.

ii. Rememberance of some specific properties (*viśeṣa dharma*) any of which may possibly be predicated to the subject.

iii. Non-perception of any of these properties or any other property which implies the presence of any of the specific properties in the subject.

---

13 Vātsyāyana, *Bhāṣya on Nyāyasūtra* 1.1.23, pp. 234, 240.

iv. Cognition of incompatibility between the specific properties, some of which may be the possible qualifier of the subject.

v. Some deficiencies or defects like greater distance or insufficient light which stand in the way of clear perception.

We shall explain these causes one by one. The cause mentioned first is the perception of the subject of doubt. It is obvious that the thing which is the subject of doubt must be known in some way, though it must be incomplete knowledge because we do not have doubts regarding objects which are unknown or completely known. Now, how much of the subject is known in case of doubt? The Naiyāyikas say that it is known as characterized by some property which is natural in the sense that the knowledge of this property does not enable us to identify the thing as a so-and-so. Such a property is common to different things, so it reminds us of more than one thing that the subject of doubt could possibly be. In the example which we have been using, the thing is perceived as characterized by some particular shape and size which is common to a man and a tree trunk. So we are reminded of two possible predicates or qualifiers, e.g. being a man and being a tree trunk.

The remembrance of the two possible predicates or qualifiers (*koṭis*) is the second causal condition. As we know, the doubt pertains to the qualifier or predicate part of the cognition, so the possible qualifiers must be presented to the perceiver. Since the qualifiers are not perceived, they are presented through remembrance. According to the Naiyāyikas, remembrance functions here as a non-physical operative relation called *jñāna-lakṣaṇā sannikarṣa* between the sense organ and the qualifiers. A doubt being a perceptual cognition there has to be a sense contact with its object. So far as the subject or qualificand is concerned, sense contact is an ordinary or physical one, but in the case of qualifiers (*koṭis*), it is a non-physical one.

In the case of doubt, possible qualifiers are remembered only but none of them is perceived to be present in the qualificand or the subject. If there were such a perception, there would have been no scope for doubt. The thing would then be perceived as a so-and-so and not as "is it this or that?". The cognition, in that case, would be of the nature of certainty. So we find that non-perception of possible qualifiers in the qualificand is another necessary causal condition of doubt. Now, the state of doubt would not have resulted unless the perceiver was aware that possible qualifiers were incompatible. If this awareness were not there, the perceiver could have taken both the qualifiers to characterize the qualificand. Since the perceiver knows that both of those qualifiers cannot characterize one and the same thing, he has a cognition which is indeterminate as to which of the qualifiers actually characterizes the thing. Therefore, awareness of the incompatibility of the qualifiers (*virodha-jñāna*) is another causal condition of doubt.

The last mentioned causal condition is the presence of some defect or deficiency which affects a knowledge situation. As we have seen in our example that a distance which is longer than the required one or insufficient light hinders clear perception of a thing and hence causes doubt.

While discussing the causation of doubt, we should take note of the fact that causal conditions of doubt include three different cognitions, viz. cognition of the qualificand, remembrance of qualifiers and cognition of incompatibility between those qualifiers. This poses a special problem for the Naiyāyikas. The Nyāya philosophers hold that a cognitive state lasts for two moments and gets destroyed at the third moment, so it is not possible for three different cognitions to coexist at any particular point in time. When the third cognition arises the first one ceases to exist. Under this situation, three cognitive states cannot assemble to produce a doubt. Two alternative solutions have been offered by the Naiyāyikas. Some say that cognition of the qualificand or subject is not necessary, a sense-contact with the qualificand would be sufficient as a causal condition of doubt. The other way to solve the problem is to admit that when qualifiers are remembered, they are remembered as incompatible, so a separate cognition of the incompatibility between qualifiers is not necessary. This solution reduces the number of causal conditions to four, while the former solution replaces the cognition of the qualificand by the sense contact with the qualificand as one of the causal conditions of doubt.

It should be mentioned here that the non-perception of the qualifiers as well as the remembrance of qualifiers are both mentioned explicitly as causes of doubt by Kaṇāda in his *Vaiśeṣikasūtra*. But Gautama in his *Nyāyasūtra* does not mention it explicitly. Vātsyāyana, the commentator of *Nyāyasūtra*, explains that the word *viśeṣāpekṣaḥ* which Gautama uses in the aphorism on *saṁśaya* (doubt) indicates it. *Viśeṣa* here means specific qualifier and *apekṣā* means being in want of and in the context of doubt they jointly mean the absence of perception of the specific qualifier. So Gautama says that the doubt is due to non-perception of the specific qualifier. But it also means indirectly that qualifiers, though not perceived, are remembered. Here, non-perception of qualifier means non-perception of any of the qualifiers which are presented to the mind through memory.

## Types of Doubt

Doubt has been divided into different kinds based on two separate principles by the Nyāya and the Vaiśeṣika philosophers. Gautama in his *Nyāyasūtra* divides doubt on the basis of special causal condition, which varies in different types of doubt. The Vaiśeṣika philosophers, on the other hand, divide doubt with reference to the object of doubt, which is either external or internal.

Let us start with the Nyāya division of doubt. Vātsyāyana, while commenting on Gautama's *sūtra* (1.1.23) on doubt, says that Gautama divided doubt into five types according to their respective specific cause. These are:

i. Doubt due to the cognition common property (*samāna-dharmopapatti*).

ii. Doubt due to the cognition of unique property (*anekadharmo-papatti*).
iii. Doubt due to hearing contradictory statements regarding one and the same subject (*vipratipatti*).
iv. Doubt due to absence of rules regarding the object of perception (*upalabdhi-avyavasthā*).
v. Doubt due to the absence of a rule regarding the object of non-perception (*anupalabdhi-avyavasthā*). Each type will be explained one by one.

The first type of doubt as mentioned by Vātsyāyana is the doubt caused by the cognition of some common property (*samāna dharma*) in the subject (*dharmī*) of doubt. Here, common means similar. For example, a thing is perceived to have a particular dimension which is similar to the dimension of a human being and a tree trunk. So the dimension here is a similar or common property. The cognition of such a property brings to the mind of the knower the remembrance of things which share that property in common. Thus, on seeing a thing with a particular dimension, we are reminded of a human being and a tree trunk. And as discussed earlier, knowing that a thing cannot be both a man and a tree trunk while there is non-perception of any specific property to determine it as a man or as a tree trunk, we are in a state of doubt to the effect "is that a man on a tree trunk?".

The second type of doubt is a doubt caused by the cognition of some unique property (*aneka dharma*) in the subject of doubt. The Sanskrit expression *aneka dharma* actually contains a suppressed word *vyavartaka* to be placed between *aneka* and *dharma*, so the full expression is *aneka vyavartaka dharma*. *Aneka* here means several kinds, *vyavartaka* means differentiator and *dharma* means property. So it means a property which differentiates its owner from things of several kinds. Several kinds again means its own kind and other kinds also. This differentiating property is, therefore, a unique peoperty of a thing which is not shared by any other thing either of its own generic class or of any other generic classes. Now if a thing is known to possess a unique property which is not found to be present in any other thing, then it gives no clue about the generic class under which that thing is subsumed; it rather leaves many possibilities open and, as a result, there is a doubt. Vātsyāyana gives an example of such doubt, a discussion of which would help us understand how this type of doubt arises. When a piece of cloth or paper is torn into pieces, a sound is produced. So the sound has the property of being produced by disjoining parts of certain things (*vibhāgajanyatva*). This property is unique to sound, it is not to be found in anything belonging to any of the classes (categories) recognized in the Nyāya–Vaiśeṣika systems. Seven categories are admitted by them, of which six are positive categories and the seventh one is negation or absence. Six positive categories are *dravya* (substance), *guṇa* (quality), *karma* (motion), *sāmānya* (universal), *viśeṣa* (individual differentiator) and *samavāya* (inherence). All producible things come under the first three categories, e.g. substance, quality and motion. The knowledge that sound is produced by disjunction leaves open the prossibility of sound being included under the class of substance or quality or motion. It may be the case that sound is a substance and by virtue of its property of being produced by disjunction, it is differentiated from other substances as well as from things belonging to the classes of quality and motion respectively. Similarly, the possibility of sound being a quality or a motion also holds. As a result, there arises the doubt to the effect "is sound a substance or a quality or a motion?".

While discussing the causal conditions of doubt, I mentioned that cognition of the subject of doubt as characterized by some neutral property is one of the causal conditions. I take both, a similar property (*samāna dharma*) and a unique property (*aneka dharma*) to be neutral properties because their presence indicates many possibilities regarding the thing's identity without specifying anyone in particular.

The third type of doubt is doubt which arises when one hears two contradictory statements regarding one and the same thing. For example, some philosopher says that the soul is eternal and another says that the soul is non-eternal, on hearing both statements, one person, who is not already committed to any particular position regarding this issue, has a doubt as to whether the soul is eternal or non-eternal since the person knows that it cannot be both. This is called *vipratipattijanya saṁśaya.*

There is some controversy among the Naiyāyikas regarding the interpretation of this variety of doubts. At the root of the controversy is the question of whether verbal statements can cause doubt. Though *vipratipatti* in the primary sense means contradictory cognitions or beliefs (*viruddha pratipatti*), in the secondary sense it means contradictory statements which express contradictory beliefs. The secondary sense has been resorted to, because, the beliefs which contradict each other are held by two different persons and as such, they cannot cause doubt in a third person's mind. So what is meant here is that two contradictory statements, made by two persons holding two contradictory beliefs respectively, cause doubt in the mind of the hearer. And a problem arises at this point. Sentences (*śabda*) can cause cognitions, but those cognitions are verbal (*śābda-buddhi*). But the standard Nyāya position is that doubt is always perceptual, there cannot be cases of inferential or verbal doubt. So the question is: what role do the sentences play in causing perceptual doubt? They say that the sentences here play the same role as that played by *samāna dharma* (similar property) and *aneka dharma* (unique property). Just as cognition of similar property or unique property reminds the knower of the possible alternative qualifiers (*koṭis*), similarly, on listening to the two contradictory sentences, one is reminded of two contradictory properties as alternative qualifiers with respect to the subject of doubt. But the doubt, in this case, is actually caused by *manas* which is an internal sense organ. Through the internal sense organ, the knower sees that both the properties cannot be true of one and the same thing and in the absence of any indicator in favour of any one of the possible alternatives he is in a state of doubt. So this type of doubt, according to the Naiyāyikas, is a case of internal perception.[14]

We may try a different interpretation of this type of doubt which seems to be plausible. It may be the case that on hearing two contradictory statements the knower has verbal cognitions of two contradictory positions and through his internal sense organ he sees that the positions being contradictory, cannot both be true. So, he has a doubt as to which position is true. (Here, of course, we are assuming that the hearer is not already committed to any particular position, he is neutral in this regard.) And since the truth or falsity of a position depends on the actual state of things, a doubt regarding this also means a doubt regarding the actual state of things. For example, on hearing two contradictory statements such as "the soul is eternal" and "the soul is non-eternal", the hearer is aware of two contradictory positions regarding the soul. Then he perceives through his internal sense organ that both the positions cannot be true as they contradict each other, so he is in a state of doubt as to which position is true, which again means a doubt to the effect "is the soul eternal or non-eternal?"

An incidental comment by Uddyotakara in his *vārttika* seems to support the above-mentioned interpretation. He says that in case of doubt caused by *vipratipatti*, the doubt is about the speakers; the hearer doubts as to which of them speaks the truth.[15] This doubt is actually an extension of the doubt regarding the truth of the positions concerned.

The fourth type of doubt is due to the absence of any rule regarding the perception of things (*upalabdhi-avyavasthā*). To explain, there is no rule that only existent things can be perceived,

---

14 Viśvanātha, *Nyāyadarśanam-Vṛtti* on *sūtra* 1.1.23, p. 238.

Viśvanātha, 1988, *Kārikāvalī-Muktāvalī* on *kārikā* 130.

15 Uddyotakara, *Nyāyavārttika* on *sūtra* 1.1.23, p. 250.

in some cases non-existent things are also perceived, as in the case of an illusion, when a snake is perceived in place of a rope. So when a thing is perceived, a doubt may arise as to whether an existent thing is being perceived or a non-existent thing; in other words, one may doubt whether the perceived thing is really there or not. For example, in a desert, if one sees a water pool one may be in doubt as to whether there is really a water pool or not, because there are cases of mirages where water is perceived when there is really no water.

The fifth type of doubt is similar to the fourth one. Here the absence of any rule regarding non-perception of things is the cause of doubt. There is no rule that a thing which is not perceived is non-existent, because, sometimes existent things also are not perceived. For example, the roots of a tree which are under the ground are not seen from above. So, there is non-perception of existent things also. As a result, when a thing is not perceived one may doubt whether the thing is non-existent or thing exists but is not being perceived due to some reasons.

According to Vātsyāyana's interpretation of the *Nyāyasūtra*, these are the five types of doubt which arise due to five different types of causes. But Uddyotakara differs from Vātsyāyana and holds that types of doubt are restricted to the first three only, the fourth and the fifth are not separate types but can be included in the first type of doubt. And, according to him, the absence of any rule regarding the object of perception/non-perception, which has been taken to be the specific cause of these types of doubt, is really included in general causal conditions of doubt. *Upalabdhi-avyavasthā* here means *sādhaka-pramāṇābhāva* i.e. absence of any evidence in favour of any one of the alternatives (*koṭis*) and *anupalabdhi-avyavasthā* means here *bādhaka-pramāṇābhāva* i.e. absence of any evidence against any of the alternatives.[16]

---

16 Uddyotakara, *Nyāyavārttika on sūtra* 1.1.23, p. 251;

Vācaspati Miśra, *Tātparyaṭīkā* on *Vārttika*, pp. 251, 253.

While discussing the causes of doubt, we have seen that non-perception of the possible qualifiers which are presented as the alternatives is a necessary condition of doubt. For example, if one perceives manhood in an object situated at a distance, then one cannot have such doubt as "is that a man or a tree trunk?" Or, if one had such doubt previously the doubt gets removed. Such doubt can also be prevented or removed even if manhood or treehood is not perceived (perception of which requires the perception of the human body which exemplifies manhood) but only, say, hands are perceived because the presence of hands implies the presence of a human body which is the exemplifier of manhood. So the perception of manhood (or, treehood) itself or the perception of hands/feet (or, branches and leaves in the case of a tree) can be regarded as evidence in favour of the assertion of one of the alternatives in the case of doubt. Therefore, the absence of such evidence (*sādhaka-pramāṇābhāva*) is one of the causal conditions of doubt.

Again, if there is some evidence against any of the alternatives (*bādhaka-pramāṇa*), then also a doubt does not occur, or, if a doubt had occurred earlier it would be removed. For example, a person who has a doubt of the form "is that a man on a tree?" regarding a thing he sees from a distance, would cease to have doubt if he finds that the thing is moving away from the place it occupied earlier, which is a sign against its being a tree. So, one of the two alternatives being cancelled, the doubt gets removed.

So, Uddyotakara holds that the absence of both perception of signs in favour of one of the alternatives and non-perception of any sign against that alternative is to be understood by the expression *upalabdhyānupalabdhyavyavasthā* and that is one of the general causal conditions of doubt. Therefore, according to him, there are only three types of doubt if the division is based on their respective special causal condition. Uddyotakara has also argued against Vātsyāyana's interpretation of *upalabdhyānupalabdhyavyavasthā* as the special cause of two different types of doubt.

Uddyotakara says that if, as Vātsyāyana holds, the absence of a rule that all perceived objects are existent and all unperceived objects are non-existent or absent were the meaning of *upalabdhyānupalabdhyavyavasthā* and were taken to be the special causes of specific types of doubt, then that position will go against common experience and would also lead to absolute scepticism. He says that we usually do not doubt the existence of a thing we perceive even though we know that sometimes non-existent things are also perceived. So Vātsyāyana's position goes against common experiences. Moreover, if the absence of the rule mentioned above were the cause of doubt, then every perception or non-perception would cause doubt regarding the existence or non-existence of the object of perception/non-perception. And such doubts would be interminable too, because the perception of specific properties which can remove a doubt would also lead to doubt about the existence of the perceived property, as a result, the previous doubt cannot be removed. Thus, no one can even be certain about the existence of any object. This would be a case of absolute scepticism. For this reason, Uddyotakara differs from Vātsyāyana and resorts to a different interpretation of Gautama's *sūtra* on *saṁśaya*.

Viśvanātha, a philosopher belonging to the modern school of Nyāya, states in his notes called *Vr̥tti* on the *Nyāyasūtra* that *upalabdhyānupalabdhyavyavasthā* as interpreted by Vātsyāyana is the cause of a doubt regarding the veridicality of a cognition (*prāmāṇya-saṁśaya*).[17] If there is no such rule that whatever is perceived is existent and whatever is not perceived is non-existent then there is a possibility that our perception of a thing may not correspond to the objective situation; the same doubt would also arise in case of the absence of perception of an object. This doubt means doubt about the truth or veridicality of our cognition: "is this cognition true or false?".

In the *Bhāṣāparicchedaḥ*, a text in Nyāya–Vaiśeṣika philosophy, Viśvanātha says that doubt about the veridicality of cognition leads

[17] Viśvanātha, *Vr̥tti* on *Nyāyasūtra* 1.1.23, pp. 242-43.

to doubt about the existence of the object of that cognition (*viṣaya saṁśaya*). For example, if a person doubts if his cognition of a water pool in a desert is true or false then he also doubts whether there is actually the water pool which he perceives to be there.[18]

Here it may be questioned as to whether both the doubts, i.e. a doubt regarding veridicality of a cognition and doubt about the existence/non-existence of the object of the cognition, should be treated as dual effects of the same cause, namely, the absence of any rule regarding existence/non-existence of the object of perception/non-perception. If that is the case then it should also be admitted that one of the effects precedes the other and the preceding effect becomes the intermediary cause (*vyāpāra*) of the ultimate effect. If Viśvanātha means to say this, then on his view *prāmāṇya-saṁśaya* (doubt regarding the veridicality of a cognition) functions only as an intermediary cause of *viṣaya saṁśaya*, i.e. doubt regarding the existence/non-existence of the object of that cognition.

Viśvanātha talks about another case where one doubt causes another doubt. He says that when one property/thing *x* is related by way of invariable co-location to another property/thing *y* then the existence of *x* somewhere implies the presence of *y* there; but if one is in doubt about the existence of *x* at a place one would also be in doubt about the existence of *y* in that place.[19] The first doubt is called *vyāpya saṁśaya* and the second is *vyāpaka saṁśaya*, and the first doubt here causes the second doubt. (In the case of the relation of invariable co-location, the relatum which is invariably co-located with the other is called *vyāpya* (pervaded) and the other relatum with which it is co-located is called *vyāpaka* (pervader).) For example, smoke is invariably co-located with fire, if one sees smoke somewhere, one infers the existence of fire there. But if one is in doubt as to whether what he sees there is smoke or not, one would also have doubted the existence of fire at that place.

---

18 Viśvanātha, *Vṛtti* on *Nyāyasūtra* 1.1.23, *Muktāvalī*, p. 738.

19 Ibid.; also *Prabhā Ṭīkā* on it. Also *Vṛtti* p. 244.

Now, both the divisions, i.e. division into *prāmāṇya-saṁśaya* and *viṣaya saṁśaya* on the one hand and division into *vyāpya saṁśaya* and *vyāpaka saṁśaya* on the other, are done with reference to the object of doubt. Doubts in each division differ from each other in respect of their objects.

In the Vaiśeṣika system, we get a different division of doubt. Praśastapāda, in his commentary on Kaṇāda's *Vaiśeṣikasūtra*, states explicitly that there are two varieties of doubt: external and internal.[20] An external doubt is a doubt concerning an external object. External objects are objects which exist out there in the external world, for example, tables, chairs, trees and animals. So when we have a doubt as to whether the thing standing at a distance is a man or a tree trunk, the doubt is an external doubt. An internal doubt, on the other hand, is a doubt regarding an internal object like cognition. Internal objects exist within an individual's mind and can be known by means of *manas* (inner organ) only. Vaiśeṣika philosophers say that a doubt that an individual sometimes has regarding the truth or falsehood of a particular piece of cognition is an example of internal doubt. They explain with the help of an example. A scientist had earlier made predictions about the time of an eclipse (solar/lunar) on the basis of astronomical calculations; once the prediction came true but the next time it turned out to be wrong; now, when he made calculations for the third time and came to a conclusion regarding the time of the forthcoming eclipse, he doubts in his mind as to whether the belief he has arrived at is true or false. They further explain that cognition is either true or false and a person who knows this fact can be in doubt about the truth or falsity of a particular cognition he owns if he anticipates the possibility of an error. In the given example, the scientist anticipates the possibility of a miscalculation as it had happened earlier and he is in a doubt about the truth of the resulting cognition. This type of doubt is called *prāmāṇya-saṁśaya*.

---

[20] *Praśastapādabhāṣya* in *Nyāyakandalī*, pp. 412-14.

Though there are some other internal objects besides cognition, e.g. pleasure, pain, desire an will, but no example of any doubt regarding these objects is given, the question of truth or falsehood does not arise in the case of these objects nor can a person be in doubt about the existence of these states of his soul. So, it is very difficult to find out what sort of doubt can arise regarding these objects if any doubt arises at all in such cases.

Regarding external doubt, Kaṇāda and his commentators admit two varieties of such doubt. In one case, the subject (*dharma*) of doubt is an external object which is being perceived at the time of doubt. In the other case, the subject of doubt is not in contact with the sense organs at the time of doubt. When we see a thing at a distance as having a certain dimension which is common to man and tree trunk, it is the first type of doubt. An instance of the second case of doubt is as follows. Suppose, we are in a forest and we see a pair of horns behind a bush, here the animal itself is not seen because it is covered by the bush but the animal is inferred from its horns and the doubt takes the form "is that animal, which has these horns, a cow or a bison?". These two animals have similar pairs of horns, so the perception of the horns accompanied by non-perception of specific properties of any of these animals causes such doubt. Here the subject (*dharma*) of doubt is the animal behind the bush which is not seen at the time when doubt occurs. So, this is the second type of external doubt.

Śaṅkara Miśra, a Vaiśeṣika philosopher, maintained that the second type of external doubt is reducible to the first type.[21] Taking the given example, he says that in that case the subject of doubt is actually the pair of horns and the form of doubt would actually be "does the pair of horns belong to a cow or to a bison?". So, in this case, the subject of doubt is not the unseen animal but the seen pair of horns.

Regarding the fivefold division of doubt on the basis of a special

---

21 *Praśastapādabhāṣya* in *Nyāyakandalī*, p. 177.

causal condition for each, as found in the Nyāya system, Śaṅkara Miśra opines that in all the cases of doubt a common or similar property (*samāna dharma*) functions as the causal condition and doubts as the effect do not differ from one another. Thus, according to him, doubts cannot be divided into different varieties in terms of their respective special causes.[22]

## Is Doubt Always Perceptual (Pratyakṣa)?

On the standard Nyāya view, every doubt is perceptual, which means doubt belongs to the class of perceptual cognition (*pratyakṣa*). We have seen that doubts are about both external and internal objects, so doubts are of both kinds: external perception and internal perception. When we have doubt of the form "is that a man on a tree trunk?". It is a case of visual (*cākṣuṣa*) external perception because it is about an external object, which we see through our eyes. On the other hand, when I doubt whether the conclusion I have reached through an inference is true or not, the doubt is a case of internal perception. It is about a piece of cognition which is an internal object (because it exists in the soul) and it is perceived through *manas*.

A view that all cases of doubts are of internal perception (*mānasa pratyakṣa*) has been mentioned by Vātsyāyana in his *Nyāyabhāṣya* and he refuted it in the *Pratyakṣa-Lakṣaṇasūtra Bhāṣya*. He says that a doubt which is about an external object cannot be a case of internal perception. The reason is that *manas* cannot have an independent or direct relation with external objects; it is related to external objects only through external senses. So external objects cannot be perceived directly by means of *manas* and therefore doubts about external objects are cases of external perception only.

Here, we may consider from a different point of view the position that doubt is always a case of internal perception and try to assess its plausibility. The position may be interpreted in

---

[22] *Praśastapādabhāṣya* in *Nyāyakandalī*, pp. 174-75.

the following way. It can be said that the object (*dharmī*) of every doubt is primarily cognition, which is also a direct object of *manas*. A doubt about an external object is usually expressed as "is that *x* or *y*?", but according to the view under consideration, the doubt would actually be of the form "do I see *x* or *y*?". That means, the primary object of my doubt is my visual perception of a thing. I am not certain about the nature of the thing I am perceiving, so I have doubt about the object of cognition which is an external thing. Now, as it is an external thing, *manas* is indirectly related to it. So even if doubt is a case of *mānasa pratyakṣa* it can be about an external object too.

The position that doubts are caused by *manas* and therefore are cases of *mānasa pratyakṣa* does not seem to be altogether implausible. If we consider the causal process through which doubt is generated, we see that the process starts with the perception of the *dharmī* of the doubtful cognition. If the doubt is about an external object, some external sense organ starts the process. For example, in the case of doubt as to whether the thing I see from a distance is a man or a tree trunk, the causal process leading to the doubt starts with the visual perception of a thing as characterized by some properties which are common to a man and a tree trunk. After this, there is a remembrance of the alternative qualifiers and an awareness of their incompatibility. Then a doubt arises. And it should be noted that it is the *manas* which is active during both the remembrance of qualifiers and the awareness of their incompatibility. So both, an external sense organ and the internal sense organ, play their role in generating doubt about some external object. Now it is to be decided which one is the main cause and which one is the auxiliary. For instance, in the case of the knowledge of absence, both a sense organ and the non-perception (*anupalabdhi*) of the counter positive (*pratiyogī*) are necessary causal conditions, but the Naiyāyikas take the sense organ to be the main or instrumental cause (*kāraṇa*).

In the case of doubt, it can be said that at the first moment of perception of the object (*dharmī*) the doubt does not occur, but only after the remembrance of the qualifiers and awareness of their incompatibility does the doubt results. So, a doubt can be treated to be similar to an after cognition (*anuvyavasāya*). First, there is a perception of an external object, then through the process of remembrance there occurs a doubt regarding the content of that perception. Though the external sense organ is a necessary condition, *manas* can be said to be the main or instrumental cause of doubt. Just because the external sense organ initiates the process of doubt, it cannot be said that it is the instrumental cause. In the case of inferential cognition too the process starts with the perception of *hetu* (probans) but either *vyāpti-jñāna*, i.e. the cognition of pervasion of probans by probandum (*sādhya*) or *parāmarśa*, i.e. the cognition of the pervaded probans as qualifying the subject (*pakṣa*) of inference is regarded as the instrumental *kāraṇa* of the inferential cognition. In the same way, *manas* can be the instrumental cause of doubt and hence doubt should be regarded as a case of internal perception. Thus, the plausibility of the position can be shown.

But it seems that the above-mentioned position did not appeal to the Naiyāyikas because they thought that when a doubt refers explicitly to an external object, it is about the external object and since an external object cannot be known without the help of an external sense organ, the doubt about it must be taken as a case of external perception.

However, the view that doubt is always perceptual, whether external or internal perception, has not been accepted by all philosophers even within the Nyāya school. There are some who hold that there are cases of verbal doubt (*śābda-saṁśaya*); some hold that there are inferential doubts too; and some others maintain that there are doubts in the form of remembrance (*smr̥ti*). They say that there is no justification in favour of the view that no non-perceptual (*parokṣa*) cognition can be doubtful.

**Possibility of Verbal Doubt (Śābda-Saṁśaya)**

We shall consider now the view according to which there are cases of *śābda-saṁśaya*. This is the position put forward by Raghunātha Śiromaṇi, a Naiyāyika of the modern school of Nyāya, in his book *Padārthatattvanirūpaṇam.*[23] He holds that the doubt which is caused by *vipratipatti vākya*, i.e. contradictory statement about an object, as mentioned in the *Nyāyasūtra*, is a case of verbal doubt.

Now, the doubt, which is said to be caused by *vipratipatti* (contradictory statement) involves some special problems. First, there arises the question: whether are there two statements about one and the same thing, contradicting each other? or, is there only a statement affirming two contradictory predicates about one and the same thing? If we follow Vātsyāyana's commentary, then it would seem that the old school of Nyāya means by *vipratipatti* two statements contradicting each other. For example, they would say, the statement "Sound is eternal" and the statement "Sound is non-eternal" are contradictory and would be considered as *vipratipatti vākya.* The modern school of Nyāya, on the other hand, is said to admit one statement with two contradictory predicates and only one subject as *vipratipatti vākya*. Viśvanātha in his *Bhāṣāpariccheda*ḥ mentions *śabdaḥ nitya na vā* as an example of *vipratipatti vākya.* Now if *vipratipatti vākya* presents two contradictory predicates (*koṭis*), one positive and the other negative, to be related to one and the same subject (*dharmī*), then the sentence is a semantically unfit (*ayogya vākya*). And on the old Nyāya theory of verbal cognition, i.e. cognition through *śabda*, semantical fitness is a necessary condition for verbal cognition. What they mean to say is that verbal cognition can be produced through a sentence if the meaning of each word in it is fit to be related to the meaning of some other word in the sentence to which it is intended to be related. In the *vipratipatti vākya* under consideration, *nityatva* and *anityatva* are intended to be related to *śabda*, but on the theory of opposition, two contradictories cannot be related to the same thing. So, this

---

[23] Raghunātha Śiromaṇi, 1976, *Padārthatattvanirupaṇam*, ed. Madhusūdana Bhaṭṭācārya Nyāyācārya, Sanskrit College, p. 61.

sentence is incapable of producing verbal cognition in the form of doubt.[24]

In reply to this, the Navya-Naiyāyikas say that actual semantic fitness is not the requirement; what is required is cognition of semantic fitness, even an erroneous or doubtful cognition of *yogyatā* (semantic fitness) will serve the purpose.[25] That means, even when two things presented by two constituent words in a sentence cannot actually be related to each other, a false belief that they can be so related, or, doubt that they may or may not be so related, enables one to have a verbal cognition from that sentence. So, the sentence *śabda nitya na vā* can produce a verbal cognition to the effect "Is *śabda nitya* or *anitya*?", with the help of a doubtful cognition of semantic competency of constituent words of the sentence. We can put it like this. From an uncertain cognition that each predicate has the possibility of being related to the subject, accompanied by the cognition of the opposition between the two predicates, a doubt as to which predicate is actually related to the subject arises.

On the other hand, the standard Nyāya analysis of the causation of doubt, in this case, is as follows. The causal process leading to a doubt starts with the two statements made by two parties in a debate, stating their respective positions which are incompatible. These two contradictory statements constitute the *vipratipatti vākya*. For example, one contender says "sound is elernal" and another says "sound is non-eternal" and these two contradictory statements are called *vipratipatti vākyas*. On hearing these two sentences, the mediator is reminded of sound which is the subject (*dharmī*) of doubt and also of the property of being eternal and the property of being non-eternal as alternative qualifiers (*koṭis*), which are incompatible. Then, by means of his mind or internal sense organ, the mediator has a perceptual doubt (*mānasa saṁśaya*) of the form "Is sound eternal or non-eternal?". So, according to this analysis, though

24 Viśvanātha, *Muktāvalī* on *kārikā* 83.

25 Gaṅgeśa, *Tattvacintāmaṇi*, Śabdakhaṇḍa, p. 285.

the causal process starts with contradictory statements, they are not the direct cause of the doubt. Therefore, the resulting doubt is not a verbal cognition (*śābda-jñāna*), but an internal perception.

This interpretation of *vipratipatti-janya saṁśāya* seems to be more reasonable than Raghunātha's interpretation of the same. Moreover, it can be said that if we appeal to our introspective awareness, we find that it does not support the conclusion that the doubt which is produced after hearing a *vipratipatti vākya* is a verbal cognition. This doubt is certainly induced by *vākya*, but not produced by it, in other words, it is *vipratipatti vākya prayojya*, but is not *vipratipatti vākyajanya*.

## Possibility of Doubt as an Inferential Cognition (Saṁśayātmaka Anumiti)

In the Navya-Nyāya literature, we find mention of some Naiyāyikas who hold that in case of a *hetvābhāsa* (defective reason) called *satpratipakṣa* (presence of counter argument), there arises a doubtful inference.[26] The case of *satpratipakṣa* is like this – the proponent offers an argument to prove his position, say, S, and the opponent puts forward another argument to prove the opposite of the position, i.e. not-*S*. In such a situation, according to the standard Nyāya view, none of these two arguments can prove its conclusion because each is inhibited by the other argument. The presence of two arguments proposing to establish two opposite conclusions causes the doubt as to whether the relation of pervasion (*vyāpti*) holds in the case of any of the arguments. So in the absence of a certain (*niścayātmaka*) cognition of the relation of pervasion, no argument can prove its conclusion. Hence no inferential cognition arises at all.

But a few Naiyāyikas of the modern school, as mentioned by Gaṅgeśa and Jagadīśa, hold that in such a situation, each of the two arguments can lead to a doubtful inference of their respective *sādhya* (probandum), though none can prove it conclusively.

---

[26] Gaṅgeśa, *Tattvacintāmaṇi*, Anumānakhaṇḍa, see *Gādādharī*, p. 1804.

Gaṅgeśa, however, rejected this position. He said that in case of a philosophical debate (*vicāra*) the mediator (*madhyastha*) who hears the arguments of the proponents and opponents with respect to a position cannot draw any inference at all in cases where the *hetvābhāsa* of *satpratipakṣa* occurs. In such a case, on hearing the proponent's argument, the mediator has the cognition that in the *pakṣa* or the subject of inference, *p*, a *hetu* or inferential mark *h*, is present, which is pervaded by the *sādhya* (the inferable property) *s*; then from the opponent's argument, he has the cognition that the same *pakṣa p* has another *hetu* $h_2$, which is pervaded by the absence of *sādhya*, i.e. *not-s*. Now, these two cognitions counteract each other, as *hetu* $h_2$ stands against proving *s* and $h_1$ stands against proving *not-s*, because the two *hetu-s* imply two contradictory properties respectively. So, no inference can be drawn in such cases. Therefore, there is no possibility of doubtful inference.

But a different suggestion can be made regarding the possibility of doubtful inference. Viśvanātha has mentioned, both in the *Nyāyasūtra Vṛtti* and *Muktāvalī*, that there is a kind of *saṁśaya* known as *vyāpaka saṁśaya* which is caused by *vyāpya saṁśaya*. He has not explained it there. It seems of that this type of *saṁśaya* can be regarded as a case of inferential doubt. It is obvious that Viśvanātha did not mean it, because of the accepted postulate that non-perceptual (*parokṣa*) cognition is always certain (*asandigdha*) in nature.[27] Still, let us explore this possibility, *vyāpya* means the *hetu* of an inference and *vyāpaka* means the *sādhya* of that inference. Now, *vyāpya saṁśaya* can be understood in two ways. First, it may mean a doubt regarding the presence of *hetu* in the *pakṣa*. Second, it may mean *vyāpyatva saṁśaya* or *vyāpti saṁśaya*, i.e. whether the *hetu* is pervaded by the *sādhya* in question. Let us take the first sense first and apply it to a case. Suppose a person sees a mass of greyish matter rising upward at a distant place. The perceiver is not sure whether it is smoke or not; it could also be dust. But still, he has a doubtful cognition that it is probably smoke. Now, if he knows that

[27] Viśvanātha, *Muktāvalī*, p. 738.

smoke has a relation pervasion with fire, then on the basis of his doubtful cognition of the presence of smoke at that place, he can have a doubtful inference of the presence of fire at the same place. So, it can be said that in this case, the doubt about the presence of *vyāpya* causes a doubt about the presence of *vyāpaka* and the resulting doubt is inferential.

If *vyāpya saṁśaya* is taken in the second sense to mean *vyāpti saṁśaya*, then also a doubtful inference of *sādhya* would be possible. If may be the case that a person is not certain that the *hetu* is pervaded by the *sādhya*, but believes that it is probably so, then that would be a doubtful cognition of *vyāpti*. Now, on the basis of that doubtful cognition of *vyāpti* or *vyāpyatva* of the *hetu*, the person can draw a doubtful or probable inference of *sādhya*. For example, if one has a doubtful cognition that manhood (*puruṣatva*) is probably pervaded by the property of being powerful (*śaktimattva*), then with regard to a particular man one can infer that the man is probably powerful.

It needs to be mentioned here that doubt in these cases should be regarded as a special type of doubt known as (*sambhāvanā*), where the probability of one of the alternatives (*koṭis*) is greater than that of the other. So, in the expression of such doubt, the less probable alternative is omitted. The expression takes the form "Perhaps it is smoke" or "probably it is a tree trunk".

In conclusion, it can be said that if explained in the above manner *vyāpaka saṁśaya* as caused by *vyāpya saṁśaya* may be regarded as a case of inferential doubt or doubtful inference. But, it has already been said that it is not the standard Nyāya position.

## Possibility of Doubtful Remembrance

Though the Naiyāyikas generally do not admit that there can be a remembrance in the form of doubt, Bhāsarvajña, a Naiyāyika of the old school, having deviant views with regard to some issues, admits this. He says in the *Nyāyabhūṣaṇam* that, since there are doubtful cognitions (*anubhavas*), the reproduction of such cognitions must also be doubtful.[28] His argument seems to be this. Every *anubhava*, i.e. non-reproductive cognition produces an impression of its object in the knower. Later, when such an impression is revived due to certain conditions, a memory cognition with the same content as that of the previous cognition (*anubhava*) results. Thus, if the previous cognition (*anubhava*) is a doubt having as its content one subject (*dharmī*) and two incompatible qualifiers (*dharma*), then the memory cognition caused by it through the impression would also have the same content and would be uncertain or doubtful.

But, there is a difference of opinion as to whether a doubt leaves behind an impression of its object. Śaṅkara Miśra, a Vaiśeṣika philosopher, says in his commentary on the *Kaṇādasūtra* that like *nirvikalpaka pratyakṣa* (non-qualificative perception) doubt also does not produce impression (*saṁskārājanakam jñānam*).[29] If that is the case, then there is no question of having doubtful remembrance, because, a remembrance is by definition a cognition produced by impression from previous non-reproductive cognition, so in the absence of impression, a doubtful cognition is not reproduced. But this position is disputed. Śaṅkara Miśra himself has mentioned a view that every qualificative cognition (*viśiṣṭa buddhi*) produces an impression, so *saṁśaya* too produces an impression. Raghunātha also in his commentary *Dīdhiti* on Gaṅgeśa's *Tattvacintāmaṇi*, mentioned the view of some philosophers who admit that memory in the form of doubt can also arise when the impressions (*saṁskāras*) of two incompatible (*virodhī*) properties are revived.[30]

To resolve this issue, we think our own individual experiences should be taken into account. Do we ever have remembrance in the form of doubt? We should search for our experience. Usually, we do not have such experience. The reason is that doubt is normally

---

[28] Bhāsarvajña, 1968, *Nyāyabhūṣaṇam*, ed. Swami Yogindrananda, Ṣaḍdarśana Prakāśana Pratiṣṭhānam, p. 13.

[29] Śaṅkara Miśra, *Upaskāra*, p. 176.

[30] Raghunātha Śiromaṇi, *Dīdhiti* in *Gādādharī*, p. 1673.

a temporary (cognition) phase of the mind that we want to and try to remove. We stop after arriving at certainty. So, doubt is subsequently replaced by a cognition which is certain in nature. It is this certain cognition which may later be remembered, but the previous state of doubt is not usually remembered. But, there may be cases of unresolved doubts. In such cases where we experienced doubts, but could not remove them, we may later remember those doubts. For example, while passing by a field in a speeding car I noticed something but could not be sure whether that was a man or a tree trunk, later when I recall that experience I may have a remembrance of the doubt I had at that time. If, on the other hand, I had removed the doubt at that time and knew that was a man, then, later I would normally remember that there was a man there and might not remember the previous doubt. But there remained the possibility that if I wanted I could remember that I was previously in doubt whether that was a man or a tree trunk. So it seems that like other non-reproductive cognition, doubt also leaves an impression and can be reproduced.[30]

To sum up, we may say that though the standard Nyāya view is that doubt is a variety of perceptual cognition only, because non-perceptional cognition can never be in the form of doubt, there are deviant opinions. After considering these views we find that they are quite reasonable and should be given due attention.

# 2

# On the Nature of Koṭi of Saṁśaya

Saṁśaya is admitted to be a kind of *apramā* (non-veridical cognition) in the Nyāya–Vaiśesika systems.[1] It is a form of indeterminate or uncertain cognition about an object which is usually expressed in the form of a question such as "Is that a man or a tree trunk?" or "Is that a man or not?". There is a difference of opinion as to whether *saṁśaya* in the former form, i.e. "Is that a man or a tree trunk?" is possible. The Navya (later) Naiyāyikas hold that *saṁśaya* always takes the latter form and not the former one. But according to the *prācīna* (earlier) Naiyāyikas *saṁśaya* in both these forms is possible. This controversy over the form of *saṁśaya* is actually a controversy regarding the nature of the *koṭis* of *saṁśaya*. Because, as we know, the form of a cognition is determined by its object; and the *koṭis* of a *saṁśaya* constitute the object of *saṁśaya*. An object of cognition can be analysed into two parts:

1. *dharmī* (subject), and
2. *prakāra* (property which characterizes the subject).

In a *saṁśaya*, the number of *prakāra* is more than one; and

---

[1] Annambhaṭṭa, 1969, *Tarkasaṁgraha with Dīpikā*, edited with *Nṛsiṁha-prakāśikā* and other commentaries, ed. Shri Satkarirama Bangiya, p. 69, Varanasi: Chowkhamba Sanskrit Series.

Viśvanātha, 1988, *Kārikāvalī-Muktāvalī*, *kārika* 129-30, ed. Sankarram Shastri, Delhi: Chowkhamba Sanskrit Pratisthan.

they are called the *koṭis* of *saṁśaya.* If the *koṭis* of a *saṁśaya* can all be positive properties (*bhāva dharmas*), then the *saṁśaya* would be *bhāva-prakāraka*, but if one of the *koṭis* is a *bhāva* (positive property) and the other is its absence (*abhāva*), then *saṁśaya* would be *bhāvābhāva-prakāraka.*[2] *Navyas* say that *saṁśaya* is always *bhāvābhāva-prakāraka* but the *prācīnas* admit *bhāva-prakāraka saṁśaya* also. My inclination is towards the *prācīna* Naiyāyikas' view and in this paper I shall try to defend that view.

Let us start with an analysis of the nature of *saṁśaya* (doubtful cognition). *Saṁśaya*, as we have already mentioned, is an uncertain or indeterminate cognition of some object.[3] In the case of *saṁśaya*, there is really no doubt regarding the subject, in the sense that the cognizer is sure of its existence, but there is uncertainty regarding its characterization. When one has a *saṁśaya* about an object, the object is apprehended but not fully and clearly, and whatever is known about it suggests a number of incompatible properties as possible predicates of it. But those properties being incompatible, all of them cannot be predicated to the thing perceived; and in the absence of the knowledge of any characteristic which shows the presence of one of the incompatible properties in the thing, the cognizer is not in a position to affirm of the thing any one of the properties in particular. Thus, he is in a state of doubt, i.e. he cannot make up his mind in favour of any of the alternatives. Therefore, the uncertain or indeterminate character of a *saṁśaya* pertains to the *koṭis*, which appear as the possible predicates of the thing perceived.

We shall now consider a concrete case of *saṁśaya* in order to

---

2 Viśvanātha, 1988, *Kārikāvalī-Muktāvalī*, Kārikā-130, p. 734.

3 Gautama, 1985, *Nyāyadarśanam: Nyāyasūtra with Vātsyāyanabhāṣya*, ed. Taranath Tarkatirtha and Amarendramohan Tarkatīrtha, p. 34 and *sūtra* 1.1.23 p. 234, New Delhi: Munshiram Manoharlal.

Śrīdhara Bhaṭṭa, 1963, *Nyāyakandalī*, a commentary on *Praśastapādabhāṣya*, ed. Durgadhar Jha, pp. 411-14, Varanasi: Varanaseya Sanskrit Visvavidyalaya.

have a better understanding of its nature. A common case of doubt is *samāna dharmajanya saṁśaya*, i.e. *saṁśaya* due to the cognition of a thing as possessed of some property that coexists with each of the *koṭis*.[4] Suppose, we perceive in insufficient light and from a distance, a figure having a height and other dimensions which are similar to those of a human being and also of a tree; we doubt "Is that a man or a tree?". This is an instance of *samāna dharamajanya saṁśaya.* Here, the perception of the height and other dimensions in the thing apprehended, bring to our mind the properties, viz. manhood and treeness as the possible predicates of the thing because both man and tree can have such height, etc. But manhood and treeness being incompatible cannot both be true of the thing perceived (*dharmī*), nor are we in a position to assert any one of these suggested alternatives. For we do not perceive either manhood itself or treeness itself in the thing perceived (*dharmī*); and we do not even perceive any other property (*vyāpya dharma*) like having hands and feet or having branches and leaves which shows or implies the presence of manhood and treeness respectively in the thing apprehended. So, we are in an indeterminate state of mind and withhold predication of any particular property to the thing apprehended (*dharmī*). This shows that the doubt is actually about the *koṭis*, which can be predicated of the subject or *dharmī.* That means the doubt is as to which of the *koṭis* can actually be asserted of the *dharmī.*

With these few words regarding the nature of *saṁśaya* we shall now proceed to discuss our problem concerning the nature of the *koṭis* of a *saṁśaya.* According to the *prācīna* Naiyāyikas, the *koṭis*

---

[4] Gautama, 1985, *Nyāyadarśanam: Nyāyasūtra with Vātsyāyanabhāṣya*, ed. Taranath Tarkatirtha and Amarendramohan Tarkatīrtha, p. 34 and *sūtra* 1.1.23 p. 234, New Delhi: Munshiram Manoharlal.

Kaṇāda, 1958, *Vaiśeṣikadarśanam* with *Rasāyana* commentary by U.T. Virrāghavācārya, Madras, *Vaiśeṣika-Sūtra* 2.2.17, pp. 88-89.

Śaṅkara Miśra, 1969, *Vaiśeṣika Sūtropaskāra*, ed. Nārāyan Miśra, pp. 172-73, Varanasi: Chowkhamba Sanskrit Series.

which appear to be possible predicates can all be positive (*bhāva)* in nature. Whereas, most of the Navya-Naiyāyikas hold that the alternatives must be one *bhāva* in nature and the other its absence (*abhāva*), e.g. manhood and absence of manhood. According to the Navyas, even when the verbal expression of a *saṁśaya* contains only positive terms as possible predicates, it is to be interpreted as a *saṁśaya* having four *koṭis*: two positive properties and absences of those properties as the other two.[5]

In order to settle the issue, we need to analyse first the sense in which *koṭis* of a *saṁśaya* are said to be *viruddha* (incompatible). Both the schools of Nyāya agree that the *koṭis* of a *saṁśaya* must be incompatible, for that follows from the very definition of *saṁśaya.* Incompatibility, from the point of view of Western logic, may mean both contrariety and contradiction. Naiyāyikas also have two senses of *viruddha*, which are similar to the senses used in Western logic. These are:[6]

1. *svarūpataḥ-viruddha*, and
2. *tadabhāvavyāpyatva-rūpa-viruddha.*

The first one, can be equated with contradiction and the second one with contrariety.

Now, if the *koṭis* of a *saṁśaya* were to be incompatible in the first sense only, then the Navya view would have to be accepted because only *bhāva* and the corresponding *abhāva* are *svarūpataḥ viruddha* (contradictory). If, on the other hand, the second sense of *viruddha* were also allowed in the case of the *koṭis* of *saṁśaya* then the *prācīna* view would also be acceptable. Because two positive properties like manhood and treeness have *tadabhāvavyāpyatva-rūpa virodha* between them, as wherever manhood is present, the

---

5 Viśvanātha, 1988, *Kārikāvalī-Muktāvalī*, *Kārikā* 129 and *Prabhā ṭīkā* by Raynarasiṁha, on this *kārikā*.

6 Gadādhara, 1970, *Tattvacintāmaṇi Gādādharī*, *Anumānakhaṇḍa*, ed. Paṇḍits Vindhyeswari Prasad and Dhuṇḍirāja Śāstrī, pp. 1804-05, Varanasi: Chowkhamba Sanskrit Series.

absence of treeness is also present, and wherever treeness is present and the absence of manhood is also present. Two properties have *tadabhāvavyāpyatva-rūpa virodha* if each exists in the same locus with the absence of the other.

But the Navyas do not allow this sense of *virodha* for the *koṭis* of a *saṁśaya*. They would argue that if the *koṭis* of a *saṁśaya* were all positive (*bhāva*), then they would be incompatible in the sense of being contrary. In that case, to know that the *koṭis* are incompatible, which is regarded as a necessary condition for *saṁśaya*, an additional knowledge will be needed, through which the incompatibility of the possible predicates will be known; because, the incompatibility between two positive properties is not apparent or evident. They are known to be incompatible only through the knowledge that each coexists with the absence of the other. If, on the other hand, one of the *koṭis* is a positive property and the other is its absence, then their incompatibility is evident. For an *abhāva* and its *pratiyogī* being incompatible, no other knowledge is needed to make their incompatibility known. So there will be economy (*lāghava*) in respect of the causal conditions of *saṁśaya*. But *lāghava* may not be a conclusive argument for the acceptability of a theory. *Prācīnas*, on the other hand, do not deny the possibility of a *saṁśaya* with positive *koṭis* only, as we in fact have such *saṁśaya*. We shall consider both the views and will try to assess which of them seems more acceptable.

We have already noted that if *virodha* between the *koṭis* of a *saṁśaya* were taken to be contrariety, than the *prācīna* Naiyāyikas view might be true. But, there are other points which we should take into consideration for the proper assessment of the views under our discussion.

The first point is that, according to the Naiyāyikas, in the case of *saṁśaya* one of the *koṭis* must be true of the *dharmī* though it is not certain which one.[7] This will be the case if the Navya view is

[7] Phanibhuṣaṇa Tarkavagīśa (ed.), *Nyāyadarśana* with Vātsyāyana →

accepted. For, of the two contradictories, one of which is *bhāva* and the other its *abhāva*, one must hold true of the subject. But if the *koṭis* were all positive, then unless *koṭis* were enumerated exhaustively, none of the *koṭis* might be true. For example, when seeing a figure with a certain height, etc. we doubt whether it is a man or a tree, we do not have in mind other possible predicates like pillarness. And it may very well be the case that the perceived thing may turn out to be neither a man nor a tree, but a pillar. So, in our example, none of the two *koṭis*, i.e. manhood and treeness, may be true of the subject. One of the positive alternatives will surely hold true of the subject only if the enumeration of *koṭis* is exhaustive. In our example, any and every property with which that particular height, etc. can coexist should be included in the *koṭis*.

Though the Navya view can accommodate easily the thesis that one of the alternative predicates in a *saṁśaya* must be true of the subject, still, the view seems to be counterintuitive and artificial. Moreover, it fails to achieve the economy, which the Navyas claim on its behalf.

The reason why it seems to be counterintuitive and artificial is that if we so decide, we can always take a positive property and its absence to be the *koṭis* of a *saṁśaya*. But, actually, the *koṭis* which are presented to the cognizers' mind are only sometimes like that. This point will be clear if we consider how a *saṁśaya* arises and how it is removed.

The type of *saṁśaya* which we are considering here is, as we have seen, caused by the cognition of *samāna dharma*. By *samāna dharma* is meant here as a property that coexists with each of

---

← *Bhāṣya*, ṭippanī, p. 131 in Bengali on Nyāyasūtra 1.1.4, Pashehimbanga Rajya Pustak Parshad, Calcutta, 1981.

Vācaspati Miśra, *Tātparyaṭīkā* in *Nyāyadarśanam*, *Nyāyasūtra* 1.1.4, p. 14.

Udayanacārya, *Tātparyapariśuddhi* on *Nyāyasūtra*, 1.1.4, pp. 145-46, ed. Anantalal Thakur, Indian Council of Philosophical Research, New Delhi, 1996.

the *koṭis*; it is not, however, a *jāti* (universal), but a property with respect to which they resemble. For example, a particular height is said to be the *samāna dharma* of the *koṭis* – manhood and treeness – because it exists in the locus of manhood and the locus of treeness. Now, if we have a *saṁśaya* of the form "Is that a man or not?", the *koṭis* are manhood and the absence of manhood. In this case, a particular height is said to be the *samāna dharma* of the two *koṭis*. That means, that particular height exists in the locus of manhood and also in the locus of the absence of manhood in the sense that they have a similar height. But what is the locus of the absence of manhood. All things except man can be the locus of the absence of manhood. But that particular height does not exist in all those things. So the locus of the absence of manhood, which is also the locus of a particular height, etc. is to be identified as a positive thing with a definite nature. Thus, we are to go beyond the mere negative character of the *koṭi*. We do have before our mind some positive *koṭi* like treeness, which is contrary to the other *koṭi*, still, for some reason we may prefer to replace it with contradictory of the other *koṭi* when we express doubt.

Similarly, if we consider the condition which leads to the removal of doubt, we shall find that we may have to go beyond the mere negative character of the negative *koṭi*. A doubt is removed only when we can assert one of the alternative *koṭis* in particular. But what enables us to be certain about one of the alternatives? It is the knowledge of the perceived thing as possessor of the *vyāpya dharmas* (specific characteristics) of one of the *koṭis*. The specific characteristics of a *koṭi* means those characteristics which exist in the locus of that *koṭi* and implies the existence of that *koṭi*.

Suppose, the doubt "Is that a man or not?" is followed by the certain knowledge "That is a non-man". In this case, how do we have the certain knowledge? The alternative *koṭi* about which we are certain is the negative one, i.e. the absence of manhood. Now, what is the specific characteristic of this alternative? The absence of manhood is present in an indefinite number of things, and the specific characteristic of each of these is definitely different. And we may find in the perceived thing (*dharmī*) the specific characteristic of a particular locus of the absence of manhood. So, we know the *dharmī* as something specific like a tree or a pillar or something else and not simply as a non-man. Thus, the negative *koṭi* is virtually replaced by a positive *koṭi.* Though specific characteristics like branches and leaves can coexist with the absence of manhood too, since it coexists with treeness, which again coexists with the absence of manhood, yet the knowledge of these specific characteristics brings to the mind first treeness and then the absence of manhood.

At this point, one may argue that if we do not perceive specific characteristics of manhood in the thing, then this non-perception will cause the perception of the absence of manhood there. Thus, the doubt can be resolved, and we have the certain knowledge that the thing perceived is a non-man.

The first thing that can be said in reply to this defence is that the non-perception (*anupalabdhi*) of the specific characteristics of each *koṭi*s is one of the causes of a *saṁśaya.* Now to say that the same non-perception of the positive *koṭi* removes *saṁśaya* by causing a certain cognition (*niścaya*) of the negative *koṭi* is to commit self-contradiction. Because, it is then asserted that the same non-perception is the cause of both *saṁśaya* and *niścaya*, with respect to the same *dharmī.*

The defender may now say that the two *anupalabdhi*s are not the same. The latter one which removes *saṁśaya* is *yogyānupalabdhi*,[8] that is, non-perception which occurs under the conditions which make clear and distinct perception of perceptible entities possible and is accompanied by an argument (*tarka*) that if the entity under consideration were present here, it would have been perceived. But the former non-perception which causes a *saṁśaya* is not of this

---

[8] Viśvanātha, *Kārikāvalī-Muktāvalī, kārikā* 62, pp. 446-50.

kind, because conditions for clear perception are absent in that case. So, there is no self-contradiction involved in this position.

Against this argument, we can say that when the conditions for clear and distinct perception obtain, one may very well perceive the *dharmī* of a *saṁśaya* as having a distinct nature and there is no need to characterize it as a non-man.

These considerations show that the Navyas may insist on having a negative *koṭi* in all the cases of *saṁśaya* but they would fail to achieve economy which they claim to achieve by this view. They argue that the *prācīna* view is less economical since the knowledge of incompatibility between the positive *koṭis* depends on the knowledge of a particular relation that one of the *koṭis* has with the absence of the other positive *koṭi*. But we find that even the Navya view is not economical either. Because, in their case, the knowledge of *samāna dharma* of the two *koṭis* and the cognition of *vyāpya dharma* of the negative *koṭi* are obtained through the knowledge of some positive property that coexists with the negative *koṭi* and is contrary to the positive *koṭi*.

Moreover, if they reduce a *saṁśaya* with two positive *koṭis* into a *saṁśaya* with four *koṭis*, two of which being positive and the other two being the negation of the positive *koṭis*, then they must also admit the knowledge of incompatibility between the two positive *koṭis* as a necessary condition for such a *saṁśaya*. For, in the absence of such knowledge, both the positive *koṭis* could have been predicated of the *dharmī*. So, we see that they would not gain anything from this reduction.

Therefore, there is no reason to prefer the Navya view which also goes against our experience. We often have a *saṁśaya* with only positive *koṭis*. There may, however, be cases where one of the *koṭis*, as it is presented to the mind of the cognizer is actually negative. This happens in the cases where the cognizer is interested in knowing only whether or not the suggested *positive* alternative is true of the *dharmī*. Let us take an example: suppose, it is evening and we have lost our way in an unknown locality. We are anxious to get somebody's help to find our way out. If at this moment we notice something standing at a distance, but cannot see clearly what it is, we will have a doubt. The doubt will take the form "Is that a man or not?". Because, at the moment we are interested in knowing only whether the thing before us is a man; and we are indifferent as to what thing it is if it is not a man. In this case also, we remember that the properties like a particular height, which we perceive in the *dharmī*, belong to human beings as well as to certain things other than human beings, but we do not have in our mind any particular thing among the things other than human beings. That means, in this case, one of the *koṭis* of a *saṁśaya* really consists of the class of those things other than human beings, which possesses that particular height, etc. (because everything other than human beings does not possess height, etc.). But none of those things was present before our mind in its individuality. So, one of the *koṭis* is really negative in this case. There are other examples of this type of doubt. For instance, when we doubt whether a particular piece of cognition is true or not; or, when we doubt whether a particular argument is valid or not, one of the *koṭis* is really negative.

So, it seems that there cannot be any such rule that the *koṭis* of a *saṁśaya* should be positive only or that one of the *koṭis* should be positive and the other negative. It will depend on circumstances and psychological factors as to which alternatives will be suggested to the cognizer who is in doubt. Therefore, the *prācīna* Naiyāyikas' view, which does not stipulate the nature of the *koṭis* of *saṁśaya*, seems more acceptable.

3

# An Analysis of the Concepts of Pramā and Pramāṇa in Nyāya

THE concepts of *pramā* and *pramāṇa* are two fundamental concepts of the Indian theories of knowledge. Among different Indian philosophical systems, several controversies centre round these two concepts. Every system has its own theory of *pramā* and *pramāṇa*. We shall concentrate here on the Nyāya theory only.

*Pramā* and *pramāṇa* are interrelated concepts. In Nyāya, the definition of *pramāṇa* has been given in terms of *pramā* and *pramā* has been admitted to depend on *pramāṇa* for its occurrence. (Though the Naiyāyikas maintain that God owns eternal (*nitya*) hence uncaused (*ajanya*) *pramā*, we are excluding such non-occurrent *pramā* from the scope of our discussion.) So, none of these concepts can be understood without reference to the other. But, when we view these two concepts in their mutual relationship, some problems crop up.

According to the definition of *pramā* as given by the Naiyāyikas, true cognition is *pramā*; *pramāṇa* is defined by them as the means of true cognition.[1] Now, if instead of viewing these concepts in

---

[1] Viśvanātha, 1988, *Kārikāvalī-Muktāvalī*, ed. Shankararam Shastri, pp. 413-14; Delhi: Chowkhamba Sanskrit Pratisthan.

Annambhaṭṭa, 1969, *Tarkasaṁgrahadīpikā* with nine commentaries →

isolation, we consider them in the background of the Nyāya theory of knowledge as a whole, then it appears that the Naiyāyikas must have meant by *pramā* something more than just a true cognition. Nyāya definitions of *pramā* and *apramā*, their definition of *pramāṇa*, and their Parataḥ prāmāṇyavāda[2] in respect of both *utpatti* (genesis) and *jñapti* (ascertainment) make up the core of the Nyāya theory of knowledge. The Parataḥ prāmāṇyavāda, with its necessary implications, adds something more to their conception of *pramā* and *pramāṇa.* We find that to be a true cognition does not seem enough to be called a *pramā*, and again to be the means of a true cognition may not be sufficient for being a *pramāṇa.*

## I

Let us start with the Nyāya conception of *pramā. Pramā* is defined by the Naiyāyikas as *yathārthānubhava*[3], which means veridical non-recollective cognition. *Jñāna* (cognition), according to them, is of two types: *smṛti* (recollective cognition) and *anubhava. Anubhava* is defined negatively as a cognition other than recollective cognition (*smṛtibhinnaṁ jñānaṁ*).[4] The Nyāya philosophers do not grant the status of *pramā* to recollective cognition. So, *pramā*, according to them, is always a non-recollective cognition (*anubhava*).

The reason why *smṛti* (recollective cognition) cannot be *pramā*

---

← on it, ed. Satkari Sharma Bangiya, p. 189, Varanasi: Chowkhamba Sanskrit Series Office.

2 Gaṅgeśa, 1974, *Tattvacintāmaṇi*, Pratyakṣa-Khaṇḍa, ed. Kamakhyanath Tarkavagish, Delhi: Motilal Banarsidass, chapters on *Prāmāṇyavāda*;

Udayanācārya, 1957, *Nyāyakusumāñjali*, ed. Padmaprasad Upadhyay and Dhundhiraja Shastri, pp. 210-33, Varanasi: Chowkhamba Sanskrit Series Office;

Viśvanātha, 1988, *Kārikāvalī* with *Muktāvalī*, pp. 740-48.

3 Udayanācārya, 1957, *Nyāyakusumāñjali*, *stavaka* 4, *kārikā* 1.

4 Annambhaṭṭa, 1969, *Tarkasaṁgraha*, p. 32.

is that a non-recollective cognition can be *yathārtha* (true) only in so far as it is an exact reproduction of a true non-recollective cognition of the same object,[5] which the knower previously had. That means, if the previous non-recollective cognition was a true one and the memory cognition is an exact reproduction of it, then memory cognition can be said to be a true cognition. But it has no independent claim to truth, its truth can be said to be borrowed from that of its cause, i.e. the previous non-recollective cognition of the same object.

Moreover, the Naiyāyikas hold that being a true or faithful copy of a previous non-recollective cognition, it cannot be true or veridical in the primary sense of the term. For, it does not correspond to its object at the time of its occurrence.[6] In the memory cognition its object is represented as what it was at the time of the occurrence of the previous non-recollective cognition, but during the time which elapsed between the moment of the occurrence of the previous non-recollective cognition and that of the present memory cognition, the object has not remained exactly the same, at least its temporal adjunct is changed. Therefore, the memory cognition cannot be said to correspond to the object at the present moment. This is, briefly, the reason for maintaining that a memory cognition cannot be *pramā.*

So far, we have been talking about the truth or veridicality (*yāthārthya*) of cognition, but we have not yet explained what truth is or what it means, for a cognition to be true. The Naiyāyikas hold that a cognition is true if it is *arthāvyabhicārī*[7] (non-discrepant with its object). It means that if a cognition represents an object as it really is, then the cognition is true. In the precise language of

---

5 Udayanācārya, 1967, *Tātparyapariśuddhi*, in *Nyāyadarśanam*, ed. Anantalal Thakur, p. 110, Darbhanga: Mithila Institute Series.

6 Ibid.
Gaṅgeśa, 1974, *Tattvacintāmaṇi*, Pratyakṣa-Khaṇḍa, pp. 843-45.

7 Vātsyāyana, *Bhāṣya on Nyāyasūtra* 1.1.4; Gautama, *Nyāyasūtra* 1.1.4.

Navya-Nyāya,[8] *tadvadviśeṣyakatvāvacchinna tat prakārakānubhava*, i.e. a non-recollective cognition the content of which consists of a property which actually qualifies the thing which appears as the subject of that cognition is true.

Let us explain the point further. According to the Naiyāyikas, every cognition, excepting *nirvikalpaka pratyakṣa* which is a non-judgemental cognition, represents a relational complex or *viśiṣṭa-viṣaya*, and the truth or falsity of the cognition depends on the actual existence or non-existence of that relational complex in the objective world.[9] For example, the cognition to the effect "The table is brown" represents a complex of the table, the brown colour and the relation of inherence (*samavāya*) between them. This cognition would be regarded as true or veridical only if such a complex exists in the objective world.

We have seen that according to the Naiyāyikas, the truth of cognition depends on the actual existence of the relational complex represented by the cognition in the objective world. We attempt to know things as they really are, and we can succeed in our attempt if some epistemic conditions are fulfilled. Epistemic conditions can be fulfilled when a *pramāṇa* is employed as a means of knowing things. We shall see in the next section that by *pramāṇa* is meant a special causal condition that is qualified by some *guṇa* (excellence) and is free from defects (*doṣa*). It is the *pramāṇa* that enables cognition to represent an object as it really is. So a *pramā* is said to be caused by *pramāṇa* (*pramāṇa-janya*).[10]

It seems that the Naiyāyikas actually believe that the truth of cognition depends on two conditions: one is the ontological condition and the other is the epistemic condition. It may be said

---

[8] Viśvanātha, 1988, *Kārikāvalī–Muktāvalī*, pp. 744-45.

[9] Gaṅgeśa, 1974, *Tattvacintāmaṇi*, Pratyakṣa-Khaṇḍa, p. 809. Viśvanātha, *Kārikāvalī–Muktāvalī*, 1988, pp. 431-32.

[10] Keśava Miśra, 1968, *Tarkabhāṣā*, ed. Badrināth Śukla, pp. 348-49, Varanasi: Motilal Banarsidass.

that the truth of cognition consists in the correspondence of the cognition with the objective situation, but this correspondence is ensured by some aspect of the way of cognizing. We shall take up this point when we come to the Nyāya conception of *pramāṇa.*

The next question which comes to our mind is: how can we know that a particular piece of cognition is *pramā* (true), i.e. how it corresponds to the object (*arthāvyabhicārī*)? We have already mentioned that the Naiyāyikas subscribe to Parataḥprāmāṇyavāda in respect of the ascertainment of *pramātva.* They hold that a piece of cognition can reveal an object but never does it reveal itself. Cognition can be revealed in the act of *anuvyavasāya* (after-perception); meaning that we can be only introspectively aware of a piece of cognition that we had. But even in that after-perception we do not know whether it is a *pramā* or *apramā. Pramātva* of a piece of cognition can be inferred from the successful activity to which it leads.[11]

Let us explain the point. The Naiyāyikas hold that all our voluntary actions are caused by cognitions. When we cognize something and also take it to be a desirable thing, we engage ourselves to attain it; similarly, if we cognize something and take it to be undesirable, we try to avoid it. Now, if our activity is successful, that is if we succeed in attaining the desired object or succeed in avoiding the undesirable object, then we infer that the cognition which led to the activity was a true one. If the cognition were not true, we could not have been able to attain the desired object as was shown by cognition. For example, if a piece of shell were presented as a piece of silver which is taken to be a desirable object, and we went to pick it for possession, we would have been unsuccessful in our activity, for only a *pramā* can lead to a successful activity (*saphala pravṛtti*).

The last point about *pramā* which I would like to mention is that

---

[11] Vātsyāyana, *Bhāṣya* preceding *Nyāyasūtra* 1.1.1.

Viśvanātha, 1988, *Kārikāvalī–Muktāvalī*, p. 753.

the Naiyāyikas do not admit *pramātva* (property of being a *pramā*) as a *jāti* (universal). They have put forward several arguments to show why no such universal can be admitted. We shall discuss briefly some of the arguments given by Udayanācārya.[12]

Udayanācārya argued that the universals which characterize cognitions can be perceived by *manas* when we have an *anuvyavasāya* of a cognition. We can perceive universals like *jñānatva* and *pratyakṣatva*, but we do not perceive *pramātva* or *apramātva*. If we could perceive it whenever we had the after-perception of the cognition which we had had, we would not have ever entertained any doubt regarding the veridicality of the cognition. But we do have such doubts. This shows that *pramātva* or *apramātva* of a cognition cannot be perceived but is to be inferred. If *pramātva* and *apramātva* were universals we could have perceived them.

Second, a universal always inheres in an individual as a whole and not in a part of it only. But sometimes, *pramātva* characterizes only a part of cognition. That is the case with *viparyaya* (erroneous cognition). The Naiyāyikas admit that even an erroneous cognition is veridical so far as the subject part of it is concerned.[13] For example, when we perceive shell as silver, we have cognition of the form "this is silver"; here, the term "this" stands for the subject (*viśeṣya*) which corresponds to the shell and is actually present before the cognizer. So there is an entity present in the objective world corresponding to the *viśeṣya* figuring in the cognition, and thus, the cognition is veridical in the subject part. But since the thing present before the cognizer does not possess silverhood, which figures as the qualifier (*prakāra*) of it in the cognition, the cognition is erroneous. So *pramātva* is found to characterize the subject part of an erroneous cognition and therefore cannot be admitted as a universal.

---

[12] Udayanācārya, 1967, *Tātparyapariśuddhi*, in *Nyāyadarśanam*, p. 109.

[13] There is an oft-quoted saying *dharmiṇi sarvam abhrāntam prakāre tu viparyaya.* It is quoted by Mathurānātha also in his *Rahasya Ṭīkā* on Gaṅgeśa's *Tattvacintāmaṇi*, see Pratyakṣa-Khaṇḍa, p. 374.

Third, *pramātva* cannot be regarded as a *jāti* because it cannot be shown to have the appropriate relationship with other universals which characterize a cognition. There is a rule that if more than one universal characterize one and the same individual, then they must be related to one another in the relation of inclusion in respect of their extension (*vyāpya–vyāpaka-bhāva*). For example, on an earth substance at least three universals inhere: *sattā* (existentness), *dravyatva* (substancehood) and *pṛthivītva* (earthness); of these *sattā* forms the widest class, which includes the class formed by *dravyatva*, which again includes the class formed by *pṛthivītva*. Now, *pramātva* can also be present in some individuals along with some universals; for example, in true perceptual cognition (*pratyakṣa pramā*) it is present along with *pratyakṣatva* and *anubhavatva* (property of being a non-recollective cognition). If *pramātva* were a *jāti*, what would be its relationship with these two? If it is admitted to form a class which is included in the class formed by *anubhavatva*, then that would preclude the possibility of memory cognition being a *pramā;* but though the Naiyāyikas do not admit memory cognition to be *pramā*, there are philosophers, e.g. the Vaiśeṣikas and Jainas, who admit memory cognition to be *pramā*. If, on the other hand, *pramātva* is admitted to form the wider class under which the class formed by *anubhavatva* comes, then each and every *anubhava* would be a *pramā*, and there could be no illusory cognition (*viparyaya*). So, *pramātva* cannot be shown to have *vyāpya–vyāpaka-bhāva* (relation of inclusion) with the universal *anubhavatva*.

How, again, would *pramātva* be related to *pratyakṣatva*? The class of *pramā* cannot be said to include the class of *pratyakṣa*, for then every *pratyakṣa-jñāna* would be *pramā*, and there could not be cases of illusory perception (*viparyaya*); nor can the class of *pratyakṣa* be said to include the class of *pramā*, for in that case, each and every *pramā* would be *pratyakṣa* (perceptual) only and *anumiti* (inferential cognition), *upamiti* (cognition by comparison) and *śābda-jñāna* (cognition by testimony) could not be *pramā*.

## II

We have already seen what a *pramā* is. The following three features of *pramā* have been identified:

i. a *pramā* is a non-recollective cognition that represents an object as it really is;

ii. a *pramā* is caused by *pramāṇa* (*pramāṇa-janya*); and

iii. a *pramā* alone can lead to successful activity (*saphala pravr̥tti janaka*).

We may now attend to the concept of *pramāṇa*. The Naiyāyikas define *pramāṇa* as *pramākaraṇam.*[14] In Indian philosophy, each of the causal conditions conducive to the production of an effect is called a *kāraṇa* and a *karaṇa* is one among them, which is regarded as a special cause. According to the great grammarian Pāṇini, *karaṇa* is *sādhakatamaṁ kāraṇam*, i.e. the most effective cause of an effect. As regards the question: which one is the most effective causal condition of an effect, there are three views current in the Nyāya system.

According to one view, that causal condition through the unique (*asādhāraṇa*) operation (*vyāpāra*) of which the effect is produced is the most effective cause and so that is the *karaṇa.*

According to the second view, that causal condition immediately after the occurrence of which the effect occurs is the most effective *kāraṇa* (*phalāyogavyavacchinnaṁkāraṇam karaṇam*).

There is a third view held by Jayanta Bhaṭṭa.[15] According to him, the aggregate of causal conditions should be regarded as the most effective *kāraṇa*, because until the aggregate of the causal conditions is complete, the production of the effect cannot be said to be inevitable.

---

14 Vātsyāyana, *Bhāṣya* on *Nyāyasūtra* 1.1.3.

15 Jayanta Bhaṭṭa, 1982, *Nyāyamañjarī*, ed. Gaurinath Sastri, vol. 1, pp. 20-23, Varanasi: Sampurnananda Sanskrit Visvavidyalaya.

Generally, the first and the second interpretations of the concept of *karaṇa* are accepted. So by *pramāṇa*, which is defined as *pramākaraṇa*, is meant that causal condition that is immediately followed by its result, i.e. a true non-recollective cognition; alternatively, it is that causal condition through the unique operation of which its result, i.e. a true non-recollective cognition, is produced.

The Naiyāyikas admit four kinds of *pramā*; so, corresponding to them, four *pramāṇas* are admitted as their respective sources. Each type of *pramā* is obtained through a *pramāṇa*. So, there are four *pramāṇas*, viz. *pratyakṣa* (perception), *anumāna* (inference), *upamāna* (comparison) and *śabda* (authority).

Now, a question arises at this point: does a *pramāṇa* always produce *pramā?* Take the case of *pratyakṣa pramāṇa* for example. According to its definition, either the sense organ or the specified operative relation of the sense organ with the object (*indriyārtha-sannikarṣa)* is to be regarded as *pratyakṣa pramāṇa*. But can we claim that whenever we perceive through our sense organ the cognition is always true? If it were the case, there would not have been instances of illusion or misperception. But we misperceive a rope as a snake, and we have an illusion of water in a mirage. In all these cases, the perceptions are produced by the sense organ through its relation with some object. So, if the sense organ or its relation with the object is the *pramāṇa*, then it does not always produce *pramā*. Is it by accident, then, that a sense organ sometimes produces *pramā* and sometimes *apramā*? The Naiyāyikas have their answer to this question. They are Parataḥ prāmāṇyavādins in respect of both the genesis and ascertainment of *pramātva* or *prāmāṇya.*

The Naiyāyikas hold that there are some causal conditions that are common to both *pramā* and *apramā;* but in order to produce *pramā*, the common causal conditions must be qualified by some *guṇa* (excellence) which is responsible for the *pramātva* of a piece of cognition. For each instance of *pramā*, there is a *guṇa* by which its *karaṇa* must be qualified. That is to say, in order to be *pramākaraṇa*, the *karaṇa* must be qualified by *guṇa.* Take the example of *pratyakṣa pramāṇa.* A sense organ or its relation with the object is the common causal condition for both veridical perception and illusion. But when the sense organ is qualified by *guṇa*, it produces *pratyakṣa pramā.* By *guṇa* in the case of *pratyakṣa* is meant nothing but the relation of the sense organ with the object, which is the actual possessor of the property, which figures as the qualifier in the resulting perceptual cognition. When we have an illusion, say, when we perceive a rope as a snake, there is the operative relation between our visual sense organ and rope which does not possess the property of snakeness, which figured as the qualifier in the illusory perception. So, due to the lack of *guṇa*, the sense organ or the sense–object relation failed to produce a *pratyakṣa pramā.* Therefore, the sense organs can be *pramāṇa* only if they are qualified by *guṇa.* There are different *guṇas* that give rise to *pramātva* in different types of *pramā.* We have already mentioned the *guṇa* which is required for *pratyakṣa pramā.* For *anumiti pramā* it is *yathārtha parāmarśa*, for *upamiti* it is *yathārthasādṛśya-jñāna* and for *śābda-jñāna* it is *yathārtha-vākyārtha-jñāna* (speaker's true cognition of the state of affairs described by the sentence uttered).[16] The later Naiyāyikas, however, maintain that the hearer's knowledge of *yogyatā* (semantic compatibility) of words uttered in a sequence that forms a sentence is the *guṇa* required for *śābda-pramā.*

Besides *guṇa*, the truth of cognition depends on another condition, i.e. absence of *doṣa* (preventing condition).[17] The *kāraṇa* of cognition must be free from defects or must not be associated with any defect which stands in the way of cognizing a thing as it really is. For example, a person with jaundiced eyes fails to perceive a white conch shell as white, instead, he perceives it as yellow even though his eyes are in contact with the conch shell, which actually possesses white colour and lacks yellow colour. Here, *pitta-doṣa*

---

16 Gaṅgeśa, 1974, *Tattvacintāmaṇi*, Pratyakṣa-Khaṇḍa, pp. 307-50; Viśvanātha, *Kārikāvalī–Muktāvalī*, 1988, pp. 740-43.

17 Ibid.

(jaundice) prevents the visual sense organ of the person from grasping the object as it really is.

So, we find that the *karaṇa*, which is neutral to truth and falsity of cognition, can acquire the status of *pramākaraṇa* only when it is qualified by the excellence (*guṇa-viśiṣṭa*) and is free from defects (*aduṣṭa* or *doṣābhāva-viśiṣṭa*).

Defects responsible for *apramā* (non-veridical cognitions) are different in different cases. The defects responsible for erroneous *anumiti*, *upamiti* and *śābda* are erroneous *parāmarśa*, erroneous *sādṛśya-jñāna* and erroneous cognition of the *vākyārtha* (meaning of the sentence) respectively. But for illusion, different specific defects are responsible for specific perceptual errors.[18] That is why even in the presence of a specific defect, cognition can be veridical in part. When a person with jaundiced eye perceives a conch shell as yellow, his perception is veridical so far as he perceives the given thing as a conch shell, but *pitta-doṣa* interferes with this perception of colour and he sees yellow colour, in place of white, in the conch shell. So the presence of a specific defect does not stand in the way of having partial veridical cognition.

## III

With this conception of *pramā* and *pramāṇa* in mind, we shall now consider a number of problematic cases of non-recollective cognition with regard to which it would be difficult to decide from the Nyāya point of view, whether they should be considered as *pramā*. We shall attend to three such cases. These cases have been mentioned and discussed at length in different texts of the Nyāya school and those of other schools also.

First, take the case of perceptual cognition, where a person perceives something to be a gem, desires to attain it, proceeds towards the place where the gem was perceived to be present and

[18] Gaṅgeśa, 1974, *Tattvacintāmaṇi*, Pratyakṣa-Khaṇḍa, pp. 307-50. Viśvanātha, 1988, *Kārikāvalī–Muktāvalī*, pp. 740-43.

finds it there.[19] Here, his activity is successful, so the cognition of the gem which led to this successful activity should be a *pramā.* But when the person went to collect the gem, he found that what came in contact with his eyes when he was at a distance was not the gem itself but its glow only. So he had actually misperceived the glow of a gem to be a gem and the perception did not correspond to the object. Therefore, the perception cannot be regarded as a *pramā.* So, the Naiyāyikas face a dilemma here. On the one hand, it would not be proper to regard a cognition to be *pramā* if it does not agree with the object; on the other hand, it would be difficult to deny *pramātva* of cognition if the activity to which it led turns out to be successful. For, if *apramā* can lead to successful activity, then the inference of *pramātva* of cognition from the success of the activity resulting from it would be invalid.

The Naiyāyikas solve the problem either by denying that the activity was really successful or by denying that the successful activity, in that case, was the result of that misperception.[20] As to why, in spite of the attainment of the gem, the activity cannot be said to be successful, the Naiyāyikas would say that the person wanted to get the thing that came in contact with his eyes and which he perceived as a gem. But the thing being the glow only, which lacks gemness, could not be obtained as a gem. So his activity was not really successful. Though he obtained the gem, it was not as a result of that illusory perception. It was really the result of a veridical perception that the person had when he reached the place

---

[19] Dharmakīrti, 1968, *Pramāṇavārttika*, ed. Dwarika Das Shastri, chapter II, *śloka* 57, Varanasi: Bauddha Bharati.

Citsukha, 1985, *Tattvapradīpikā*, ed. Swami Yogindrananda, Varanasi: Saddarshan Prakashan, p. 358.

[20] Gaṅgeśa, 1974, *Tattvacintāmaṇi*, Pratyakṣa-Khaṇḍa, p. 263, Phanibhusan Tarkavagish added a footnote on this point in the edition of *Nyāyadarśana* with Bengali translation and explanation by himself, published by Paschimbanga Rajya Pustak Parsad, Calcutta, 1981, vol. I, p. 4.

where he had earlier located the glow. Since the glow emanated from a gem, the gem was present nearby, and the person could perceive it when he reached the place. And his success in getting the gem was actually the result of this latter perception which was veridical.

Let us now turn to two other problematic cases of cognition, one of which inferential cognition, and the other is verbal cognition (*śābda-jñāna*). The case of inferential cognition is like this. A person misperceives steam to be smoke, and on the basis of his knowledge that smoke is pervaded by fire, he infers the presence of fire at the place where he perceived smoke.[21] Then he goes over to that place and finds that there is fire but no smoke; what he perceived as smoke was steam only. In this case, the inferential cognition to the effect "There is a fire there" corresponds to fact and so it must be regarded as a *pramā*. But can its *karaṇa* be regarded as *pramāṇa*? The Naiyāyikas explained only the *karaṇa* here cannot be a *pramāṇa*. The reason is as follows.

The *guṇa* required for the generation of *pramātva* of an *anumiti* (inferential cognition) is *yathārtha parāmarśa*, i.e. veridical cognition of the *pakṣa* as qualified by the *hetu* which is pervaded by the *sādhya*. The *parāmarśa* is immediately followed by the *anumiti*. Now unless the *parāmarśa* is true, the *anumiti-karaṇa*, which is either the *parāmarśa* itself or *vyāpti-jñāna* (cognition to the effect that the *hetu* is pervaded by the *sādhya*), cannot be characterized by the *guṇa*. And a *parāmarśa* cannot be true unless the *hetu* actually characterizes the *pakṣa* and it itself is actually pervaded by the *sādhya*. In the case we are considering, the *parāmarśa* is not true because the *hetu* is not present in the *pakṣa*. Here smoke is the *hetu*, but it is not present at the place where the presence of fire is inferred. So, the *anumiti-karaṇa* here is not characterized by the *guṇa* and hence should not be regarded as *pramāṇa*.

---

21 Śrīharṣa, 1979, *Khaṇḍanakhaṇḍakhādya*, ed. Swami Yogindrananda, pp. 73, 211, Varanasi: Saddarshan Prakashan Pratisthan.

But the case is further complicated if smoke is also present at the place where fire and steam are present.[22] In that case, the *parāmarśa* corresponds to the fact and hence should be regarded as true. But is this *parāmarśa* really true i.e. *yathārtha*? For though the smoke was present there, the person did not perceive the real smoke, instead, he perceived steam to be smoke. That means, in his cognition the thing which appeared as the subject (*viśeṣya*) was steam, which did not possess smokeness, but the property which appeared as the qualifier (*viśeṣaṇa*) was smokeness. But, a *pramā* must be *tadvadviśeṣyakatvāvacchinna tatprakāraka anubhava*, which means that the property which appears as the qualifier in the cognition must be possessed by the thing which appears as the subject in the same cognition. This truth condition has not been satisfied by the *parāmarśa* which we are talking about. *Parāmarśa* is a direct cognition that is produced by sense–object contact. In our present case, though both smoke and steam were present, the cognizer's eyes were in contact with the steam, so steam was the subject where smokeness was wrongly attributed. In the absence of smokeness in the steam with which the eyes were in contact, there is the absence of *guṇa*, viz. *viśeṣaṇavad viśeṣya sannikarṣa*, i.e. sense-contact with the thing which is the possessor of the property which appeared as the qualifier. Thus, the *parāmarśa* being false, the *kāraṇa* of *anumiti* lacks the *guṇa* required for *anumiti pramā*, so though the *anumiti* turns out to be true, it cannot be said to be *pramāṇa-janya* (caused by *pramāṇa*).

The third problematic case is the case of true verbal cognition (*śābdabodha*) which a hearer has on hearing *bhrāntapratāraka vākya*, that is, a sentence uttered by a person who intentionally makes false statements to deceive people but is under delusion while uttering the present sentence.[23] For example, the deceiver had been under the impression that a particular meeting was to be held at 12 noon;

---

22 Śrīharṣa, 1979, *Khaṇḍanakhaṇḍakhādya*, pp. 73, 211.

23 Gaṅgeśa, 1974, *Tattvacintāmaṇi,* Pratyakṣa Khaṇḍa, pp. 348-50.

but in order to deceive a person who wanted to know the time of the meeting, he told that it was to be held at 2 p.m. and in fact the meeting was scheduled to be held at 2 p.m. So the verbal cognition that the hearer had from hearing the deceiver's sentence was a veridical one. But the sentence which produced this cognition was not an *āpta-vākya*, i.e. utterance of a trustworthy person, hence it was not a *pramāṇa.* The *guṇa* responsible for the truth of verbal cognition is the speaker's knowledge of the meaning of the sentence. The deluded deceiver, who was the speaker, did not have the true cognition of the sentence meaning, instead he had *doṣas* (defects) like deceitfulness and error. So the cognition, though veridical, was not obtained through a *pramāṇa.*[24]

In all these cases where the *kāraṇa* is either vitiated, i.e. defective, or lacks the relevant *guṇa* (excellence), but the cognition which results from it is non-discrepant with the object (*arthāvyabhicārī*) since it is found to have led to successful activity, the question arises as to whether the cognition, which is non-discrepant with the object, should be regarded as *pramā* in spite of the fact that it is not produced by a *pramāṇa?* Or, if it is accepted as a *pramā* then should its *kāraṇa* in spite of being defective or lacking in excellence be regarded as *pramāṇa*, since it is *pramākaraṇa*? Both these alternatives seem to be in conflict with the Nyāya conception of *pramā* and *pramāṇa.*

---

24 Though Gaṅgeśa does not make an explicit reference to the speaker (*āpta*) in his definition of *śābda-pramāṇa*, he mentions that a sentence in order to be *pramāṇa* must be caused by the true cognition of the state of affairs, which it describes (*arthatattva jñāna janyaḥ*). He defines *śābda-pramāṇa* as *prayogahetubhūta arthatattvajñānajanyaḥ-śabdaḥ pramāṇam.* So even according to Gaṅgeśa's definition of *śābda-pramāṇa* the sentence uttered by a deluded deceiver cannot be regarded as *pramāṇa*, because it is not produced by the true cognition of the state of affairs described in the sentence. So even though the cognition the hearer has on hearing that sentence corresponds to fact, it cannot be said to be *pramāṇa-janya.*

## IV

After analysing the concepts of *pramā* and *pramāṇa*, and studying the problematic cases where it is difficult to decide whether a particular cognition should or should not be regarded as a *pramā*, we may make the following observation.

If we take a comprehensive view of the Nyāya theory of knowledge comprising their notion of *pramā* and *pramāṇa*, both in respect of the genesis of *pramātva*, as well as ascertainment of it, we shall find that a distinction needs to be drawn between a *pramā* which is obtained through some *pramāṇa* and any *yathārthānubhava* irrespective of the means of obtaining it. The Naiyāyikas, however, did not explicitly admit such a distinction. But, on the basis of some indirect evidence, we can argue that admitting this distinction would not be incompatible with the Nyāya theory of knowledge. The Nyāya definition of *pramāṇa* implies a causal relation between *pramāṇa* and *pramā.* Accepting this causal relation, the Naiyāyikas cannot allow the occurrence of a *pramā* without a *pramāṇa.* They avoided including the property of *pramāṇa-janyatva* or *guṇa-janyatva* in the definition of *pramā* as it would have involved circularity,[25] but they must have meant the property of *pramāṇa- janyatva* to be an essential property of *pramā.* So, where that property is absent, the cognition should not be regarded as a *pramā*, even if it is a *yathārthānubhava.*

The claim to *pramātva* made on behalf of a piece of cognition should be justified both by its result, i.e. successful activity as well as by its cause, i.e. *pramāṇa.* A cognition should not be regarded as a *pramā* unless it is shown to be produced by some *pramāṇa*

---

[25] By *guṇa* is meant here *pramājanaka asādhāraṇa kāraṇa*, i.e. the specific causal condition leading to the production of *pramā*. So, *guṇa* being defined in terms of *pramā*, to define *pramā* in terms of *guṇa* would involve circularity. For the definition of *guṇa* and *doṣa* in the context of *pramā* and *apramā*, see Annambhaṭṭa's *Tarkasaṁgrahadīpikā* (1969), pp. 368-69.

though it might turn out to be true (*yathārtha*) in case the activity to which it led was successful. So, a true cognition produced by some improper means should not be given the status of *pramā*, since its claim is only partially justified, i.e. justified by its result but not by its cause.

As regards the question how the Naiyāyikas would account for the veridicality of a cognition which is not produced by a *pramāṇa* the following reply may be given. The exceptional cases where a cognition seems to be true accidentally (*kākatālīya-saṁvāda* or *yāddṛcchika-saṁvāda*) the Naiyāyikas would account for the truth as having been caused by *adṛṣṭa*, i.e. imperceptible results of past deeds of the knower.[26] In Nyāya, admission of an imperceptible cause is permissible only if the perceptible cause is not available for explaining the occurrence of an event.

26 N.S. Rāmānujatātācārya, delivered a lecture entitled "Prāmāṇya-vādasya tulanātmakadṛṣṭya Vicāraḥ" as Pandit Panchanan Shastri Memorial Lecture, 1983, organized by Prasthana Mimamsa at Jadavpur University, Calcutta. Prasthana Mimamsa also published the text of his lecture in a booklet. There, he has mentioned this solution.

# 4

# How to Ascertain the Truth of a Cognition

## The Nyāya Position on Prāmāṇya-jñapti

Pramā and *pramāṇa* are two fundamental topics of Indian epistemology. *Pramā* means knowledge or veridical cognition, and *pramāṇa* is the source of knowledge. *Prāmāṇya* is an essential property of both *pramā*, i.e. the veridical cognition, and *pramāṇa*, which is the means of *pramā*. Since it is the property of these two distinct things, *prāmāṇya* is used in two senses in two cases:

a. *prāmāṇya* means *pramāṇatva* or validity in the case of a *pramāṇa;*

b. *prāmāṇya* means *pramātva*, i.e. veridicality or truth in the case of a *pramā*.

*Prāmāṇya* can be established when *pramātva* of the cognition which it produces is established because a means of cognition cannot be regarded as valid (*pramāṇa*) unless the cognition it produces is a *pramā*. So, the question arises as to how to ascertain that a particular piece of cognition is veridical or *pramā*. *Pramātva* or veridicality means agreement with the object, i.e. *yathārthatva* (*artha-avyabhicāritva*). That is to say, a cognition is veridical or *pramā* if it reveals an object as the object actually is.[1] On the other hand,

---

[1] Vātsyāyana, *Bhāṣya* on 1.1.4, *Nyāyadarśanam*, ed. Tārānātha Nyāyatarkatīrtha and Amarendramohan Tarkatīrtha, 1985, p. 113, New Delhi: Munshiram Monoharlal.

if a cognition reveals an object as what it actually is not, then that cognition is non-veridical (*ayathārtha*); it is called *apramā* and it has the property of *aprāmāṇya*. Theories formulated by different schools of philosophy regarding this issue of ascertainment of *prāmāṇya* and *aprāmāṇya* are known as Prāmāṇyavāda *jñaptipakṣa*. This is the topic of this essay. I shall discuss the Nyāya theory known as Parataḥprāmāṇyavāda as against the Mīmāṁsā theory of Svataḥprāmāṇyavāda.

Theories regarding *prāmāṇya-jñapti* are about the ways of knowing whether a piece of cognition is veridical or not. Now, to know the veridicality or non-veridicality of cognition, we must be aware of the cognition itself, because cognition is the locus (*dharmī*) of the property (*dharma*) of *prāmāṇya* or *aprāmāṇya*, which we want to ascertain. So the first question is: how are we aware of the cognition that we have? The next question is: When we are aware of a cognition are we aware of the veridicality of that cognition also? or, a separate cognition reveals its veridicality? Those, who maintain that the *prāmāṇya* of a cognition is revealed at the time when cognition itself is revealed, are the Svataḥprāmāṇyavādins.[2] On the other hand, the Parataḥ prāmāṇyavādins hold that when we are aware of a cognitive state, we do not know whether it is veridical or not, for knowing that we need a separate cognition, which proves the veridicality of the cognition.[3]

To state the issue of ascertainment of *prāmāṇya*, it should be mentioned that three different objects of cognition are involved here:

---

[2] Viśvanātha, *Kārikāvalī-Muktāvalī*, ed. Shri Shankar Ram Shastri, Delhi: Chowkhamba Sanskrit Pratirthan, 1988; *Muktāvalī* on *kārikā* 136, pp. 747-50.

[3] Annambhaṭṭa, 1963, *Tarkasaṁgraha* and *Tarkadīpikā*, ed. Athalye, Bodas and Pusalker, Bombay Sanskrit Series, pp. 55-56.

Keśava Miśra, *Tarkabhāṣā* with explanation in Hindi by Badrināth Śukla, pp. 194-96.

i. Cognition of an object *x*;
ii. cognition of the cognition of *x*; and
iii. cognition of the veridicality of the cognition of *x*.

Our purpose is to ascertain the veridicality of the cognition of *x*.

According to the Mīmāṁsakas, who are Svataḥ-prāmāṇyavadins, the *prāmāṇya* of a cognition is revealed by the same cognition that reveals the cognition which is the locus of *pramātva* (*pramātva svāśraya grāhakasāṁgrīgrāhya*). That means, they hold that both the cognition of *x* and its veridicality are cognized in the same act of cognition. But Mīmāṁsā philosophers differ among themselves as to how a cognition of an object is known. According to the Prābhākara school of Mīmāṁsā, a cognition reveals itself along with its veridicality. They, like the Advaita Vedāntins, hold that *jñāna* (cognition) is *svaprakāśa* (self-revealing). A cognition reveals not only its object but also reveals itself along with its *prāmāṇya* and also the knower. That means, the cognition of *x* reveals *x*, which is the object and also reveals itself as a *pramā*. Therefore, according to the Prābhākara school, the cognition which is *svaprakāśa* reveals all three, i.e. its object, itself and its *prāmāṇya* at the same time.[4]

The Bhāṭṭa school of Mīmāṁsā holds that *jñāna* can be known by means of *anumāna* (inference), because a cognition is imperceptible. According to them, we cannot be directly aware of our cognitive states. Through inference, a cognition is known along with its property of *pramātva*. So, here too, one and the same cognition reveals the cognition of an object *x* and its veridicality. To state very briefly, Kumārila holds that a cognition is imperceptible (*atīndriya*), but every cognition produces a property called *jñātatā* (cognizedness/knownness) in its object. This property of *jñātatā* is perceptible. For example, when I see a jar (*ghaṭa*), the property of *jñātatā* is produced in it. After that moment, I see the jar as a cognized jar (*jñāta ghaṭa*). On the basis of this property of *jñātatā* in a jar which I perceive, I can infer that I had a cognition of the

---

4 Viśvanātha, *Kārikāvalī-Mūktavalī*, pp. 749-50.

jar and not only that, I also infer the cognition of the jar to be a veridical one or *pramā*. So according to Kumārila the way of knowing the *prāmāṇya* of a cognition is an inference based on *jñātatā* (*jñātatāliṅgaka-anumāna*).[5]

There is a third version of Svataḥprāmāṇyavāda held by Murārī Miśra, another Mīmāṁsā philosopher. According to him, a cognition is known by mental perception, which is called *anuvyavasāya* (after-cognition). And that mental perception reveals the veridicality of the cognition also.[6]

Considering all three versions of Svataḥprāmāṇyavāda we find that the Mīmāṁsakas in general hold that when a cognition is known, it is known as *prāmā*. The reason for this is that according to them a cognition originates as *pramā* unless some defect hinders its veridicality. Similarly, when a cognition is known, it is known as *pramā* unless a *bādhaka-jñāna* (sublating cognition) arises, or, presence of some defect is known.

The Naiyāyikas, who are Parataḥ prāmāṇyavādins, hold that *jñāna* is *parataḥprakāśya*, it is revealed in a mental perception known as *anuvyavasāya*. But, they deny that the veridicality of the cognition is also revealed by that *anuvyavasāya* as the Mīmāṁsā philosopher Murārī Miśra held. According to Nyāya, veridicality of a cognition is known by means of another cognition which is inferential. So the Nyāya position is this:

1. We have a cognition of *x*;
2. we have a mental perception that we have the cognition; and
3. we have an inferential cognition to the effect that the cognition of *x* which we had was true.

So, here *x* and its cognition and veridicality of that cognition are known in three different states of cognition.

---

5 Viśvanātha, *Kārikāvalī-Mūktavalī*, p. 748.

6 Ibid., pp. 748-49.

## I

Before entering into the discussion of the Nyāya philosophers' arguments in favour of their theory about the ascertainment of *prāmāṇya* (truth of a cognition), we need to answer a relevant question. It may be asked whether there is any need to ascertain the truth or veridicality of a cognition. The answer is simple – if there is doubt regarding the truth of a cognition, the doubt needs to be removed by ascertaining the veridicality of the cognition. For, doubt about the veridicality of a cognition causes doubt regarding the existence or about the nature of the object of that cognition. So, removal of doubt is necessary by ascertaining the truth.

But a second reason is also given to show the need for ascertaining *prāmāṇya*. It has been said by the Indian philosophers that there are persons who undertake actions like sacrificial rites to acquire other-worldly results as prescribed by the Vedas and, for this, the person needs to know the veridicality of the cognition generated by the Vedic sentence. This is because one has to have an unshaken will (*niṣkampa pravṛtti*) to perform the sacrificial act which involves a lot of labaour, austerity and cost. To have an unshaken volition towards such acts, knowledge of the truth of cognition that causes the volition is necessary.[7] For example, there is a Vedic injunction (*vidhivākya*), which says – a person desirous of attaining *svarga* (heaven) should perform the sacrifice called Agnihotra. One needs to know the truth of the cognition produced by this Vedic sentence before undertaking the act of sacrifice. In mundane cases, we may have shaky volitions from cognitions, the veridicality of which is doubted. For example, one may have doubt about a piece of land as to whether it is fertile, still one may want to have the benefit of doubt and sow that land. But this does not happen in the case of scriptural actions.

It has been said that doubt regarding the veridicality (*prāmāṇya*-

---

[7] Gaṅgeśa, 1974, *Tattvacintāmaṇi*, Pratyakṣa Khaṇḍa, ed. Kamakhyanath Tarkavagish, pp. 282-83, Delhi: Motilal Banarsidass.

*saṁśaya)* occurs in cases of some cognitions. The Nyāya philosophers use this point to formulate their argument in favour of Parataḥ prāmāṇyavāda. The Naiyāyikas argue that Svataḥprāmāṇyavāda excludes the possibility of a doubt regarding the veridicality of any cognition. For, doubt can arise if the following conditions are fulfilled:

i. the subject (*dharmī*) of the doubt must be known;
ii. possible alternative predicates (*koṭi/dharma*) must be remembered; and
iii. there must be the absence of certain knowledge (*niścaya)* of any of the predicates (*koṭi*) to be the one belonging to the subject.

Now, in the case of doubt regarding the truth of a cognition, the cognition is the *dharmī*, veridicality and non-veridicality are the alternative predicates (*koṭis*). On the theory of *svataḥ-prāmāṇya* when the cognition, which is the subject, is known, its veridicality is also known. So, along with the *dharmī*, one of the *koṭis* is also known to belong to the subject. Thus, there is no scope for doubting. But, the Naiyāyikas argue that we do have such doubt at times, so the possibility of doubt must be kept open. Therefore, Parataḥ prāmāṇyavāda, which accommodates *prāmāṇya-saṁśaya* by maintaining that veridicality of a cognition is not known at the time when the cognition itself is known, should be accepted.[8]

The Naiyāyikas clarify the cases of occasional doubt regarding the veridicality of a cognition. They say that we do not usually have a doubt regarding the veridicality of the cognitions about those objects which we are familiar with. They call it *abhyāsadaśāpanna-jñāna*, which means cognitions that we have in familiar or accustomed situations. We have repeated cognitions of many objects which we use in our day-to-day activities of life. We frequently have cognitions of things like water, drinks, food items, bed, tables, chairs, books, papers and pens in our daily life, and we

[8] Viśvanātha, *Muktāvalī*, pp. 141-43.

do not entertain any doubt about the truth of such cognitions. But the Naiyāyikas point out that when we have the very first cognition of a new thing with which we were not already acquainted, it is called *anabhyāsadaśāpanna-jñāna*,[9] in such cases we do have a doubt regarding the veridicality of those cognitions. For example, let us suppose, you are visiting a new country where you were given some fruits which you had never seen or eaten before and were told that those fruits are nutritious and tasteful. In such a situation, you would normally have a doubt about the veridicality of the cognition which you acquired from others' words about those fruits. That means, you would doubt whether those are really nutritious and tasteful. You will then try to ascertain the veridicality of that cognition by some means. We shall presently discuss the way of ascertaining the truth of such first time cognitions according to the Nyāya. But once the truth of a cognition about some object *x* is ascertained, the subsequent cognition of *x* that we may have, would not normally be doubted because *x* then becomes familiar and its repeated cognitions are, what is called, *abhyāsadaśāpanna-jñāna*.

Let us now see how according to the Nyāya the first time cognition of a thing is verified, or how its truth is known. The Naiyāyikas say that inference (*anumāna*) is the means of ascertaining the veridicality of a cognition. The inference is made on the basis of the success of the volition or action (*saphala pravṛtti*) which is caused by the cognition, the veridicality of which we want to ascertain.[10] Let us explain the matter. All the actions that we perform are meant to attain some of our ends. For example, our act of drinking water

---

[9] Annambhaṭṭa, *Tarkasaṁgrahadīpikā*, p. 55.

Rāmānujatātācārya, 1993, *Prāmāṇyavādasya tulanātmaka dṛṣṭaya vicāraḥ*, presented a paper organized by Prasthana Mimāṁsā in Calcutta, p. 16.

[10] Vācaspati Miśra, *Tātparyaṭīkā* in *Nyāyadarśanam*, p. 9.

B.K. Matilal, 1986, *Perception*, pp. 164-66, Oxford: Oxford University Press.

is for quenching our thirst. When I see a glass of water I believe that this is water and this will quench my thirst, so I drink it. If I am satisfied after drinking it, that would mean that my volition or action of drinking water is successful. This proves that the cognition of water, which was a cause of my action was veridical. If it were not veridical, my action of drinking water would not have been successful. If what I saw as a glass of water was not really water but something else looking like water (which was an illusion), then it would not have been possible to drink it and to have quenched my thirst. This instance is a case of cognition under a familiar situation or *abhyāsadaśāpanna-jñāna*, where usually verification of the truth of the cognition is not required. Let us then take the case of first time cognition of a thing or *anabhyāsadaśāpanna-jñāna*. Suppose, I am thirsty and I have been given a drink that I have not tasted before. In that case, I may have a doubt as to whether that drink will quench my thirst, yet I drink it; because we have mentioned earlier that for having a volition the truth of cognition which causes the volition need not always be known; so, from a doubtful cognition also, volition can take place in case of mundane actions. After taking the drink if I felt satisfied, then my volition was successful and the cognition that, that particular drink can quench thirst, was proved to be true or veridical.

The form of inference as given by Viśvanātha in *Muktāvalī*, is like this:

> This piece of cognition is veridical, because it produces successful volition, if a cognition is not veridical, it cannot produce successful volition, just as a non-veridical cognition cannot.

In this inference, a piece of cognition about a particular thing *x* is the subject of inference (*pakṣa*), *prāmāṇya* is the probandum (*sādhya*) and being the cause of successful volition (*saphala pravṛtti janakatva*) is the probans (*hetu*). This inference is based on the negative relation of pervasion (*vyatireka vyāpti*) between *hetu* and *sādhya* established by agreement in absence between probandum and probans supported by an instance (*dṛṣṭānta*). To take this present case of inferring veridicality of a cognition (*prāmāṇyānumāna*), the relation of pervasion employed here is of the form "where there is absence of *prāmāṇya*", there is absence of successful volition, as in a non-veridical cognition of a mirage (*marīcikā*) as water. On the basis of this *vyatireka vyāpti*, it is inferred that a cognition that produces successful volition is veridical. Thus, a first-time cognition of any object can be verified as true by this type of inference on the basis of successful volition. But when we have cognition of the same thing for the second, third and many more times, we do not need to prove the veridicality of those cognitions by means of this type of inference.

The Naiyāyikas hold that if we need to ascertain the veridicality of the cognitions which we repeatedly have under familiar situation (*abhyāsadaśāpanna-jñāna*), then we shall have recourse to another type of inference based on the ground of likeness (*tajjātīyatva*) with another cognition previously verified as true.[11] The Naiyāyikas say that when we have repeated cognitions like $C_1$, $C_2$, $C_3$ about the same or similar objects, if $C_1$ has already been proved as true on the basis of successful volition, we can argue that $C_2$, $C_3$ are also true because they are similar to $C_1$ as having the same content (*samānākāra*). For example, if I repeatedly have a cognition of the form "this is a glass of water", then excepting the first cognition, any other piece of cognition of the same form can be inferred to be veridical on the ground that it belongs to the same kind of cognition which has been proved as veridical. This inference, as shown by Vācaspati Miśra, can be formulated in this way:

> This piece of cognition of water is veridical, because it belongs to the same kind as that of the previous cognition of water which has been known to be veridical.

We see that according to the Naiyāyikas, these two are the ways

---

[11] Vācaspati Miśra, *Tātparyaṭīkā* in *Nyāyadarśanam*, p. 9.

B.K. Matilal, 1986, *Perception*, pp. 164-66.

by which the veridicality of a cognition can be inferred. One form of the inference is for the first cognition of an object which they called *anabhyāsadaśāpanna-jñāna* and the other form of inference is for cognitions under familiar situations or *abhyāsadaśāpanna-jñāna*.

## II

Let us now consider some objections raised by the Svataḥprāmāṇyavādins against the Nyāya position that the *prāmāṇya* can be known by means of a separate cognition which is inferential (*anumiti*). The main objection raised against this position is that it is vitiated by the fallacy of infinite regress (*anavasthā doṣa*).[12] The Svataḥprāmāṇyavādins argue that the inference by means of which the veridicality of a cognition is to be proved, must itself be veridical, otherwise, it cannot prove the truth of another cognition. So, the question of ascertaining the veridicality of the inferential knowledge arises. For proving the veridicality of that inferential cognition another inference would be needed. The same question of proving the veridicality would also arise with regard to the second inference and a third inference would be required for that purpose. In this way, the process will go on infinitely. As a result, veridicality of no cognition can be ascertained.

The Naiyāyikas reply to this charge of infinite regress (*anavasthā*). Their argument is based on the following three tenets:

i. It is not necessary that veridicality of each and every cognition should be ascertained.

ii. Ascertainment of veridicality (*prāmāṇya-niścaya*) is necessary only when there is *prāmāṇya-saṁśaya* about a particular piece of cognition.

iii. A *prāmāṇya-saṁśaya* does not occur in case of each and every cognition.

Let us have some elaboration on the third tenet mentioned

[12] Vācaspati Miśra, *Tātparyaṭīkā* in *Nyāyadarśanam*, p. 9. B.K. Matilal, 1986, *Perception*, pp. 164-66. Rāmānujatātācārya, p. 16.

above. We have already seen that the Naiyāyikas argued in favour of Paraḥprāmāṇyavāda by citing the case of *prāmāṇya-saṁśaya* and showing that Svataḥprāmāṇyavāda does not leave the scope for such doubt. At the same time, they also hold that *prāmāṇya-saṁśaya* does not occur in all cases of cognition. They say that such doubt occurs in some cases and we may feel the need to remove that doubt by ascertaining the veridicality of the cognition in those cases. They argue that, that we do not have doubt about the veridiciality of every cognition is proved by the fact that we do have cognitions of innumerable objects in our lifetime; if every piece of cognition were doubted we would have confined ourselves to one cognition of one object followed by an unending process of doubting and ascertaining the veridicality of each of the cognition in the series.

They argue further that there is at least one cognition where there is no scope for doubt; that is the last cognition which one would have in one's life. Being the "last" cognition, it cannot be succeeded by any cognition whatsoever, thus, the possibility of doubting its veridicality is ruled out, because doubt is a form of cognition. Hence, they justify their third tenet, viz. *prāmāṇya-saṁśaya* is not a universal phenomenon.[13] From the third tenet the other two tenets also follow. And with the help of these three tenets, the Naiyāyikas defend their theory of *parataḥprāmāṇya* from the charge of infinite regress.

The Naiyāyikas deny the possibility of infinite regress by arguing that the inferential cognition by means of which the veridicality of a cognition is ascertained, need not itself be verified to be true, because its veridicality may not be doubted. In case such doubt arises, a second inference may be needed to verify the first one, but there is no chance that this process of verifying the truth would go on infinitely. It is not possible to doubt each and every cognition, because the admission of universal doubt would make our practical life impossible. So, in the cases where the doubt is removed by ascertaining the truth or falsehood of the cognition by

[13] Gaṅgeśa, *Tattvacintāmaṇi*, Pratyakṣa Khaṇḍa, pp. 278-79.

means of an inference, there is no question of having an unending series of inference for verification of the truth of the cognition.

Vācaspati Miśra, however, has given a different answer to the charge of infinite regress in this context. In his *Tātparyaṭīkā* he says that *anumāna* has *svataḥ-prāmāṇya*, which means, it is self-verifying. When we make an inference on the basis of a valid probans (*sat hetu*) which is known to have invariable concomitance with the probandum (*sādhya-avyabhicārī*), the inference is valid. And when we have *anuvyavasāya* (mental perception) to the effect "I infer the *sādhya* on the basis of the *hetu* which has been known to have invariable concomitance with the *sādhya*" we know that the inference is valid or veridical. So, there is no need to make another inference to ascertain its validity and therefore there is no possibility of *anavasthā*.[14]

The later Naiyāyikas, however, interpreted Vācaspati's view that the veridicality of *anumāna* is self-verified in a slightly different way. They say that what Vācaspati meant is that there is no scope for doubting the validity of an inference. In the absence of the apprehension of its being non-veridical (*aprāmāṇya-śaṅkā-virahāt*) its veridicality is considered self-established (*svataḥ- evaprāmāṇyam niściyate*). The later Naiyāyikas have admitted that there are a few more cases of cognition where due to the absence of doubt, their veridicality can be considered as self-established.[15]

---

[14] Vācaspati Miśra, *Tātparyaṭīkā*, p. 9 in *Nyāyadarśanam*.

[15] Udayanācārya, 1911, *Tātparyapariśuddhi*, pp. 117-18 in *Saṭikanyāya-vārttikatātparyapariśuddhi*, ed. Siva Candra Sarvabhauma, Calcutta: Asiatic Society.

Udayanācārya said that there are three types of cognition, the veridicality of which is beyond doubt. These are *anumiti* (inferential congnition), *anuvyavasāya* (mental perception) and *dharmī-jñāna* (cognition of the thing which appears as the subject in a cognition). He claimed that Vācaspati Miśra intended to include all these when he said that *anumāna* is self-verifying.

## III

Now, we shall see how the Naiyāyikas establish their theory of *parataḥprāmāṇya* as against Murārī Miśra's version of *svataḥ-prāmāṇya*. The Naiyāyikas hold that a cognition can be known by a subsequent *anuvyavasāya*, but the veridicality of the cognition is not known by the same mental perception. For ascertaining the veridicality of a cognition, an inferential cognition is needed. Murārī Miśra, a Mīmāṁsā philosopher, on the other hand, held that a cognition and its truth, are both known by the same *anuvyavasāya*. So, it may be questioned why did the Naiyāyikas differ from Murārī Miśra in their opinion in this regard? How would they justify their position?

Let us first have an idea about Murārī Miśra's position. He being a Svataḥprāmāṇyavādin holds that the veridicality of a cognition is known at the same time when the cognition itself is known. He does not admit cognition to be self-revealing (*svaprakāśa*), but holds that every cognition is invariably known by a succeeding *anuvyavasāya*. This *anuvyavasāya* has for its object the preceding cognition, which is called *vyavasāya*. Now this *vyavasāya*, along with its own object, becomes the object of *anuvyavasāya*. For example, if I have a cognition to the effect "this is silver", the subsequent mental perception will be of the form "I am aware that this is silver". Murārī Miśra being a Mīmāṁsaka subscribes to the view that every cognition is naturally (*svabhāvataḥ*) veridical unless some blemishes vitiate it and make it non-veridical. So, the cognition to the effect "this is silver" is veridical and that means, in this cognition a piece of silver is revealed as silver. Here, the subject term "this" stands for a thing that possesses silverness and the predicate term "silver" means silverness which is ascribed to the subject. To know silver as silver is a *pramā*. Now, when this *vyavasāya* is revealed by the *anuvyavasāya* to the effect "I am aware that this is silver", this amounts to knowing that I know silver as silver. And that is the same as knowing that my cognition of the silver is a *pramā*. Thus, *anuvyavasāya* reveals the veridicality of the cognition along with the cognition itself.[16]

The Naiyāyikas' opinion, on the other hand, is that the *anuvyavasāya* of a cognition does not reveal the veridicality of the cognition, because in that case there could be no doubt regarding the veridicality of a cognition (*prāmāṇya-saṁśaya*). But, we do have a doubt regarding the veridicality or truth of a cognition. This point has already been discussed in this chapter.

The Naiyāyikas further argue that since a cognition is either veridical or non-veridical, if, the *prāmāṇya* of a cognition is known in its *anuvyavasāya*, then the non-veridicality of a cognition should also be known in *anuvyavasāya*. In that case, no volition or action will follow from the cognition which is non-veridical. For example, if I see a glass of water and in the subsequent *anuvyavasāya* I become aware that my cognition of water is non-veridical, i.e. I see non-water as water, then I will not make any effort to drink it. But, in fact, many of our actions follow from non-veridical cognitions also, unless we are aware that the cognition is non-veridical.

The Naiyāyikas also explain their position as to why the *prāmāṇya* or *aprāmāṇya* of a cognition cannot be revealed in the *anuvyavasāya* of that cognition. Suppose, I have a cognition to the effect "this is silver", here this refers to a thing that is present before (*purovartī*) the knower. Now the thing, that is present before me, may be a thing possessed of silverness or it may be a thing which does not possess silverness. If it actually possesses silverness, then the cognition of it as silver would be *pramā*. If on the other hand, the thing present before me is a shell, it does not possess silverness and the cognition of it as silver would be *apramā*. So, both the possibilities are open as "this" is a neutral term, which stands merely for something which is present before the knower. And the Naiyāyikas hold that after having the cognition to the effect "this is

---

[16] Pañcānana Śāstrī, 1963, *Muktāvalī Saṁgraha* on *Muktāvalī Ṭīkā*, in *Bhāṣāparicchedaḥ* (Bengali edn), p. 524, Sanskrit Pustak Bhandar.

silver", if we have its *anuvyavasāya* in the form "I am aware that this is a silver", I only know that I am aware of a thing, which is present before me, to be possessed of silverness.[17] This does not amount to knowing silver as silver. Therefore, veridicality or otherwise of the cognition is not known in *anuvyavasāya*; for knowing the *prāmāṇya* or *aprāmāṇya* of any cognition we shall have to depend on *anumāna*.

To conclude, let us sum up the Nyāya theory of *parataḥprāmāṇya-jñapti* (way of ascertaining the veridicality of a cognition). The Naiyāyikas say that since a cognition can be either *pramā* or *apramā*, sometimes a doubt about the veridicality of a cognition arises. In that case there is the need to ascertain the veridicality of the cognition which is under doubt. According to the Nyāya, though a cognition itself can be known by means of its *anuvyavasāya*, its *prāmāṇya* cannot be known in the *anuvyavasāya*. The same is true of the *aprāmāṇya* of a cognition also. So they hold that *anumāna* is the way of ascertaining the veridicality of a cognition. They have shown two types of inference that can establish the veridicality of a cognition. One type of inference which is based on causation of successful volition (*saphala pravṛtti janakatva*) taken as the inferential ground (*hetu*) is meant for proving veridicality of a cognition under unfamiliar situations (*anabhyāsadaśāpanna jñāna*). And the second type of inference based on likeness to previous cognitions (*tajjātīyatva*) as the inferential ground or *hetu* can be employed in cases of cognition under familiar situation. The Naiyāyikas further maintain that there is no need to establish the veridicality of each and every cognition as doubt regarding the veridicality does not arise in every case. There is no need to prove the validity of the inference which proves the veridicality of a cognition, if there is no scope for doubting that inference.

---

17 Rāmānujatātācārya, p. 28.

# 5

# Some Problems Concerning Smṛti

Smṛti (memory) is an important topic of Indian theory of knowledge. According to Indian philosophers, we have basically two types of *jñāna* (cognitive states): *anubhava* (experience) and *smṛti*. By *anubhava* they mean all the types of cognitions that we acquire through different sources of knowledge like *pratyakṣa* (perception), *anumāna* (inference) and *śābda* (verbal testimony). And by *smṛti* they mean recollective cognitions which are only the reproduction of past cognitions belonging to the class of *anubhava*.[1] Some Naiyāyikas, however, admit that we can also have recollective cognition from a recollection itself, *smṛti*, though the first recollection is always from *anubhava*. *Smṛti* is also accepted to play a role in the causation of different types of *anubhava* and for this reason, it is important in the Indian theory of knowledge. In this essay, I shall deal with some problems regarding *smṛti* from the point of view of the Nyāya epistemology.

Let us start with a brief account of origination of *smṛti* according to the Nyāya theory. They define *smṛti* as a cognition which is caused solely by means of *saṁskāra* (impression) that is left behind by a past experience or *pūrvānubhava*. On their theory, every *anubhava* is an

---

1 Viśvanātha, *Kārikāvalī*, *kārikā* 51.

Annambhaṭṭa, *Tarkasaṁgraha*, with *Dīpikā*, ed. Shri Satkariram Bangiya, p. 32, Varanasi: Chowkhamba Sanskrit Series Office, 1969.

event which occurs in time, it originates at one moment, stays till the second moment and gets destroyed at the third moment, but it leaves behind an impression (*saṁskāra*, technically named *bhāvanā*) of its object in the soul of the knower.[2] This impression remains stored in the soul and can produce a recollection of the same object in the knower at anytime, if it is revived under some appropriate conditions. From this account, it is also clear that the knower and the rememberer are the same person. No one can remember what was experienced by any other person. A person can only remember his own experiences. The reviving conditions are called *udbodhaka*, because they activate the impressions to cause recollection. For example, if I had known earlier two persons, say, *x* and *y*, to be good friends and later, if I see one of them, say *x*, I will remember *y*; here the event of seeing *x* functions as the reviving condition, because *x* is one of the relata of the (friendship) relation holding between *x* and *y*. There are many such reviving conditions. In Gautama's *Nyāyasūtra* (3.2.41) twenty-seven reviving conditions are enumerated and Vātsyāyana in his *Bhāṣya of Nyāyasūtra* mentions that there are many more *udbodhaka*s that can be added to those twenty-seven reviving conditions which are enumerated in the *Nyāyasūtra*.[3]

As we know, cognitions are also divided into two classes – veridical (*pramā*) and non-veridical (*apramā*) on the basis of their truth value. So, the question arises whether a recollective cognition belongs to the class of *pramā* or *apramā*. The Naiyāyikas' initial answer to this is that it can be veridical or true if it fulfils two conditions. First, if it is an exact reproduction of the previous *anubhava* which causes it. That means, the content of the recollective cognition must be exactly the same, neither more nor less than the content of the previous *anubhava*, which is its cause. Second, the previous *anubhava*, which is the cause of recollective

[2] Viśvanātha, *Kārikāvalī*, *kārikā* 51. Annambhaṭṭa, *Tarkasaṁgraha*, p. 32. Viśvanātha, *kārikā* 160 and *Muktāvalī* on it.

[3] Vātsyāyana, *Bhāṣya* on *Nyāyasūtra* 3.2.41, p. 880.

cognition, must itself be true or veridical. If the *anubhava* of an object is true, then the recollection being an exact reproduction of it (*yathānubhava*) would also be true. Likewise, a recollective cannot be *yathārtha* (true) if the past *anubhava* which caused it was not true. Being an exact reproduction of a non-veridical *anubhava*, recollective cognition would also be non-veridical (*ayathārtha*). That means the truth of recollection is dependent on the truth of the past cognition, which is its cause. And for this reason, the Naiyāyikas hold that even if a recollective cognition is true, it cannot be granted the status of *pramā*. It is considered as *yathārtha* in a weaker sense, in a sense being *yathānubhava* i.e. an exact representation of the past experience. A cognition that is true in its own right can only be regarded as *pramā*, so a recollective cognition is not a *pramā*.[4]

But the final opinion of the Naiyāyikas, as stated by Udayanācārya, is that a recollective cognition, i.e. *smṛti*, cannot even be *yathārtha* in the true sense of the term. A recollection brings to the knower's mind an object which was experienced in the past, but is not present at the moment of recollection. Now a cognition to be veridical must be *yathārtha*, which means it must agree with its object. But a recollective cognition fails to agree with its object because in recollection, the object is presented as it was at the time of previous experience of the object; since that time has elapsed, the object is not in that state at the present time; so, the recollection cannot correspond to the object at this moment; in other words, it does not present the object as it is at this moment; therefore, it cannot be regarded as *yathārtha*.[5]

Now, if, on the Nyāya theory of knowledge, *smṛti* cannot be true at all, then a serious problem would arise. The Nyāya account of the causation of three types of *anubhava* or non-recollective cognition,

---

4 Udayanācārya, *Nyāyakusumāñjali*, *stavaka* 4, *kārikā* 1 with *Kusumāñjaliparimāla Ṭīkā* by Haridas Bhattacharya, p. 156.

5 Udayanācārya, 1911, *Tātparyapariśuddhi*, pp. 191-95, Calcutta: Asiatic Society.

viz. inferential cognition (*anumiti*), cognition by comparison (*upamiti*) and testimonial cognition (*śābdabodha*), shows that in each case *smṛti* is included in the set of their causal conditions. For (*anumiti*), the recollection of the relation of pervasion (*vyāpti smṛti*); for knowledge by comparison (*upamiti*), recollection of the statement of similarity (*atideśa vākya*) and for cognition by verbal testimony (*śabda*), the recollection of things meant by words (*padajñāna-janya-padārthasmṛti*) are needed as causal conditions. Now a question may be raised: if recollections are untrue, then will they not vitiate the cognitions that are produced with their help? It that is true, then, how can resulting cognitions be veridical and *pramā*?

We can try a solution to this problem. It can be said that only particular entities change over a gap of time, but universal properties or relations do not change with time. The relation of pervasion (*vyāpti sambandha*), the similarity between two classes of entity and the meaning relation between words and things are universal relations. And the recollection of these is considered as causal conditions of *anumiti*, *upamiti* and *śābdabodha* respectively. So, if the original cognitions, i.e. *anubhava* of these relations, are true, their recollection would also be true if reproduced correctly. When one perceives that the smoke is pervaded by the fire, or hears that the bison (*gavaya*) is similar to the cow, or knows that the word "cow" denotes an animal qualified by cowness, one is having knowledge of some universal facts which do not change with time. In the case of *vyāpti sambandha*, we know that smoke, as qualified by smokeness, is pervaded by fire as qualified by firehood. So, this is a universal relation that holds between smoke and fire at any time. *Upamāna pramāṇa* depends on the knowledge of similarity holding between two classes of entities like cow and *gavaya*. This similarity also holds universally between any cow and any bison for all the times. And a meaning relation between a word and a thing, say, the word "cow" and an animal possessing cowness holds for all time. Whenever the word "cow" is uttered, it would be taken to mean an animal possessing cowness. All these relations are unchanging. Therefore, at the time of remembering them, they can be said to be the same as they were at the time of the previous cognition (*anubhava*) of them. So, recollection, even though was not granted the status of *pramā*, cannot vitiate the cognition, which is causally dependent on them.

Another problem regarding *smṛti* that I would like to bring up here is about the form and the object of recollective cognition. It has been said that *smṛti* is always about a previously known object (*pūrvānubhūta-viṣaya-viṣayaka*). And it has also been said that the content of *smṛti* cannot be more or less than the content of the previous cognition, which is its cause; they have exactly the same content. This is quite obvious because the previous cognition becomes its cause through the impression (*saṁskāra*) of its content. Since no cognition can produce an impression of anything more than its object, *smṛti*, which is caused by the impression, cannot be about anything more than what was previously cognized.

And again, since cognition leaves behind impression of the whole of its content, its recollection should also be about the whole of it and not less than that. So *smṛti* is said to have the same content as its cause, i.e. the past cognition (*anubhava-samāna-viṣayaka smṛti*). It should however be mentioned here that though a recollection can never include in its content anything that was not in the content of the past cognition, a recollection can sometimes be partial, losing a part of the content of the past cognition. In such cases, the content of recollection is less than that of the past cognition. This happens either because a part of the impression does not get revived due to some reasons; or because a part of the impression is destroyed due to a long time gap or due to some disease afflicting its owner. This is called *pramuṣṭaviṣayā smṛti*.[6] It is actually a case of partial forgetting, which we experience sometimes in our life. However,

---

[6] Keśava Miśra, 1968, *Tarkabhāṣā*, with Hindi commentary, ed. Badrināth Śukla, p. 26, Vanarasi: Motilal Banarsidass.

it is held that a recollection normally has the same content as that of the past *anubhava*, which causes it.

Let us now ask what we actually remember when we have a recollection of a previously known object? Is it the object as such or object as previously experienced by me. For example, suppose I visited the Taj Mahal, a famous monument, in the past, and now, on hearing someone talking about it, I remember that monument. Now, do I remember simply the Taj Mahal or remember it as the Taj Mahal seen by me? It seems that the knower is somehow conscious of his previous experience along with the remembered object. It may be that we are not explicit about it and merely say "That Taj Mahal", but the recollection seems to include the past experience too. If this is admitted, then it would follow that the content of memory includes something more than what was the content of previous experience (*pūrvānubhava*). For, the past experience which left the impression was not a past experience at the time of its occurrence. Hence, its object, which was known at that time, was not previously known (*pūrvānubhūta*). But, if the object, while being remembered, is remembered as previously known, then the object of memory and the object of previous experience which causes the memory do not have an equal content. So this would be a problem for the Naiyāyikas. This problem would not have arisen had the Naiyāyikas admitted that every cognition is self-revealing (*svaprakāśa*). In that case, every experience would leave the impression of itself along with its object, and the memory cognition, having the same content as the previous experience, could take the form of "that thing which was previously known".

Advaita Vedāntins and Prābhākara Mīmāṁsakas, who subscribe to the theory of Svaprakāśavāda, can say that the previous experience which causes recollection includes in its content both the object and itself. For them, there would be no problem in admitting recollection to include the previous experience of the object in its content. But the Naiyāyikas are Parataḥprakāśavādins. They maintain that a cognition cannot reveal itself; it can be known by another cognition which is an internal perception called *anuvyavasāya*. Cognition of an object is called *vyavasāya* which can be known by a subsequent *anuvyavasāya*. This *anuvyavasāya* reveals the first cognition along with its object. So, it seems that on the Nyāya epistemology, if recollective cognition has to include the previous knownness of its object in its content, then it must be caused by *anuvyavasāya*, rather than by *vyavasāya*. But, this also would not be acceptable to the Naiyāyikas, because they do not admit that every cognition must necessarily be known; in other words, they deny *avaśyavedyatva* of cognition.[7] That means, there remains the possibility that there can be cognitions of which the knower is not conscious or aware. So, it cannot be admitted that *smṛti* is always caused by *anuvyavasāya*. In that case, past cognition of an object cannot enter into the content of every recollective cognition.

In Vātsyāyana's commentary on the *Nyāyasūtra*, we find a discussion about the object of *smṛti*.[8] There, Vātsyāyana states that the object of recollection is not limited only to the thing which was previously known; it may include the previous cognition and the knower also. He explained that we have recollective cognition in four forms:

1. I knew that thing;
2. I have knowledge of that thing;
3. That thing has been known by me; and
4. that thing has been the object of my knowledge.

All these forms of recollection show that the knower, knowledge and the known thing – appear in the content of recollective cognition. However, in his discussion, the commentator does not mention whether every recollective cognition takes all the three, viz. the knower, known and knowledge within its content. Usually,

---

7 Vardhamānopādhyāya, *Nyāyanibandhaprakāśa* on Udayana's *Tātparyapariśuddhi*, p. 49, Calcutta: Asiatic Society, 1911.

8 Vātsyāyana, *Bhāṣya* on *Nyāyasūtra* 3.1.14, *Nyāyadarśanam*.

the form of recollective cognition is mentioned as "that thing" referring to the thing, which was known in the part, in contrast with the form of cognition as "this thing", which occurs when the thing is present before the knower. Apparently, the recollective cognition of the form "that thing" does not include the past knowledge and the knower within its content.

Considering the epistemological tenets of the Nyāya school, which we have discussed earlier; viz. cognition, is revealed by another cognition (Parataḥprakāśavāda) and that every cognition need not be cognized (*avaśyavedyatvābhāva*) by the knower; it seems that the Naiyāyikas would not accept the position that *smṛti-jñāna* is always of the form "I knew that thing", including - the knower, known and knowledge in its content. In some cases we have the recollection of the thing only. Maybe, later we can also remember our past experiences too. So it might be that on hearing something about the monument Taj Mahal, I could remember just that monument, its image only appearing in my mind; later. I could further recall my past act of knowing it.

It may, however, be argued that it has been accepted by the Naiyāyikas that in every recollective cognition, the object is remembered as "that thing", meaning thereby that the thing was there in the past. Thatness (*tattā*) is considered the qualifier of the object of memory. By the property of (*tattā*), the object of memory is distinguished from the object of perception where the object is present before the knower at the time of perception. In perception, the object is mentioned as "this thing". Thisness or *idantā* qualifies the object of perception.

Now, the point is: does not *tattā* mean the property of being the object of past experience (*pūrvānubhūta viṣayatva*)? And then the past experience must have entered into the content of recollection, otherwise, how could one remember it as a thing known in the past?

But, there is another aspect to the problem. It will be difficult to explain how *tattā*, in the sense of being the object of past experience, becomes a part of the recollective awareness. For, the experience, which gives rise to recollective cognition, was not past at the time of its occurrence. The *anubhava* and its object, all were present. So the *saṁskāra* left by the previous experience cannot include *tattā*, which is taken to mean "being the object of past experience". And if, in the absence of the impression of *tattā*, there is recollective awareness which includes *tattā*, then it is to be admitted that *anubhava* and the memory cognition resulting from it do not have the same content, rather the memory cognition includes something more. *Tattā* was not experienced previously, still it becomes a part of the content of the memory cognition.

The Naiyāyikas solve this problem by denying that *tattā* means the property of being the object of past experience. They hold that memory cognition does not exceed the content of the previous experience (*pūrvānubhava*) by adding a new property of *tattā*. The same thing which was experienced as "this" is remembered as "that". The change in the use of expression (*śābda-prayoga*) is due to the fact that memory cognition is caused by impression (*saṁskāraja-jñāna*). For the same reason, *pratyabhijñā* (recognitive awareness), which is caused partly by *saṁskāra*, takes the form "*this* is *that* Devadatta" meaning thereby this is the (same) Devadatta (whom I had known previously). *Pratyabhijñā* being a perceptual experience (*pratyakṣa anubhava*), it contains the word "this" in its expression; and being caused partly by impression also, it contains the word "that". What is known through sense-object contact is presented as "this" and what is known through impression (*saṁskāra*) is presented as "that". So to be produced by *saṁskāra* is the cause of the use of the word "that" with regard to the object remembered, though objectwise there is no difference between recollective awareness (*smṛti*) and non-recollective awareness (*anubhava*). It is a fact that from an *anubhava* of the form "this is a pot", we do not have remembrance of the form "this pot"; nor is there an experience of the form "that pot" corresponding to the remembrance "that pot". From the impression left by the experience of the form "this pot", the remembrance of the same object, along with the properties and the time of the occurrence of the experience, results; but the word "that" instead of "this" is used in the verbal expression of the remembrance. Gaṅgeśa in his *Tattvacintāmaṇi*[9] gives this solution to the anticipated objection that a recollective cognition includes something more to its content, which was not in the content of the previous *anubhava*. By admitting the sameness of the content of both the remembrance and the previous experience which the cause of remembrance, Gaṅgeśa also justified the Nyāya view that *smṛti* is a non-veridical cognition (*ayathārtha-jñāna*). Since in memory cognition, its object is presented as it was at the time of previous experience, the memory cognition does not correspond to the object as it is at the time of the occurrence of the recollection. The difference consists in respect of the time which qualifies the object at the time of the occurrence of two different cognitions, viz. experience and recollection.

[9] Gaṅgeśa, 1974, *Tattvacintāmaṇi*, Pratyakṣa Khaṇḍa, p. 843, Delhi: Motilal Banarasidass.

# 6

# Perceptual Cognition as Direct Awareness

PRATYAKṢA-JÑĀNA (sense perception) is the first and foremost form of awareness. Our knowledge begins with sense perception. This form of awareness is regarded as direct or immediate awareness.[1] So a perceptual cognition can be characterized as:

i. a cognition that is produced by the contact between our sense organ and an object; and
ii. it is immediate or direct (*sākṣāt*).

Whichever cognition is considered to be a perception must possess these two characteristic. But there is a problem regarding the second characteristic. If immediacy means being produced by sense-object contact without the mediation of any state of cognition, then perhaps only *nirvikalpaka pratyakṣa* would be regarded as perceptual cognition. Starting from a determinate perception (*savikalpaka pratyakṣa*) of the form "This is *x*", each variety of perception is in fact produced by the sense organ through an intervening cognition of some kind.

Let us take the following cases of perception (*pratyakṣa*):

1. *Savikalpaka pratyakṣa* (determinate perception),

---

[1] Keśava Miśra, 1968, *Tarkabhāṣā*, with Hindi translation by Badrināth Śukla, p. 64, Varanasi: Motilal Banarsidass.

2. *pratyabhijñā* (recognitive awareness),
3. *saṁśaya* (doubt),
4. *bhrama* (illusion),
5. *parāmarśa* (special cause of inference), and
6. *abhāva pratyakṣa* (perecption of the absence of some object).

In all the above instances, perception is mediated by a memory cognition at least. The perception of absence is preceded by a *tarka* (indirect argument) also, besides a memory cognition. The first determinate cognition of a thing, say, a cow, as "This is a cow" is preceded by an indeterminate perception of cowness, the qualifying property, though in later cases, perception of the same kind of the thing may be mediated by a memory cognition of cowness.

## I

We shall analyse each case of perception one by one to show the role of memory cognition in each case.

### Savikalpaka Pratyakṣa (Determinate Perception)

When we perceive something as characterized by some property, e.g. "This is a table", this perception is called a determinate perception. It is a qualificative cognition (*viśiṣṭa buddhi*), the content of which is analysable into three elements: the qualificand (*dharmī/viśeṣya*), the qualifier (*dharma/viśeṣaṇa*) and relation (*saṁsarga*) between the two. This sort of cognition requires a prior cognition of the qualifier property.[2] So, immediately after our eyes come in contact with a table, we cannot have a perception of the form "This is a table", in between the sense-object contact and the determinate perception, there has to be a cognition of the qualifier tableness. If the perceiver had previously perceived a table, then on the present occasion, he can have a memory cognition of previously perceived tableness as

[2] Viśvanātha, 1988, *Kārikāvalī-Muktāvalī*, ed. Shankararam Shastri, p. 431 (*Muktāvalī* on *kārikā* 58), Delhi: Chowkhamba Sanskrit Pratisthan.

soon as his eyes come in contact with a table. After that, he can perceive the thing in contact with his eyes as a table, i.e. as qualified by tableness. But if the perceiver perceives a table for the first time, there is no possibility of having a memory cognition of tableness, so to explain this case, the Naiyāyikas have admitted a state of indeterminate cognition (*nirvikalpaka pratyakṣa*) where the qualifier property as such is perceived immediately after the sense-object contact, which in turn causes the qualificative cognition.[3] What they mean is that when a perceiver's sense organ comes in contact with an object, say, a table, which is actually a object-complex, comprising an entity, a property, and a relation between two, all the three elements, viz. table, tableness and their relation, are given to the senses and are grasped by a sense organ separately, in an unrelated way. At the next stage, they are perceived as connected. That means, at the first stage, we have an indeterminate perception that functions as a cause of the determinate perception. So we see that in the case of determinate cognition, either an indeterminate cognition or a memory cognition plays the role of an intermediary between the sense organ and perception.

## Pratyabhijñā (Recognitive Awareness)

*Pratyabhijñā* is the awareness of the sameness of an object of the present experience with the object of a past experience. This is considered by the Naiyāyikas to be a case of sense perception.[4] When we have such a perception as "This is that person whom I met in the office", we recognize the person to be the one who was the object of my past experience; the adjective "that" stands for the object of past experience (*tattā*). Suppose, I met the person at a previous time in a different location and at present I perceive the person in another place, how can the object which was perceived previously, be the object of our perception? Our sense organs can

---

[3] Gaṅgeśa, 1974, *Tattvacintāmaṇi*, Pratyakṣa Khaṇḍa, p. 817, Delhi: Motilal Banarsidass.

[4] Ibid., pp. 562-63.

be in contact with only such objects which are present before the perceiver, so no property having reference to the past time and distance place is related to the sense organ at the present time and place. So, how can such perception take place? The Naiyāyikas hold that on seeing the person who is present before the perceiver, impression left behind by the past experience of the person is revived, and the perceiver remembers his past experience. Through this memory cognition, the property of *tattā* is connected to the sense organ, which is in contact with the object (the person in this case) present before the perceiver.[5] Thus, the object (the person) is perceived as characterized by both the properties of thisness (*idantā*) and *tattā* and the cognition is expressed as "This (what is present before) is that (previously seen) object". This perception clearly depends on the preceding memory cognition through which the property of thatness is related to sense organ.

## Saṁśaya (Doubt)

Doubt is a form of cognition, according to Indian philosophers. It is the opposite of the state of cognition which is known as certainty (*niścaya*). The Naiyāyikas hold that doubt is always perceptual. When we perceive a thing but are not sure whether the thing is *x* or *y*, we have a doubtful cognition, which is usually expressed, in an interrogative sentence "Is it *x* or *y*?" Here we do not perceive either of the properties *x*-hood or *y*-hood, but what we perceive

---

5 Gaṅgeśa, 1974, *Tattvacintāmaṇi*, Pratyakṣa Khaṇḍa, p. 839. There is however a difference of opinion between the old and the new schools of the Nyāya as to whether the impression (*saṁskāra*) or the memory cognition (*smṛti*) is the cause of *pratyabhijñā*. The *navya* (new) school accepts memory cognition to be the cause, whereas the *prācīna* (old) school takes impressions to be the cause. I have followed the new school in this case.

Raghunātha, 1976, *Padārthatattvanirūpaṇam*, ed. with Bengali translation by Madhusūdana Nyāyācārya, p. 49, Calcutta: Sanskrit College.

suggests these two properties as alternatives, which cannot be present together in a thing.[6] If we could perceive either *x*-hood or *y*-hood as the qualifier, we would have a cognition, which is of the nature of certainty as "This is *x*" or "This is *y*". That means when we are in a position to assert one predicate in particular, excluding the possibility of its denial, we have a certain cognition (*niścaya*).

Let us now see how a doubtful cognition is caused. Suppose I see from a distance a thing with a medium height and width standing upright; it looks like either a man or a tree trunk. Now the property of being a man and the property of being a tree trunk are incompatible; hence, both of them cannot be perceived to be present there; neither any one of these properties is perceived to be present in exclusion of the other because in that case there would have been a certain cognition predicating one property to the subject. How do then these properties appear to qualify the subject alternately. These properties, which figure as predicates in a doubtful cognition, are technically called *koṭi*s. The Naiyāyikas explain that on seeing some property like a particular dimension which is common to both a man and a tree trunk, the perceiver is reminded of these properties, viz. being a man and being a tree trunk. These properties are thus related to the sense organ through memory and appear to the person to be present there in the perceived object. But the perceiver being aware of the incompatibility between the two properties, cannot ascribe both to the present object but ascribes them alternately and therefore is in a state of doubt or uncertainty. So in case of doubt too, memory acts as a causal condition, by presenting *koṭi*s to the perceiver's sense organ.

**Bhrama (Illusion)**

According to the Naiyāyikas an illusory perception or misperception is a case of perceiving a property as qualifying a thing that does

---

6 Gautama, 1985, *Nyāyadarśanam* with Vātsyāyana's *Bhāṣya* and other commentaries, pp. 234-40, New Delhi: Munshiram Manoharlal.

not actually possess it.[7] For example, when we perceive a thing, which is actually a piece of rope, to be a snake, we erroneously apply the property of snakeness to a thing where it is absent. So, it is a case of misperception. But the question is: how can snakeness, which is not present in the thing that is in contact with our sense organ, be the object of perception? As we know, perception can be only about objects which are present before the perceiver. The Naiyāyikas say that snakeness which is a property of real snakes has been perceived by the cognizer in the past at some other place. Impressions of past experience are stored in the cognizer's soul. Now, when our eyes come in contact with a piece of rope, its similarity with the snake causes a remembrance of snake/snakeness due to the revival of the impressions of past experience of snake and snakeness. This memory cognition functions as the operative relation (*sannikarṣa*) between the sense organ and snakeness. This operative relation is a non-physical relation and is given the name *jñāna-lakṣaṇā sannikarṣa*, which means an operative relation that is identical with a cognition of the object.[8] So, there being a physical operative relation between the eyes and the object present before (which is actually a piece of rope) and snakeness being related to the eyes through *jñāna-lakṣaṇā sannikarṣa*, there arises an illusory perception ascribing snakeness to an object which does not possess it. So, we find that memory cognition intervenes between the sense-object contact and the illusory perception.

## Parāmarśa

*Parāmarśa* is a perceptual cognition which is the immediately preceding causal condition of an inferential cognition. According to the Naiyāyikas, the inferential process is like this. Suppose a person knows that wherever smoke is present, fire is also there. This sort of relation between two things is known as *vyāpti sambandha* (relation of pervasion). Now the person, who knew this relation,

---

7 Gaṅgeśa, 1974, *Tattvacintāmaṇi*, Pratyakṣa Khaṇḍa, p. 401.

8 Viśvanātha, 1988, *Kārikāvalī-Muktāvalī*, pp. 466-67.

sees smoke coming out of a hill, and the sight of smoke reminds him of the relation of pervasion which the smoke has with the fire. That means, he has a memory cognition of the relation of *vyāpti*. After this, he sees the smoke on the hill, not simply as smoke but as characterized by the property of being pervaded by the fire. Thus, he has the perception to the effect "The hill has the smoke which is pervaded by the fire" and this perception is called *parāmarśa*. Previously, he had the perception to the effect "The hill has smoke", then he had the remembrance that the smoke is pervaded by the fire, after which he had the perception called *parāmarśa*. Immediately after that, an inferential cognition to the effect "The hill has fire" follows.[9] So we find that sense contact with smoke, which is the *hetu* (inferential mark), mediated by the memory of the relation of pervasion, which the smoke (*hetu*) has with the fire (*sādhya*) gives rise to the perceptual cognition called *parāmarśa* which finally causes *anumiti* (inferential cognition).

## Perception of the Absence of a Thing

According to the Naiyāyikas, *abhāva* (absence) of something is a real thing; just as a table is real, its absence too is real. If a table is present somewhere in the world, its absence also is to be found somewhere in the world. For example, a table is present in one room of a house, but there is no table in another room. And the Naiyāyikas hold that just as we can perceive a table, we can also perceive the absence of a table. The absence of a perceptible thing is perceivable.

Let us now see how, according to the Naiyāyikas an absence is perceived. By perception of an absence is meant perception of the absence of something at some place. The thing which is absent is called the counterpositive (*pratiyogī*) and the place where the absence is located is the *adhikaraṇa* (locus of the absence). So, an absence is perceived along with its *pratiyogī* and *adhikaraṇa*.

For the perception of an absence, the following causal conditions are to be fulfilled:

[9] Viśvanātha, 1988, *Kārikāvalī-Muktāvalī*, pp. 471-73.

i. Sense contact with the locus.

ii. Memory cognition of the counterpositive.

iii. Non-perception of the counterpositive accompanied by an indirect argument (*tarka*) to the effect "if it (the counterpositive) were present here, then it would have been perceived" (because all other causal conditions are fulfilled).[10]

There is something paradoxical about the perception of absence, as an absence is perceived along with its counterpositive, but non-perception of the counterpositive is a condition for perception of an absence. Therefore, it turns out that there should be both perception and non-perception of the counterpositive. But how is that possible? The solution to the problem is that non-perception here is meant that the counterpositive is not perceived through normal (*laukika*) sense–object contact; the perception of the counterpositive here is a case of extraordinary perception where a memory cognition of the counterpositive connects it with the sense organ. So, the point is that an absence is perceived as qualified by its counterpositive, but the counterpositive is not present in the locus of the absence, hence, there is no normal sense contact with it. The counterpositive is, however, remembered due to some reason like need and expectation. (For example, on entering a room, I may look for a table because I need it to keep my things on. Or, in a classroom, I may look for a blackboard as it is expected to be there. Thus, in these cases, we remember the counterpositives and find that they are absent.) Now the perceiver's sense organ, which is in contact with the locus of the absence, gets related in a non-physical way (*alaukika sannikarṣa*) to the counterpositive by means of this rememberance (*jñāna-lakṣaṇā sannikarṣa*). Therefore, there is an extraordinary perception of the counterpositive which qualifies the absence.

The Naiyāyikas have also said that non-perception of the counterpositive to be effective in causing perception of the absence

---

[10] Viśvanātha, 1988, *Kārikāvalī–Muktāvalī*, pp. 446-48.

must be accompanied by an indirect argument (*tarka*). So, besides memory cognition of the counterpositive, another cognition in the form of *tarka* precedes the perception of an absence.

## II

After considering the six varieties of perception mentioned above, we find that each of them is caused by at least one cognition which intervenes between the sense-object contact and the resulting perception. There are a few other cases of perceptual cognition which are also causally dependent on memory.

This leads us to think about the concept of immediacy, which is considered as an essential characteristic of perceptual cognition. It is clear from the above discussion that immediacy cannot be taken to mean not to be mediated by any state of cognition or, in other words, not caused by some cognition (*jñāna ajanyatva*). What does it mean them?

Śrīharṣa, a Vedāntin, in his book *Khaṇḍanakhaṇḍakhādya*, which is a critique of the Nyāya-Vaiśeṣika theories of *pramāṇa*, has considered a number of ways in which immediacy can be interpreted and have shown that none stands to reason.

Śrīharṣa seems to have taken into account all possible interpretations of the concept of *sākṣāttva* and has argued against each of them. Let us consider here one or two interpretations of *sākṣāttva* (immediacy) from Śrīharṣa's text *Khaṇḍanakhaṇḍakhādya*. These are the following:[11]

> *avyabahitārtha pramātvam sākṣāttvam* ।
>
> or
>
> *avyavahitadhītvam sākṣātdhītvam* ।
> *jñānājanya jñānatvam pratyakṣatvam* ।
> *Jñānsaya jātibhedaḥ kaścitsākṣāttvam* ।

---

[11] Śrīharṣa, 1979, *Khaṇḍanakhaṇḍakhādya*, ed. Swami Yogindrananda, pp. 336, 344-45, Varanasi: Ṣaḍdarśanaprakāśa Pratiṣṭhānam.

Śrīharṣa explains the first sense of *sākṣāttva* as *avyatahita-arthapramā*, which literally means the knowledge of an object which is not separated. It is apparent that the meaning is incomplete. Separation is a relative term that expects another term from which the thing is said to be not separated. Now, what is this thing from which the object of knowledge is not separated? To say that the object is not separated from the sense organ is only a roundabout way of saying that the object is in contact with the sense organ. An immediate or direct cognition would then mean nothing more than a cognition that is about an object which is in contact with the sense organ.

He says that if immediacy means this, then our inferential cognition about our own eyeballs would be an immediate cognition since the visual sense organ is situated in the eyeball, and hence the eyeballs are in contact with the sense organ. But we cannot perceive our own eyeballs. Therefore, this meaning of immediacy unduly applies to some non-perceptual cognition, and for that reason, it is not acceptable.

Śrīharṣa considers a slightly different version of the same meaning, e.g. an immediate or direct cognition is one which the knower has when no other object stands as an obstruction between the knower and the object of knowledge. For example, if no curtain is drawn on the window of my room, I can have an immediate cognition of things outside. But this interpretation of immediacy also suffers from the defect of over coverage. The Nyāya–Vaiśeṣika philosophers admit some all-pervasive objects like space and time, which according to them, are imperceptible. Since they are all-pervasive, nothing can stand as an obstruction between them and the knower. So, a non-perceptual cognition of time or space can be called an immediate cognition; thus, there is an over coverage (*ativyāpti*).

There is a still different way of understanding *avyavahitatva*, which was considered by Śrīharṣa. It may mean "not being preceded by a cognition of something which is required for the cognition of the given object". It may be understood by contrasting it with a case of mediate cognition or *vyavahitadhī*. Take the case of an inferential cognition. We infer fire from smoke, and this cognition is invariably preceded by a cognition of smoke which is the inferential mark, without the cognition of which no inference can take place. So this is a mediate (*vyavahita*) cognition. Its opposite, i.e. not being preceded by such a cognition, which is necessary for causing the perception, would be *avyavahitatva* (immediacy).

But Śrīharsa points out that this interpretation of immediacy would be too narrow as it would not apply to some cases of perceptual cognition like the cognition of some relative qualities like farness, nearness or being younger, being older, or being distinct. To know something is far or near, we must have a cognition of the thing from which it is far or near. So such cognition is invariably preceded by a cognition of the other thing with reference to which farness or nearness of the thing is cognized. Therefore, such a perceptual cognition cannot be immediate if immediacy is taken in the sense as interpreted here.

Immediacy, if understood in the second way – as *jñānājānya* (*jñāna-ajanya*) – i.e. not being caused by any cognition, will not be acceptable for the simple reason that even the simplest form of determinate perception is caused by cognition and hence would lack immediacy in this sense. We have already discussed this point while considering *savikalpaka pratyakṣa*. We have seen that every determinate cognition presupposes a cognition of the qualifier, i.e. the property to be predicated to the subject of the determinate perception. So, it is causally dependent on some cognition, which means it is *jñānajanya*.

### III

From the above critical analysis by Śrīharṣa, it is clear that immediacy cannot be defined in terms of direct or unmediated occurrence of the perceptual cognition. But the Nyāya–Vaiśeṣika philosophers maintain that as long as a cognition is caused and preceded by sense-object contact, even if it is also preceded by some other causal condition, it is a direct or immediate awareness. The intervening causal condition does not remove the sense-object contact, so the contact continues to be there till the cognition is produced. Hence, it is a direct product of the sense-object contact.

The Nyāya-Vaiśeṣika philosophers hold that all such cognitions, which are the direct product of sense-object contact, possess a universal (*jāti*), which is named *sākṣāttva.* This *jāti* is admitted on the basis of the uniform cognition of the form *aham sākṣāt karomi* (I am directly aware of it).[12] After having known an object, say, a pot through sense organs, we may have an introspective awareness (*anuvyavasāya*) of that cognition and that introspective awareness takes the form "I am directly aware of a pot" (*aham ghaṭam sākṣāt karomi*). In case of other types of cognition like inferential or verbal cognitions we have introspective cognition of the form "I infer so and so", or, "I am having a verbal cognition of so and so". Thus, corresponding to each type of cognition the Nyāya-Vaiśeṣika philosophers admitted a *jāti*, like *pratyakṣatva* or *sākṣāttva, anumititva, upamititva* and *śābdatva.* Now, every *jāti* is a simple unanalysable property (*akhaṇḍa dharma*). So, in this case too, *sākṣāttva* is an unanalysable property. Therefore, it cannot be defined in terms of other properties. But, perceptual cognition can be defined in terms of *sākṣāttva jāti,* since this *sākṣāttva jāti* is the exclusive property of *pratyakṣa-jñāna.*

Śrīharṣa considers *jñānasya jātibhedaḥ sākṣāttva* as one of the interpretations of *sākṣāttva* and rejected that too. We shall have here a brief discussion of Śrīharṣa's objections against it.[13]

The first objection raised by Śrīharṣa against *sākṣāttva jāti* is that this *jāti* cannot be a property of all perceptual cognitions. It fails to be present in some specific cases of perceptual cognition. The

---

12 Gaṅgeśa, 1974, *Tattvacintāmaṇi*, Pratyakṣa Khaṇḍa, p. 443.

13 Śrīharṣa, 1979, *Khaṇḍanakhaṇḍakhādya*, pp. 446-48.

case cited by him is an introspective cognition of the knowledge of atomic particles (*paramāṇu*). Atoms are not perceptible because of their smallest size, but we can infer them. After having an inferential cognition (*anumiti*) of atoms, we can also have an introspective awareness (*anuvyavasāya*) of the cognition of atoms. Since introspective awareness is a perceptual cognition, it possesses the universal *sākṣāttva* and the cognition of atoms (*paramāṇu*), being a part of the introspective awareness, should also possess *sākṣāttva*. But, can it be admitted that the cognition of imperceptible atoms possess *sākṣāttva jāti?*

To this objection, an answer can be given from the Nyāya point of view. Though atoms are imperceptible and cannot be in contact with external sense organs, at the time of introspective awareness of the inferential cognition of atoms, atoms are related to the internal sense organ (*manas*) through the non-physical relation (*alaukika sannikarṣa*) named *jñāna-lakṣaṇā sannikarṣa*. Introspective awareness as *anuvyavasāya* being an internal perception *mānasa pratyakṣa*, has *sākṣāttva jāti* and its object, i.e. the cognition of atoms can have *sākṣāttva* as being a part of it. But the point is that only with respect to a cognition that is caused by physical sense-object relation (*laukika sannikarṣa*), we can have introspective cognition of the form *aham sākṣāt karomi* (I directly perceive). So in the case of *paramāṇu* and its cognition, due to the absence of *laukika sannikarṣa*, we do not have an awareness of the form "I directly perceive atoms". Instead, we have the cognition "I am inferentially aware of atoms (*annuminomi*)" or "I know (*jānāmi*) atoms".

Another objection that is raised by Śrīharṣa is that there is partial overlapping of the loci of *sākṣāttva* with the loci of the property of *parokṣatva*; and in such circumstances, none of the two properties can be granted the status of *jāti.* The property of *parokṣatva* should reside in all non-perceptual cognitions and *sākṣāttva* should reside in all perceptual cognitions, but the two should never share a common locus. If such a thing happens, then that prevents those properties from being considered as a *jāti*. This is known as *jāti-bādhaka* (preventing condition) named *sāṅkarya*. And this condition of *sāṅkarya* holds in the case of *sākṣāttva*. Śrīharṣa says, when we infer the existence of a property (*sādhya*) in a thing (*pakṣa)* that is being perceived by us, the property of *parokṣatva* is present in the *sādhya* part of the cognition, but *sākṣāttva* is present in the *pakṣa* part of it. So, *sākṣāttva* and *parokṣatva* are present in one and the same cognition. This is a case of overlapping of their loci.

One possible reply to this objection may be that *parokṣatva* is not a *jāti*, but *sākṣāttva* is; *parokṣatva* is merely the absence of *sākṣāttva*. And partial overlapping of the locus of *sākṣāttva* with the locus of *parokṣatva*, which is not a *jāti*, does not stand in the way of *sākṣāttva* being regarded as a *jāti*. The reason is that the relation between any two universals can be either of incompatibility or of inclusion; for example, cowness and horseness are mutually exclusive or incompatible properties that cannot coexist, but animalhood and manhood have the relation of inclusion. Animalhood includes manhood, because man is a subordinate class under the class of animals. If there were partial overlapping of loci of two universals, then none of the above relations could hold between them. Now, in the case under consideration, *parokṣatva* not being a *jāti*, partial overlapping of its locus with the locus of *sākṣāttva* cannot nullify *jātitva* (universalhood) of *sākṣāttva*.

But this reply is not considered to be satisfactory by Śrīharṣa. He says that there is no justification for granting the status of a *jāti* to *sākṣāttva* and denying it to *parokṣatva*. It could also be the reverse; i.e. *parokṣatva* could be a *jāti*, and *sākṣāttva* would be the absence or negation of *parokṣatva*.

Some of the Naiyāyikas belonging to the Navya (modern school of) Nyāya, however, do not consider *sāṅkarya* or overlapping of loci of two (*jātis*) as a preventing condition of *jātitva* (*jāti-bādhaka*).[14] But, this cannot be treated as a strong defence in favour of the Nyāya position.

---

14 Viśvanātha, 1988, *Kārikāvalī-Muktāvalī*, *Dīnakarī Ṭīkā* on it, p. 105.

At this point, we may try to find out if there is some other way of defending the Nyāya position by overcoming the charge that *sāṅkarya jāti-bādhaka* stands in the way of admitting *sākṣāttva* as a *jāti*. It has been shown that in cases of some inferences where the subject of inference (*pakṣa*) and the inferential mark (*hetu*) are being perceived by the inferer, though the predicate (*sādhya*) is inferred, there is an overlapping of the properties of *sākṣāttva*. Let us take an example. A person sees a hill and also sees that the smoke is coming out of that hill. He previously experienced that where there was smoke, there was fire. On remembering this relation of co-presence which is the relation of *vyāpti* (pervasion), the person has another cognition, which is called *parāmarśa*, to the effect "the hill has smoke which is pervaded by fire (*vahnivyāpya dhūmavān parvataḥ*)". From this cognition follows the inferential cognition of the form "the hill has fire". Now it is alleged that this cognition in the predicate part (*sādhya*), i.e. having fire is inferential and hence *parokṣa*, but in the subject part, i.e. the hill, it is perceptual or *sākṣāt-jñāna*. Therefore, in one and the same cognition both *sākṣāttva* and *parokṣatva* are present. In reply, it can be said from the Nyāya point of view that, when the inferer sees the hill and the smoke which is coming out of the hill, it is a perceptual cognition, no doubt. But, through *vyāpti-jñāna* and *parāmarśa*, when the inference takes place, the hill as such is not known, but it is known as qualified by the fire (*vahniviśiṣṭa parvataḥ*); that means the hill at that time was a part of the object complex, "the hill having conjunction with the fire" and that object complex was not given to the senses because there was no sense contact with the fire which is the *sādhya* or the inferable property. So, the object complex as a whole is inferred. In one single act of knowing, the hill (*pakṣa*), the fire (*sādhya*), and their relation of conjunction are known, and that act of knowing is inferring. Therefore, it cannot be said that the cognition is partially perceptual and partially inferential. Therefore, there is no *sāṅkarya* (partial overlapping) of the locus of *sākṣāttva* with *parokṣatva*.

To conclude, let us sum up the Nyāya-Vaiśeṣika position regarding the concept of direct awareness (*sākṣāttva*). According to them, *sākṣāttva* is a *jāti* which is established on the basis of the internal perception of the form "*aham sākṣātkaromi*" (I am directly aware of) which we have about every cognition that is produced by the sense-object contact (*indriyārtha-sannikarṣa*). So direct awareness (*sākṣāt-jñāna*) means a *jñāṇa* having *sākṣāttva jāti*; and *pratyakṣa-jñāna* is a cognition which is produced by sense-object contact and is characterized by *sākṣāttva jāti*.

# 7

# Salient Features of the Nyāya Theory of Object-Perception

To talk about the perception of an object, we must first be clear about the notion of an object. The term object, I think, is not used in precisely the same sense in the two expressions, viz. "object of perception" and "perception of object". On the Nyāya view, at least, the term "object" in the first expression has a broader meaning which includes the perceiver or the subject who perceives and the perceptual cognition itself, besides perceptible external entities. But in the expression "perception of object", "object" seems to be contrasted with the subject and the cognitive state of perception. It thus excludes the perceiver, the perceptual cognition and other internal states, which can be perceived only as characterizing the owner subject. So, "object" here would mean only external entities and perception would mean external perception. According to the Nyāya school, perceptible external objects include substance (*dravya*), quality (*guṇa*), motion (*karma*), universal (*jāti*), the relation of inherence (*samavāya*) and absence (*abhāva*) of these entities. We perceive substances like trees, buildings, tables and chairs, qualities like colour, taste, smell and size, movement of fans, cars, etc. In addition to these, we perceive universals like tableness, redness and motionhood, which are present respectively in substance, quality and motion; we perceive the relation of inherence that connects these entities with their appropriate relata. And the Naiyāyikas hold that we also perceive the absence of these entities at different places. But all substances, all qualities, all movements, all universals and all absences are not perceivable. Even those which are perceivable are not always perceived. So we are to consider which entities are perceptible, what are the conditions for their perceptibility and how their perception is caused.

According to the Nyāya theory, the following are the conditions for the perceptibility of different objects.

*Conditions for the Perceptibility of Substance*[1]

a. A substance must have a large size (*mahat-parimāṇa*); by large size is meant a size other than infinitesimal size (*aṇu parimāṇa*).
b. A substance must possess manifest colour (*udbhūta-rūpa*). This condition has been modified by the new school of Nyāya, which holds that a substance must possess either manifest colour or manifest touch for being perceptible.

Atoms and dyads of earth, water, air and fire are excluded from the class of perceptible substances because they do not satisfy the first condition. *Manas* fails to fulfil any of the conditions and hence is imperceptible. *Ākāśa*, *dik* (space), *kāla* (time), *ātman* and *manas* fail to fulfil the second condition; hence, they are imperceptible. So, of the nine substances, only medium-sized substances belonging to earth, water, fire and air are perceptible. Regarding the perceptibility of air, there is a difference of opinion between the old and new schools of Nyāya. According to the old school, air is imperceptible because it does not have colour, which is a condition for the perceptibility of substances. But the followers of the new school of Nyāya say that a substance is perceptible if it has either manifest colour or manifest touch, and air has manifest touch, so it can be perceived.

---

[1] Viśvanātha, 1988, *Kārikāvalī-Muktāvalī*, ed. Shankararam Shastri, p. 431, *kārikās* 56, 58, Delhi: Chowkhamba Sanskrit Pratisthan.

*Conditions for the Perceptibility of Quality*[2]

a. A quality to be perceptible should be located in a substance having large size.

b. A quality must be manifest (*udbhūta*). These two are the conditions for perceptibility of any quality. The Naiyāyikas admit two types of qualities: specific (*viśeṣa guṇa*) and generic (*sāmānya guṇa*). Smell, taste, colour, touch and sound are instances of specific (*viśeṣa*) quality of external substances, and size, number, conjunction, disjunction, etc. are instances of generic (*sāmānya*) quality of all substances. For the perceptibility of generic qualities, an additional condition is to be fulfilled;

c. The locus substance of a generic quality must be perceived.

We should note that perception of the locus substance has not been regarded as a condition for the perception of specific qualities.

*Conditions for the perceptibility of motion, universals and inherence:*[3] They must be located in a perceptible (substance) entity.

*Condition for the perceptibility of absence (of a thing):*[4] The counter correlative of the absence must be perceptible.

Now these are the conditions that must be fulfilled by the object for being perceived. In addition to these, an object in order to be perceived must be present at the time of perception and be suitably proximate to the subject or perceiver; because, objects, which are too far or too near, cannot be perceived visually. Since an object which is present (being both *vartamānakālika* and *purovartī*) can only be perceived, the object itself is regarded as a cause of perception.

Next, we shall consider what are the causes of perception of objects.

---

2 Viśvanātha, 1988, *Kārikāvalī-Muktāvalī*, p. 431, *kārikās* 52-54.

3 Ibid., *kārikā* 55.

4 Ibid., *kārikās* 61-62.

*Causes of Perception of Objects*[5]

1. The most important cause of perception is the sense organ. There are five external sense organs through which we perceive objects. There are some fixed objects for each sense organ, or to put it in the other way, each object is knowable through some specified sense organ/s only. These specifications are as follows:
    a. Substances are perceived only through visual and tactile sense organs.
    b. Of the specific qualities, colour is perceived by visual sense organ, smell by olfactory sense organ, taste by gustatory sense organ, touch by tactile sense organ and sound by auditory sense organ.
    c. Generic qualities are perceived by visual and tactile sense organs (because they can be perceived only if their loci substances are perceived and substances are perceivable by only these two senses).
    d. Motion is also perceived by these two senses because it is always perceived along with its locus substance. We perceive a fan or a car moving, but never a movement as such.
    e. A universal is perceived by the same sense organ by which its locus is perceived. Substance, quality and motion are the loci of universals and each sense organ, being capable of perceiving one or other of these entities, is also capable of perceiving universals.
    f. The relation of inherence (*samavāya*) is also perceived by all the senses because its relata are perceived by them.
    g. An absence is perceived by the same sense organ by which its counter-correlative is perceived. Hence, all

[5] Viśvanātha, 1988, *Kārikāvalī-Muktāvalī, kārikās* 58-61, p. 431.

the sense organs are capable of perceiving some absence or other.

2. Now a sense organ by its mere presence cannot produce a perception. So, an equally important causal condition is that there should be an appropriate operative relation (*indriyārtha-sannikarṣa*) between the sense organ and the object. There are six specified relations between sense organ and object which cause perception. For the perception of substances it is contact (*saṁyoga*); for perception of quality, excepting sound and for perception of motion, it is contact - inherence combination (*saṁyukta samavāya*); the same relation is required for perception of universals present in a substance, for perception universals present in quality and motion the relation is contact combined with the relation of inherence at two stages (*saṁyukta–samaveta-samavāya*). Sound is perceived through the relation of inherence (*samavāya*) between the auditory sense organ and sound. The universal of soundness is perceived through the relation of inherence with the inherent (*samaveta samavāya*). For the perception of inherence (*samavāya*) and absence (*abhāva*) the required relation is (*viśeṣya–viśeṣaṇa-bhāva*) qualificand–qualifer relation.[6]

3. But the sense–object relation is not a sufficient condition for the causation of perception, according to the Nyāya philosophers. They hold that there should also be a contact between mind (*manas*) with the sense organ.[7] In spite of there being sense–object relation a perceiver would fail to perceive the object if he/she is unmindful, i.e. if his/her attention is on something else. This shows that the sense organ must be assisted by the *manas* in order to produce perception.

---

6 Annambhaṭṭa, 1963, *Tarkasaṁgrahadipikā*, ed. Athalye, Bodas and Pusalker, Bombay Sanskrit Series, No. LV, pp. 31-32.

7 Gautama, *Nyāyasūtra* 1.1.4 and 1.1.16.

4. For perception of an object through visual sense organ, another causal condition is required and must be satisfied, viz. the presence of adequate light.

So we see that an object can be perceived only if it satisfies the conditions of perceptibility and is related to the appropriate sense organ by any of the specified operative relations, while the sense organ is also connected with the *manas.*

But the Naiyāyikas would add that for the occurrence of a perceptual cognition of the form "This is a table" or "This piece of cloth is red" besides these causal conditions an intervening cognition in the form of an indeterminate perception (*nirvikalpaka pratyakṣa*) is required.[8] They even admit that in some other cases of perception, there is an intervention of a recollective cognition. And, according to them, the perception of absence is preceded by a thought in the form of indirect argument (*tarka*). Thus, according to the Naiyāyikas, though perception is a form of direct awareness, every perception, except the indeterminate perception, is mediated by some cognitive state.

While talking about the perception of objects we shall consider only the determinate perception of objects (*savikalpaka pratyakṣa*) which we can be introspectively aware of and which we can communicate to others by expressing in language. For example, when I see a table, I express it by saying "This is a table" and I can also be aware of my seeing a table. In this perception, I see a thing as qualified by tableness. This is a qualificative cognition, which has for its object a qualificand, a qualifier and their relation, in the given example, a table which is present before me is the qualificand, the universal tableness is the qualifier and their relation is the relation of inherence.

In this chapter I shall deal with certain problems regarding the perception of substance. On the Nyāya view, we can perceive substances like tables, trees and buildings. But the Buddhist doubts

---

[8] Viśvanātha, 1988, *Kārikāvalī-Muktāvalī*, *kārikā* 58, p. 431.

whether it is at all possible to perceive a substance. They say that when we say that we see, say, a building what we actually see is only a portion of the building, the portion which we are facing and it is never possible to perceive all the sides of the building at a time. So our cognition of the building is either an inferential cognition which we derive from the perception of a part; or, the cognition of the building may be obtained by putting together the results of perception, inference and remembrance, that is, by joining through memory piecemeal perceptions and inferences of different parts of the building. In neither case, it is a perception of the building. The same would be true in the case of perception of any substance whatsoever.[9]

The Naiyāyikas however do not find it problematic to explain the possibility of the perception of substances. This is because of their ontological position regarding the concept of a whole and the relation between the part and the whole. They do not consider the whole to be only an aggregate of parts, as the Buddhists do, but according to them the whole is a product of its parts. It is a new entity constituted by parts and inheres in each part. So the relationship between the two is that of (material) cause and effect, and also of locus and located. This being the Nyāya conception of the substantive whole, they hold that when our sense organ is in contact with a part of a substance it is also in contact with the whole, so when we see or touch a part of a substance we see/touch the substance whole too. Sense contact with all the parts of a substance is not necessary for the perception of a substance. Sense contact with any part of a substance causes sense contact with the substance and if other conditions are fulfilled, the substance is perceived. So, according to the Nyāya theory, we never perceive only a part of a substance but whenever we perceive a part we perceive the whole too.[10] Actually, in this theory, there are two consecutive

---

9 Gautama, *Nyāyadarśana*, 2.1.31-32.

10 Gautama, *Nyāyadarśana*, with *Bhāṣya sūtra* 2.1.33.

perceptions, one of the part and the other of the whole, and, it seems that depending on the context, one of the perceptions is predominant. But due to the unbroken succession of the two and the predominance of one of the two, we behave as if we have only one perception. So, while standing in front of a building, we say that we see the building in case we were searching for the building, or, we say that we see the front of the building in case we came to inspect the building. So the Naiyāyikas do not find any problem in explaining the perception of substances.

We shall now consider another issue concerning the visual perception of substance. We have already said that a substance can be perceived either by the visual sense organ or by the tactile sense organ. And to cause the perception, the sense organ must be in contact with the substance. Now contact between two things requires (as a condition) close proximity between them. This condition is fulfilled in the case of perception by the tactile sense organ; we can know by touch only those things which are very close to our body so that there is no gap between the object and the tactile sense organ which is present in skin spreading all over the body, both inside and outside. But it is not so in the case of visual perception. We perceive through our eyes objects situated at a distance; not only that, we cannot see an object if it is too close to our eyes. So, how is visual perception caused in the absence of contact between the object and the visual sense organ? The Naiyāyikas say that there is indeed a contact between the visual sense organ and the object, situated at a distance. They have their explanation as to how this is possible. In the Nyāya theory, the visual sense organ is a kind of light (*tejas*) located within *kṛṣṇasāra* (pupil). It being a kind of light, emanates rays, which reaches the object situated at a distance straight in front of the eyes. Thus, through its rays, it comes in contact with the object and produces perceptual cognition of the object. The Nyāya explanation of the process of visual perception is just the opposite of the scientific explanation, which says that light reflected from the object enters into the eye to make visual perception of the object possible.[11]

But against the Nyāya explanation, it may be said that the thesis of the travelling of the eye-rays from the eyeball to the object cannot be proved because eye-rays are not perceived. We can perceive sunrays, and we can perceive rays emanating from a lamp or a candle but we do not perceive eye-rays, if they were there they should have been perceived. To this, the Nyāya reply is that the visual sense organ is devoid of manifest colour which is why it and its rays are imperceptible. But the visual sense organ is a kind of light and has rays as is seen in cats. Eye-rays of the cat is perceptible because they have manifest colour. If the visual sense organ of humans had manifest colour, then it would not need the aid of external light for perception of its object, as we know that cats can see things in the dark without the aid of external light. In the case of a human's visual sense organ it is to be inferred. If the human eyes do not have rays, they cannot be in contact with the object which is located at a distance. In that case there would be two possibilities – either visual perception would be impossible or visual perception would be possible without sense–object contact. The first possibility is denied by our experience. We do have visual perception. Regarding the second possibility the Naiyāyikas observe that if perception without sense–object contact were possible, then any object situated anywhere could be perceived; one could even see things that are at the other side of the wall. But that is not the case. The absence of the visual perception of an object, which is covered by or obstructed by some opaque thing, shows that visual perception is not possible unless there is sense–object contact. Therefore, it is to be inferred that the visual sense organ reaches the object through its rays but fails to reach it if there is obstruction by some opaque substance.[12]

---

11 Gautama, *Nyāyadarśana* 3.1.32, 34, 42-44.

12 Ibid. 3.1.46.

If we assess the Nyāya position regarding the perception of substance as a whole, it seems to appeal to common sense. The common people believe that we perceive a substance as a whole, say, a table, even though we are looking at the top of the table. We do not think that we perceive the top only and inferring the table. The Naiyāyikas justify their position in terms of their metaphysical theory of Avayavīvāda, which is about the creation of a composite substance and the relation of the whole with its parts. Their theory, however, was disputed by the Buddhist philosophers, but we are not considering it here.

To defend their position on visual perception of substances, we find that the Naiyāyikas have used their metaphysical theory regarding the origin and the nature of sense organs. According to their theory, the visual sense organ is a product of *tejas* (fire element) and so it has light rays; and light rays can travel to a substance situated at a distance. From this position it follows that a contact can be made between the visual sense organ and the substance which results in the visual perception of the substance. This metaphysical theory is apparently not supported by the common sense and it has been opposed by many philosophers. But the argument put forward by the Naiyāyikas seems to be in order. It cannot be denied that visual perception cannot occur without sense–object contact, as otherwise it could be possible to perceive a substance which is obstructed from sight by some opaque thing. Since visual perception of substance occurs, the visual sense organ must be admitted to have contact with substance. But it is a fact that a substance, if it is in close contact with the physical organ of the eye, cannot be perceived. So the visual sense organ must somehow be in contact with a substance situated at a considerable distance. The reasoning is in order so far, but the explanation as to how the visual sense organ comes in contact with a substance as has been offered by the Naiyāyika may not be acceptable to all.

# 8

# Validity Is Not Enough

In the West, logic and epistemology are regarded as two separate but closely related branches of philosophy. Logic deals with inference which is accepted as a source of knowledge and knowledge is the subject matter of epistemology. Since a major portion of our knowledge is obtained through inference, epistemology depends on logic for justification of the knowledge claim made on behalf of some of the beliefs. If a belief is true and can be shown to be the conclusion of a valid inference, then it would be considered knowledge. So, a theory of inference, which logic is to provide us with, must take into account the requirements of epistemology.

A theory of knowledge demands such a theory of inference which will take care of the truth-giving aspect of inference, in addition to the consistency or validity of reasoning. By the truth-giving aspect of inference, we mean its role in discovering or proving a truth. It is something different from the truth-preserving or truth-transmitting aspect of inference because an inference, in spite of being truth-preserving, may not give the truth in the conclusion. In formulating a theory of inference, logic must recognize an ideal of what inference should be if it is to be a way of knowing. If in making inference what we want is not merely that the conclusion follows from the premises but also that we get the truth in the conclusion, then the theory of inference must lay down conditions of truth as well as conditions of consistency or validity. Validity divorced from truth or mere formal validity is not enough for an inference if it is to be a way of knowing. So, a theory of inference which combines truth with validity would be in order. Such a theory of inference alone can serve the purpose of epistemology properly.

In India, philosophy had been a comprehensive study. Therefore, Indian philosophy does not admit of branching into metaphysics, logic, epistemology, etc. There, we find indeed a division of the subject matter of philosophy into *pramāṇa* (means of knowledge) and *prameya* (object of knowledge); and corresponding to these, a theory of *pramāṇa* and a theory of *prameya*. The theory of *pramāṇa* may roughly be equated with logic and epistemology in brackets. The theory of *prameya*, on the other hand, may be regarded as the Indian counterpart of metaphysics.

Each Indian philosophical system has its own *pramāṇa* theory and *prameya* theory. A general observation which may be made about Indian theories of *pramāṇa* is that almost all the philosophical schools in India accept *anumāna* (inference) to be a source of knowledge and none of the theories of inference propounded by them is a purely formal one, i.e. not concerned with the actual truth value of either the premise or the conclusion, rather every Indian theory of inference lays down conditions for correctness of the inferential process in such a way that fulfilment of those conditions ensures the truth of both the premise and the conclusion.

In the present chapter we shall consider only the Nyāya theory of inference to show that it is a theory of inference which is fit to serve the purpose of a theory of knowledge. We have chosen the Nyāya theory of inference in particular because the Nyāya school, especially the Navya (modern) school, is well known for its *pramāṇa* theory.

## I

To begin with, we shall point out some basic differences that the Nyāya theory of inference has from the theory of inference in Western formal logic.

In Western formal logic, validity is conceived as something which is independent of truth. In a theory of pure formal logic an inference can be valid without yielding a true conclusion and an inference can yield a true conclusion without being valid.

Even when a semantical concept of validity is used in formal logic, formal logic is not concerned with the actual truth or falsity of the premise or conclusion. It recognizes merely that a false conclusion cannot follow validly from true premises. So, according to the theory of Western formal logic, if the premises are true and the rules of inference are valid, then the conclusion must be true. But it never says that if an inference is valid, then its conclusion must be true, or that, if the conclusion is true, then the inference which led to the conclusion must be a valid one.

The Nyāya theory of inference, on the other hand, rests on a notion of validity on which validity without truth is impossible. According to the Nyāya theory, a valid inference is sure to yield a true conclusion; and the condition for the validity of an inference, on their theory, coincides with the condition for the truth of the premises, so a valid inference contains only true premises. So, in the Nyāya theory of inference, a valid inference with either false premises or false conclusion is not possible. Thus, Nyāya provides a theory of inference which establishes valid inferences to be invariably a source of true belief or knowledge, and thus proves itself to be adequate for epistemology.

The Nyāya school admits four *pramāṇas*[1] of which *anumāna* is one. They also admit that the greater part of our knowledge comes through inference.[2] Now from the very definition of *pramāṇa*, i.e. a *pramāṇa* is the means to true cognition (*pramākaraṇam pramāṇam*),[3]

---

1 Gautama, 1985, *Nyāyadarśanam* ed. Tārānātha Nyāyatarkatīrtha and Amarendramohana Tarkatīrtha, see *sūtra* 1.1.3, New Delhi: Munshiram Manoharlal.

2 Vātsyāyana, *Bhāṣya* on *Nyāyasūtra* 1.1. 5, in *Nyāyadarśanam*.

3 The Nyāya philosophers give a causal account of knowledge. →

it follows that an *anumāna* in order to be a *pramāṇa* must lead to a true cognition.

According to the Naiyāyikas, an inference can necessarily yield a true conclusion if it is a valid one. And the inference is valid only if the *hetu* (inferential mark) is a legitimate (*sat*) one. They have mentioned a number of characteristics which a *hetu* must have if it is to be a *sat hetu.* We shall elaborate on that point later. What we should note here is that the two conditions of yielding a true conclusion and having a legitimate inferential mark must both be fulfilled to make an inference a *pramāṇa.* And, normally, none of these two conditions can be fulfilled without the other being fulfilled too. If the conclusion to which an inference leads is false then the inferential mark could not be a legitimate one and, in that case, the inference is not a *pramāṇa* but a *pramāṇābhāsa* (pseudo *pramāṇa*). If on the other hand, the *hetu* is legitimate then the conclusion drawn on the basis of it is true and the inference would be a *pramāṇa.*

Before proceeding further with the Nyāya theory of inference, we should discuss briefly a few preliminaries about *anumāna* as well as some terminological matters.

In Indian epistemology as such, an inference is not analysed into premise/s and conclusions. The Indian epistemologists maintain that an inference, which is a cognitive process, admits of a causal analysis. In an inference, a number of cognitive states function as

← According to them, a number of causal conditions conjointly give rise to a *pramā*. Among these causal conditions (*kāraṇas*), one which is the most effective is called the instrumental cause (*karaṇa*) and that is technically called *pramāṇa.* As regards the question of which condition is the most effective, there are two prominent views:

i. that causal condition which through some operation produces the effect, viz. *pramā,* is the most effective condition and hence the *karaṇa*; and
ii. that condition, immediately after the occurrence of which the effect, viz. *pramā*, is produced is the *karaṇa.*

causal conditions which lead to another cognitive state which is the effect. Now, this effect in the relevant case is called *anumiti*, which is roughly what is normally called a conclusion in Western terminology. The causal conditions are all called *anumāna*, though sometimes in a technical sense, only one among those causal conditions is singled out and called *anumāna*.[4] This will be explained later.

If we look into the internal structure of the cognitive states which constitute the entire inferential process, we shall find that every *anumāna* involves three elements: *pakṣa* (subject of inferential cognition), *sādhya* (inferable property which is to be predicated of the subject); and *hetu*. The typical expression of an *anumāna* is: "*p* has *s* because of *h*", here *s* is inferred to be present in *p*, on the basis of *h*. So *p* is the *pakṣa*, *s* is the *sādhya*; and *h* is the *hetu* which bears the inferential relation with the *s*, i.e. the inferable property. It is by virtue of this inferential relation that *h* can serve as an inferential mark for *s*. The inferential relation is known as the relation of *vyāpti* (pervasion). If a thing *X* is related to another thing *Y* in such a way that wherever *X* is present *Y* is also present then *X* is pervaded by *Y*. In that case *X* can function as the *hetu* for *Y*.

The psychological process of *anumāna* according to the Nyāya philosophers is like this. Let us consider the commonly used instance of an inference, viz. the inference of a fire on a hill on the basis of smoke. The inferer first perceives smoke coming out of a hill; this perception reminds him of the truth that smoke has the relation of pervasion (*vyāpti*) with fire, something which he had ascertained earlier. This remembrance leads to another perception,[5]

---

4 Uddyotakara, *Nyāyavārttika*, on *Nyāyasūtra* 1.1.5 in *Nyāyadarśanam*.

5 *Parāmarśa*, i.e. the cognition to the effect that the subject of inference (*pakṣa*) possesses such a property (which is the *hetu* as is pervaded by the inferable property (*sādhya*) is generally a perceptual cognition according to the Naiyāyikas). But it is a bit different type of perception indeed, for it is produced not merely by the relation (*sannikarṣa*) between the sense organ and the object but has the remembrance of the relation of pervasion (*vyāpti smṛti*) →

where the inferer perceives that the hill possesses such smoke as is pervaded by fire. From this, he concludes that the hill has fire.

So the inferential cognition to the effect that the hill has fire is preceded by three cognitions:

---

← as one of its causal conditions. An account of the way in which *parāmarśa* occurs is as follows. The knower's sense organ is in contact with the *pakṣa* (say, a hill) as well as the *hetu* (say, smoke) and as a result, has a perceptual cognition to the effect that the *pakṣa* (hill) possesses the *hetu* (smoke); this perception causes the remembrance of the relation of pervasion which all the members of the class of smoke (which is the *hetu* in this example) have with fire (which is the *sādhya*), as previously experienced by the knower. Through this remembrance, a non-physical relation (*alaukika sannikarṣa* called *jñāna-lakṣaṇā*) is established between the knower's sense organ and the property of being pervaded by fire (*sādhya*), which the instance of smoke present in the hill, possesses as being a member of the class of smokes. Thus, the knower perceives that the hill (*pakṣa*) is possessed of the smoke (*hetu*) which is pervaded by fire (*sādhya*), though fire itself, which is a relatum of the relation of pervasion, in this case, is not perceived at that time.

An alternative explanation as to how a *parāmarśa* arises is also given (see Gaṅgeśa, *Tattvacintāmaṇi*). After having the perception of the *pakṣa* as possessed of *hetu* and having remembered the relation of pervasion which smoke has with *sādhya*, the knower by means of his/her inner sense organ (*manas*) directly apprehends that the smoke which is present in the hill is also, as a member of the class of smoke, pervaded by fire. In this case also, the remembrance of the relation of pervasion establishes a non-physical relation between the knower's inner sense organ (*manas*) and the property of being pervaded by fire and thus makes the perception possible.

In the first explanation, it was a case of external perception, whereas, according to the second explanation, it was a mental (*manas*) perception, but in both cases, it has remembrance as one of its causal conditions. Gaṅgeśa maintains that in most cases *parāmarśa* is a case of mental perception.

i. the perception of smoke in the hill;
ii. the recollection to the effect that smoke stands in the relation of pervasion with fire; and
iii. the perception that smoke, as is pervaded by fire, characterizes the hill.

The second cognition, viz. the recollective cognition of the relation of pervasion, however, depends on a previous non-recollective cognition of the relation. But, this non-recollective cognition of the relation of pervasion, though presupposed, does not form a part of the actual process of inferring.

Now, the three cognitions mentioned above are the causal conditions which lead to inferential cognition. The first cognition is named *pakṣadharmatā-jñāna*, the second one *vyāpti-jñāna* and the third *parāmarśa*. These three cognitions have a partially common object, viz. the *hetu*. The same *hetu*, which was perceived to be present in the *pakṣa* (cognition I), is remembered to be pervaded by the *sādhya* (cognition II); this again leads finally to perceive the *hetu* as characterized by the relation of pervasion with the *sādhya* to be present in the *pakṣa* (cognition III). It is also clear that these cognitions are causally related; the first cognition causes the second one and that again causes the third, after which the inferential cognition (*anumiti*) results.

Now, besides these causal conditions which constitute the actual inferential process, the Naiyāyikas talk about some other conditions which should be fulfilled before an inferential process can make a start. We may call them preconditions for an inference. They are the conditions for the possibility of making an inference. These conditions are as follows:

i. The *pakṣa* (subject of inferential cognition) must not be known to the inferer to possess the *sādhya* (inferable property);[6]

[6] The Naiyāyikas admit *pakṣatā* as a necessary condition of *anumiti* and it means the absence of the knowledge of *sādhya* in the *pakṣa*, accompanied by the absence of desire to infer the same *sādhya* in the →

ii. the *pakṣa* must not be believed by the inferer to possess the absence of *sādhya*; and

iii. the *pakṣa* should not be believed by the inferer to be allegedly characterized by some *hetu* having the relation of pervasion with the contradictory of the *sādhya*.

We find that the three preconditions for an inference, which have been mentioned above are negative. The non-fulfilment of any of these negative conditions implies that the corresponding positive condition holds and, in that case, the inference cannot take place. Let us see why.

Take the first condition first. Its non-fulfilment means that the *pakṣa p* is known to possess the *sādhya s*. In such a situation there is really no scope or need for making an inference to obtain the knowledge that *p* has *s*. The Naiyāyikas have, however, conceded that in such a situation if the inferer has a special desire to draw an inference to know the same thing which has been already known, the inference can take place. Normally, an inference is made with a view to knowing something which is not already known.

Let us now come to the second condition. The non-fulfilment of this condition implies that the *pakṣa p* is believed to possess the absence of the *sādhya s*. Having this belief, viz. *p* has non-*s*, the inferer cannot make an inference to reach the conclusion that *p* has *s*. The rationality of thought excludes the possibility of such a situation.

The non-fulfilment of the third condition would halt, at least temporarily, the process of inference. For, if the inferer is aware of the supposed presence of some *hetu* having the relation of pervasion with the absence of *sādhya*, in the *pakṣa*, then he/she cannot proceed to infer the presence of the inferable property in the same subject of inference without refuting the alleged possibility

---

← same *pakṣa*. See Annambhaṭṭa, 1976, *Tarkasaṁgrahadīpikā*, Section 49, pp. 196-200, ed. and tr. Gopinath Bhattacharyya, Calcutta: Progressive Publishers.

of the contradictory conclusion. So, we find that unless the above conditions are fulfilled, no inference can take place.

We now come to the conditions for the validity of an inference. In the Nyāya theory of inference, conditions for validity are meant those conditions which make the inference both legitimate (*sat*) and, also, a source of knowledge. The Naiyāyikas talk about two sets of conditions one to ensure that the *hetu* is legitimate and the other that the conclusion is true. But, actually these two sets of conditions are related in such a way that the fulfilment of the conditions for the legitimacy of the *hetu* ultimately leads to a true conclusion.

Let us first see what is the condition for the truth of the conclusion, i.e. the inferential cognition. According to the Naiyāyikas, an inferential cognition is true if its immediately preceding causal condition, viz. the *parāmarśa*, that is, the cognition that the *pakṣa* is characterized by the *hetu* which has the relation of pervasion (*vyāpti*) with the *sādhya*, is true. This is so because the Naiyāyikas hold that true cognition can be produced only by a means which is qualified by some *guṇa* (excellence).[7] In the case of inferential cognition, the means is the *parāmarśa* and its truth is the stipulated excellence.[8]

---

7 Gaṅgeśa, 1974, *Tattvacintāmaṇi Pratyakṣa Khaṇḍa*, ed. Tarkavagish, Kamakhyanath, pp. 308-09, Delhi: Motilal Banarsidass.

8 Ibid., pp. 327 and 341. The Naiyāyikas, however, recognize some cases of inference where despite the falsity of *parāmarśa* the resulting inferential cognition is true. For example, someone misperceives steam as smoke and seeing (mistakenly) that smoke is coming out of some place and remembering that smoke is pervaded by fire, comes to believe that the place possesses such smoke as is pervaded by fire. This belief, which is called *parāmarśa*, is false here since that place actually possesses steam and not smoke. But from this belief, the person concludes that there is fire in that place and on verification, the inferential belief is found to correspond to fact. So, according to the Nyāya definition of *pramā*, it should be regarded as *pramā*. This certainly poses some problems for them →

Now, the *parāmarśa* cannot be true unless the other two cognitions, viz. *pakṣadharmatā-jñāna* and *vyāpti-jñāna*, which precede the *parāmarśa* and are among the causal conditions of *anumiti*, are also true. If we call these causal conditions premises, we can say that the truth of the premise is the sufficient condition for the truth of the conclusion, i.e. the inferential cognition.

The other set of conditions is required to be fulfilled in order that the inference is legitimate, that is to say, the *hetu* of the inference is *sat*. A *hetu* is legitimate if and only if it possesses five characteristics,[9] viz.:

1. *pakṣa-sattva* (to be present in the *pakṣa*);
2. *sapakṣa-sattva* (to be present in a thing other than the *pakṣa*, where the presence of the *sādhya* is known for certain);
3. *vipakṣāsattva* (should not be present in a thing where the *sādhya* is known to be absent);
4. *abādhitatva* (contradictory of the *sādhya* must not be known to be present in the *pakṣa*); and
5. *asatpratipakṣitatva* (a *hetu* tending to prove the contradictory of the *sādhya* must not be present in the *pakṣa*).

In our example of the inference of fire in a hill on the basis of smoke, the hill is the *pakṣa*, the kitchen is a *sapakṣa* and the *hetu* smoke is present in both the hill and the kitchen. A lake would be

← so far as their theory of *parataḥprāmāṇya* regarding the origin of *pramā* is concerned. They have to face this question: if a *pramā* can be caused by a false *parāmarśa*, then how can that *pramā* be said to be caused by the required *guṇa* (excellence). The Naiyāyikas have attempted to answer the question by conceding that the required excellence (*guṇa*) for giving rise to a true inferential cognition (*anumiti pramā*) might not be the same in all cases.

[9] Jayanta Bhaṭṭa, 1982, *Nyāyamañjarī*, a commentary on the *Nyāyasūtra* of Gautama, ed. Gaurinath Sastri, Varanasi: Sampūrṇananda Sanskrit Viśvavidyālaya. See part I, pp. 164-65.

Viśvanātha, *Vṛtti* on *Nyāyasūtra* 1.2.4 in *Nyāyadarśanam.*

a *vipakṣa* and smoke is not present in it. The hill is neither known to be characterized by the absence of fire nor is some *hetu* which is pervaded by the absence of fire found to be present in the hill. So the *hetu* of this inference has all the five characteristics of a legitimate *hetu*. But, there are certain types of inference the *hetu* of which cannot and need not have all the five characteristics, four of which suffice in such cases. In order to grasp these details we are to have an idea of the Nyāya classification of inference.

The Naiyāyikas first divide inferences into two kinds: *svārthānumāna* (inference for one's own self) and *parārthānumāna*[10]

---

[10] By *parārthānumāna* (inference for others) two things are meant:

i. an argument, that is the verbal expression of an inferential process, which one person employs to convince others of his position; and
ii. the inferential process which takes place in the mind of the person who hears the argument.

If stress is given on *parārtha* (for others), the first sense seems to be the primary sense; if, on the other hand, emphasis is on *anumāna* (inference), the second sense should be the primary sense.

It is in the context of a philosophical debate (*vicāra*) between two parties holding opposite positions regarding something that *parārthānumāna* is employed. The argument has a definite form. It is a compound sentence comprising five component sentences (*pañcāvayava vākya*). It starts with the statement of the position and ends with the assertion of the position, the other three sentences which occur in-between state the reasoning process. This five-membered conjunctive sentence, when heard by a person holding the opposite position or by a mediator (*madhyastha*) who is neutral, generates in the mind of the hearer an inferential process through which the same conclusion is reached. Thus, through *parārthānumāna* one can convince others of one's position or can prove one's position. From the point of view of the person employing a *parārthānumāna*, it is a way of proving, whereas from the point of view of the person for whom it is employed it is a way of knowing.

(inference for others). *Svārthānumāna* is a way of knowing, but *parārthānumāna* is something more, it is a way of proving a position. In this chapter, however, we are concerned with *svārthānumāna* (inference for one's own self) only.

Each of these two kinds of inference can again be of three types:[11]

a. *anvaya-vyatirekī*,
b. *kevalānvayī*,
c. *kevala-vyatirekī*.

Though, there is a difference of opinion regarding the principle of this division, still it can roughly be said that, if both a positive instance of the *hetu* being accompanied by the *sādhya* and a negative instance of the absence of *sādhya* being accompanied by the absence of *hetu* can be found, then the inference with such a *hetu* belongs to the type (a) above. An example of this type of inference is the inference of fire from smoke, because, smoke is found to be accompanied by fire in the kitchen and the absence of fire is also found to be accompanied by the absence of smoke in the lake. If only a positive instance of the concomitance of the *hetu* with the *sādhya* can be found, then the inference with such a *hetu* belongs to the type (b). An example of this type of inference is: A horse is nameable, because it is knowable, just as a man is. Since, as the Naiyāyikas maintain, every real thing is knowable and nameable, no instance of the absence of nameability being accompanied by the absence of knowability can be found. And if only the negative instance of the concomitance of the absence of the *sādhya* with the absence of the *hetu* can be found then the inference with such a *hetu* belongs to the type (c). The following inference belongs to this type. A substance differs from other things because it has substancehood. Here, no locus of substancehood other than substance can be found, but all the substances are included in the

---

[11] Gaṅgeśa, 1970, *Tattvacintāmaṇi*, Anumāna Khaṇḍa with *Dīdhiti* and *Gādādharī*, ed. Vindhyeswari Prasad Dvivedi, Varanasi: Chowkhamba. See *Kevalānvayīprakaraṇam*.

*pakṣa*, hence only a negative instance of the concomitance of the absence of the difference from things other than a substance with the absence of substancehood is found.

Now, of the five characteristics of a legitimate *hetu* as mentioned above, the *hetu* of an inference of type (a) should have all of them; the *hetu* of an inference of type (b) should have four of them excluding only *vipakṣāsattva* (not being present in a thing where the *sādhya* is known to be absent), because in that type of inference the *sādhya* is such that nothing can be found to have its absence. The *hetu* of the inference of type (c) should have the four characteristics excluding only *sapakṣa-sattva* (being present in a thing other than *pakṣa* where the presence of the *sādhya* is known for certain), for in such an inference, the *pakṣa* alone is the locus of the *sādhya*.

So we find that having either five or four of the characteristics mentioned above makes a *hetu sat*. And we have already said that according to the Nyāya theory, an inference with a legitimate *hetu* would yield a true conclusion.

Each of the five characteristics of a legitimate *hetu* has either direct or indirect bearing upon the truth of the conclusion of an inference. Let us see how.

As pointed out earlier, an inferential cognition, i.e. the conclusion of an inference, is true if the *parāmarśa*, which causes it, is true. A *parāmarśa* is the cognition to the effect that the *pakṣa* (subject of inference) is characterized by the *hetu* (inferential mark) which is pervaded by the *sādhya* (inferable property). The *parāmarśa* is true if and only if *pakṣadharmatā-jñāna* (cognition to the effect that the inferential mark characterizes the subject of inference) and *vyāpti-jñāna* (cognition to the effect that the inferential mark is pervaded by the inferable property) are true. These are again true if and only if

i. the inferential mark exists in the subject of inference (*pakṣa-sattva*), and

ii. the inferential mark exists in a thing (other than the subject of inference) which is known to be a locus of the inferable property (*sapakṣa-sattva*) and/or the inferential mark does not exist in anything which is known to be characterized by the absence of the inferable property (*vipakṣāsattva*).

The characteristic of *pakṣa-sattva* is the truth-condition of *pakṣa-dharmatā-jñāna.* The characteristics *sapakṣa-sattva* and *vipakṣāsattva,* on the other hand, are disjunctively the truth conditions of *vyāpti-jñāna.* And, since the truth of *pakṣadharmatā-jñāna* and *vyāpti-jñāna* is a necessary condition for the truth of *parāmarśa*, the truth of the inferential cognition (the conclusion of the inference) ultimately depends on the three above-mentioned characteristics of the *hetu.* If the *hetu* of an inference possesses those three characteristics, the inference is sure to yield a true conclusion.

The last two characteristics of a legitimate *hetu*, i.e. *abādhitatva* and *asatpratipakṣitatva*, seem to have direct relevance to the truth of the conclusion (*anumiti*). Like any other cognition, inferential cognition can be regarded as true according to the Naiyāyikas if it corresponds to the objective situation. For example, if we infer that a particular hill possesses fire, then that inferential cognition can be regarded as true if that particular hill actually possesses fire. Now, this is not possible unless the *hetu* is *abādhita* and *asatpratipakṣita.* If a *hetu* was *bādhita*, then the objective situation would be such that the inference drawn on the basis of such a *hetu* could not correspond with it. To be *bādhita* is to be contradicted, but when a *hetu* is said to be *bādhita*, what is contradicted is not the *hetu* itself but the proposition which is to be drawn on its basis. That means, the contradiction of the conclusion is true and it corresponds with the objective situation, hence the conclusion from a *bādhita hetu* cannot correspond to the objective situation. In our example, the *hetu*, i.e. the smoke would be *bādhita* if that particular hill did not possess fire. That means, it is contradictory to the proposed conclusion which corresponds to the objective situation and is thus true and so the proposed conclusion itself, i.e. "That hill possesses fire" cannot be true.

If a *hetu* is *satpratipakṣita*, then there is no certainty that the conclusion drawn from it would be true. A *hetu* is said to be *satpratipakṣita* if another *hetu* which is capable of proving the opposite conclusion can be found. In such a case, only one of the contradictory conclusions can be true, so there is the possibility of the conclusion, which is drawn on the basis of the first *hetu*, being false. So in order to ensure the truth of the conclusion, a *hetu* must possess the characteristics of *asatpratipakṣitatva.*

It may be pointed out here that if the inferer entertains a belief that the *hetu* upon which he is going to draw an inference is not *abādhita* and *asatpratipakṣita*, then he cannot proceed with his inference. That means, if the inferer believes rightly or wrongly that the *hetu* he is employing is *bādhita* and/or *satpratipakṣita*, then he would refrain from drawing the inference. If a *hetu* is believed to be *bādhita*, it would be logically inconsistent to use such a *hetu* for drawing an inference. For, an attempt to draw a conclusion which is already contradicted, on the basis of some evidence (*pramāṇa*), cannot be rationally justified. Similarly, to proceed to draw a conclusion when one is aware of the presence of some premise (*hetu*) tending to yield just the opposite conclusion is not rationally justifiable. One can proceed with the inference only after being convinced that the premise (*hetu*) which has been alleged to prove the opposite conclusion is incapable of proving it. That is the reason why we have taken the absence of the belief that the *hetu* is *bādhita* and also the absence of the belief that the *hetu* is *satpratipakṣita* to be preconditions for an inference.

We may now sum up the points made so far about the Nyāya theory of inference.

First, the Nyāya theory of inference upholds a different notion of validity, such that an inference cannot be valid without leading to a conclusion which is actually true. A purely formal concept of validity is not found in Indian logic. But, still, if we look for a corresponding concept in the Nyāya theory of inference, we may say that on the Nyāya theory any inference that can be expressed in the following schema may be treated as formally valid:

The *pakṣa* has the *hetu*,

The *hetu* is pervaded by the *sādhya*,

∴ The *pakṣa* has the *sādhya*,

provided the *hetu* in the premises 1 and 2 stands for things belonging to the same class and the *sādhya* in the premise 2 and in the conclusion stands for things belonging to the same class. But the Indian logicians are not interested in this sort of validity, it would be a trivial concept for them. Any possible inference in their system of logic belongs to this form, even fallacious arguments have the same form. Only an inference which belongs to this form and has a legitimate (*sat*) *hetu* is valid in their sense of the term and leads invariably to a true conclusion.

Second, it specifies three sets of conditions:

i. Conditions for the very possibility of an inference or pre-conditions;
ii. causal conditions of an inference; and
iii. conditions for the validity of an inference.

Third, the conditions for validity, as formulated in the Nyāya theory of inference, are truth-ensuring. So, in this theory, every valid inference has a true conclusion as well as true premises. The Nyāya philosophers' argument, in brief, is as follows:

> An inference cannot be valid unless its *hetu* is legitimate. An inferential mark cannot be legitimate unless it satisfies the five (four in some cases) conditions for legitimacy enumerated by the Nyāya philosophers, or, in other words, unless the *hetu* possesses the five characteristics of a legitimate *hetu*.

If the *hetu* is *sat*, then the premises are true. And the premises being true, the conclusion which follows from them must also be true.

Thus, with the fulfilment of the condition of the legitimacy of a *hetu*, which is the same as the condition for the validity of an inference, the truth of the premises as well as the conclusion is guaranteed.

## II

An inference, in order to be a way of knowing, must not only be capable of yielding a conclusion which is actually true, but it must also effect some progress in knowledge. The inferer must know something new by drawing an inference. Of course, by "knowing something new" is not meant any objective novelty;[12] that means, it is not required of an inference that to be a way of knowing an inference must have an object which was not known before; what is required is that through the process of inference, the inferer should gain some knowledge in conclusion, in the sense that conclusion was not known to him when he knew the premises.

[12] In some schools of Indian philosophy, an objective novelty, in the sense of knowing something which was not known to the knower (*anadhigatārthaviṣayakatva*), is one of the defining characteristics of *pramā*. But the Naiyāyikas reject this view of knowledge. They maintain that it is not necessary for a *pramā* to be about some object which was hitherto unknown, for there are admittedly some cases of *pramā* where this condition cannot be satisfied, for example, omniscient God's knowledge is such, because at no point of time nothing can be unknown to Him.

That the Naiyāyikas do not admit objective novelty to be an essential characteristics of *pramā* is evident also from their theory of *pramāṇa-saṁplava*, i.e. one and the same object may be known by means of different *pramāṇas* at different time; that means, even when an object is known with the help of one *pramāṇa* it may be known through another *pramāṇa*. So, a subject can have knowledge (*pramā*) of an object which is already known to him/her.

Moreover, the Naiyāyikas cannot be said to claim objective novelty in the conclusion of an inference, because they hold that a subject can draw a conclusion which is already known, if he/she has a special desire for that. See note 6 on p. 134.

We have to consider now whether, on the Nyāya theory of inference, such epistemic progress is possible. We have seen that an epistemic progress can be made by an inference, if the knowledge of the premises does not presuppose or include the knowledge of conclusion; or, in other words, what is known in conclusion had not been known in the premises. Apparently, the process of inference as analysed in the Nyāya theory of inference does not leave any scope for epistemic progress. Let us explain why.

We have seen that it is possible to infer *s* on the basis of *h* only if *h* is related to *s* by the relation of *vyāpti* (pervasion) and the inferer is aware of that relation. This is clear from the inclusion of the cognition II (*vyāpti-jñāna*) in the set of causal conditions leading to the inferential cognition (*anumiti*). If we want to infer, say, fire (*s*) from smoke (*h*), smoke should be related to fire by the relation of pervasion, meaning that wherever smoke is found, there fire is to be found; and we should also have a cognition of that relation. Now, this relation of *vyāpti* is a universal relation holding between all the members of the class of smokes and the members of the class of fires such that each member of the class of smokes is accompanied by some member of the class of fires. Here, the smoke, which is the *hetu*, is regarded as the subjunct (*anuyogin*) of the relation of *vyāpti*, and the fire, which is the *sādhya*, is the adjunct (*pratiyogin*) of that relation. So, the *hetu* is that which is pervaded and the *sādhya* is that which pervades. Now, so far as the relation of *vyāpti* is concerned, the *hetu* smoke and the *sādhya* fire are taken as the class of smoke (*sakala-dhūma*) and the class of fire (*sakala-vahni*) respectively, though in an actual inference a particular instance of smoke and a particular instance of fire figure as the *hetu* and the *sādhya* respectively. It must be admitted that when the inferer ascertains the universal relation of *vyāpti* holding between the members of two classes, viz. smoke and fire, he is also aware of the particular instance of fire which is to be inferred because a relation cannot be cognized without cognizing the relata at the same time and that particular instance of fire belongs to the class of fires which is one of the relata. So, it can be alleged that the conclusion is already known at the time of knowing the premises. The same objection, which has been raised against the syllogism like "All men are mortal, Socrates is a man; therefore Socrates is mortal" seems to hold in this case also. Thus, how can there be an epistemic progress in the Nyāya theory of inference?

To be clear about the problem as well as the solution as regards epistemic progress in inference on the Nyāya theory, we have to consider first the way of ascertaining the relation of *vyāpti*.

According to the Nyāya thinkers, the universal relation of pervasion is ascertained by perception (*pratyakṣa*), aided by some indirect argument (*anukūla tarka*),[13] which helps to remove any doubt concerning the invariability of the relation or to remove a mistaken certainty that there is no such invariable relation in the case under consideration.

Let us explain. Taking the inference of fire from smoke as an example, we shall explain how to ascertain that smoke is related to fire by the relation of pervasion. One forms a belief concerning the relation of *vyāpti* holding between the *hetu*, i.e. the smoke and the *sādhya*, i.e. the fire, when one perceives at least one case of concomitance between smoke and fire without coming across any case of absence of concomitance between the two and without entertaining any belief to the contrary. If one has an apprehension as to the possibility of there being some cases of absence of concomitance, such a belief acts as an inhibitor to the belief concerning the relation of *vyāpti* between the two. But, if there is no such belief to the contrary, one can form a belief regarding the relation of *vyāpti* under consideration and based on that belief one can draw an inference.

Now it may be questioned as to how it is possible to establish the universal relation of *vyāpti* by observing only one particular

---

[13] See Varadarāja, *Tārkikarakṣā*, Reprint from *The Paṇḍit*, 1903. Gaṅgeśa, *Tattvacintāmaṇi*, Anumāna Khaṇḍa, *Tarkaprakarṇam*.

instance of concomitance? That is, by observing only one case of the concomitance of smoke and fire in, say, a kitchen, how can one believe that there is a relation of pervasion between all the members of the class of smokes and the members of the class of fires, such that wherever smoke is present, fire is also present. It may be mentioned here that it is not the case that every member of the class of smokes is pervaded by every member of the class of fires, but by some member or other. In symbols:

$$(x)\ [x \in S \supset (\exists\, y)\ (y \in F \cdot x \text{ is concomitant with } y)].$$

The Naiyāyikas solve this problem by having recourse to a special type of perception. They hold that whenever we perceive a particular, we also perceive the universal which characterize it, e.g. when we perceive a smoke, we perceive smokeness too. For, to perceive a smoke means to perceive something as smoke, which again means to perceive it as characterized by smokeness. They also hold that when a universal, e.g. smokeness, is being perceived in any particular, the universal or its cognition functions as an operative relation (*sannikarṣa*) between the relevant sense organ and all the particulars which exemplify the universal smokeness. This is a non-physical operative relation (*alaukika sannikarṣa*) known as *sāmānya lakṣaṇā sannikarṣa.*[14] Thus, when our sense organ is in contact with only one instance of smokeness, we can perceive, in a special way, all the instances of smokeness, albeit not in their particularity, but only as the exemplifiers of the universal smokeness. Therefore, the Naiyāyikas argue when only one instance of smoke is present before us, we can have a special type of perception of *all* smokes and can believe that *all* smokes are pervaded by fire, i.e. every instance of smoke is accompanied by fire. The Naiyāyikas have also conceded that just as we can form a belief about *all* smokes being pervaded by fire when we have that special type of perception of *all* smokes, one can also doubt as to whether or not *all* smokes are accompanied by fire. This doubt stands in the way of ascertaining

[14] Gaṅgeśa, *Tattvacintāmaṇi*, Anumāna Khaṇḍa, *Sāmānyalakṣaṇā-prakarṇam.*

the invariable relation of *vyāpti*. So, unless this doubt is removed, the belief that there is a relation of pervasion between smoke and fire cannot be justified.

The inferer himself may have such doubt, or someone else may raise it. In any case, if one's belief regarding the relation of *vyāpti* in a particular case of inference is shaken or challenged, one has to dispel the doubt that the relation of *vyāpti* may not hold in that case. This can be done with the help of a *tarka* (an indirect argument). In an indirect argument, the denial of the belief under consideration is taken as a supposal, and it is shown that the supposal leads to a consequence which is unacceptable. If, for example, one doubts whether smoke is pervaded by fire, then the indirect argument may be like this: if smoke were not pervaded by fire (that means, if smoke could be found in places where fire was absent), then smoke would not have been caused by fire. This shows that the denial of the relation of pervasion in this case would lead to the denial of the accepted causal relation between the fire and the smoke. This is not welcome, so the belief about the relation of pervasion is reinstated.

In some cases, however, a doubt as to whether or not the relation of pervasion holds between a particular *hetu* and a particular *sādhya* may not be entertained at all. In such cases, the absence of the doubt is said to be self-evident (*svataḥsiddha*), for, to entertain such a doubt is to make practical life impossible. So, no one can entertain such a doubt. For example, no one can doubt whether eating satisfies hunger or can hold the contradictory belief that eating does not satisfy hunger because that would lead to a belief–behaviour contradiction.

Thus, either by removing the doubt or a contradictory belief concerning the relation of pervasion or by showing that no such belief or doubt can be entertained at all, the belief in the relation of pervasion can be justified.[15]

[15] Gaṅgeśa, *Tattvacintāmaṇi*, Anumāna Khaṇḍa, *Vyāptigrahopāya-prakaraṇam.*

We may now come back to the question of epistemic progress. From what we have discussed about the relation of pervasion and its ascertainment, it should be clear that the cognition of the relation of pervasion includes the cognition of the relata which, in our example, comprises all the members of the class of smoke and members of the class of fire. So, when the inferer has the cognition of the relation of *vyāpti* he already knows the *sādhya*, viz. fire and hence there seems to be no scope for epistemic progress. As we have seen, the particular instance of fire which is to be inferred is also admitted to be perceived in a special way along with all the members of the class of fire, when we see a particular smoke to be accompanied by a particular fire in a kitchen.

In spite of this, the Naiyāyikas would argue, their theory of inference permits epistemic progress. In the inferential cognition or the conclusion of the inference the inferable property figures as the qualifier of the *pakṣa* (subject of inference). For example, we infer fire in a hill; that means, fire is inferred as existing in a particular hill or as qualifying that particular hill. But while ascertaining the relation of pervasion between smoke and fire, the fire is known only as the pervader (*vyāpaka*) of smoke. So what is inferred in the conclusion was not known before, that is, at the time of ascertaining the relation of *vyāpti*, hence there is definitely progress in knowledge for the inferer.

It may be questioned at this point, whether the conclusion was not known to the inferer when he had the cognition III, i.e. *parāmarśa*, which was the final causal condition to be followed immediately by the inferential conclusion (*anumiti*). Such an apprehension arises, because in the cognition called *parāmarśa*, the three elements of inference, viz. the *pakṣa*, *sādhya* and *hetu*, are revealed in their mutual relationship. If we take our stock example of the inference of fire from smoke, the *parāmarśa* would reveal the hill (*pakṣa*) as characterized by such smoke (*hetu*) which is pervaded (*vyāpya*) by fire (*sādhya*). In this cognition, therefore, the fire, which is the *sādhya*, having been known as the pervader of smoke which characterizes the hill, is implicitly known to characterize the hill. So in the conclusion, nothing new is known. The apprehension is that in the passage from *parāmarśa* to *anumiti*, there is no epistemic progress, for, when the inferer knows that the hill which he sees, possesses such smoke as is pervaded by fire, he also knows that the hill has fire. To this what can be said first is that since the former (*parāmarśa*) implies the latter (*anumiti*), it is true that to know the former is to know in a way the latter, but still there is some difference between the two cognitions. In the *anumiti* the inferable property or *sādhya*, i.e. the fire qualifies the subject of inference or *pakṣa* directly, whereas, in the *parāmarśa*, fire qualifies the *pakṣa* only indirectly, as the pervader of smoke which qualifies the *pakṣa* or the subject of inference directly. For, in the latter cognition the *pakṣa* is qualified by the *hetu*, i.e. smoke, which again is qualified by the relation of pervasion with the *sādhya*, i.e. fire, and so fire, which is the adjunct of the said relation, figures in this cognition as the qualifier of the *pakṣa*. Thus, since the two cognitions are different in respect of their content, despite the *sādhya* forming a part of the content of both cognitions, it can be claimed that in the passage from *parāmarśa* to *anumiti* something new is known.

The second way of solving the problem may be this. It may be argued that *parāmarśa* should not be regarded as a premise of the inference, but only a step through which the conclusion is reached. To explain, for drawing an inference, viz. "The hill has fire because it has smoke", two basic items of information are necessary,[16] viz:

1. that the *hetu* has the relation of pervasion with the *sādhya*, and
2. that the *hetu* is present in the *pakṣa*.

So, these two may be treated as premises of an *anumāna*. But the actual inferential process includes a few more steps. The first

[16] Keśava Miśra, 1968, *Tarkābhāsa*, with Hindi tr. Badrināth Śukla, Varanasi: Motilal Banarsidass, p. 120.

item of information, viz. the information regarding the relation of pervasion is retained in the mind of the inferer in the form of a disposition (*saṁskāra*). On having the second bit of information the disposition gets revived and gives rise to the recollection (*smṛti*) of the relation. This recollective cognition forms a part of the actual inferential process, so the first item of information reproduced in this way is one of the premises of an *anumāna*. As we have stated earlier, three cognitions, viz. *pakṣadharmatā-jñāna*, i.e. the cognition that the *hetu* is present in the *pakṣa*, *vyāpti-jñāna* or the recollection of the relation of pervasion holding between the *hetu* and the *sādhya* and *parāmarśa*, i.e. the perception that the *pakṣa* is characterized by such a *hetu* which is pervaded by the *sādhya*. These are the causal conditions which lead to the inferential cognition to the effect that the *pakṣa* is characterized by the *sādhya*. We have also seen that the first cognition leads to the second one and the second cognition leads to the third, which finally leads to the conclusion. Now, on our proposed solution to the problem of epistemic progress, the first two cognitions should be taken as premises, but the third cognition, which is in a sense a product of the two previous cognitions, should be regarded as a step through which the conclusion is reached. Though, according to the Nyāya theory, the third cognition, i.e. the *parāmarśa*, is not an inference from the other two cognitions, yet it is a perceptual cognition which connects or synthesizes two previous cognitions and, hence, could not have occurred unless these cognitions had occurred. The content of this cognition includes the contents of both of its preceding cognitions. On the Nyāya view, *parāmarśa* is considered an intermediary operation (*vyāpāra*) through which the second cognition, i.e. *vyāpti-jñāna* produces the *anumiti*. This shows that it would not be incompatible with the Nyāya position if *parāmarśa* is regarded as a step[17] in the inferential process rather

---

[17] This proposal of treating *parāmarśa* as only a step in the inferential process and not as a premise may not, however, be accepted in some cases of inference. Indian logicians admit that in some cases an →

than a premise. An acceptance of this interpretation would keep off the charge that the inferer knew the conclusion when he had known the premises and hence there is no epistemic progress. Actually, it is through the *parāmarśa* that the implication of the premises is finally drawn.Therefore, epistemic progress through inference is not excluded by the Nyāya theory of inference.

To conclude, we can say that what has been discussed so far vindicates our claim that the Nyāya theory of inference is well suited to epistemology; the ideal that it recognizes is validity united with truth and it lays down the conditions for attaining this ideal.

---

← inference is drawn on the basis of a verbal cognition (i.e. a cognition that one has on hearing a sentence) in the form of *parāmarśa* (*śābda-parāmarśa*). For example, on hearing the sentence "The hill has smoke which is pervaded by fire" a person has a verbal cognition to the effect that the hill, which has been referred to, possesses smoke which is pervaded by fire. On the basis of this *śābda-parāmarśa* the person infers that the hill in question possesses fire. In this case, neither *pakṣadharmatā-jñāna* nor *vyāpti smṛti* precedes the inferential cognition, but *parāmarśa* alone precedes it. So, in this case, *parāmarśa* should be treated as the premise from which the inferential conclusion follows.

# 9

# Types of Inference in Indian Logic

IN INDIAN philosophical systems, *anumāna* (inference) has been accepted as a *pramāṇa*, i.e. as a means of *pramā* (knowledge). The inference is classified into different types under various classification schemes in different systems. Each of these schemes takes into account a different characteristic of an inference, and based on that the classification is done. For example, in some schemes the classification is based on the nature of *sādhya* (inferable entity); in some others, the classification is based on the nature of the relation *vyāpti* on which an inference is drawn. As a result, one and the same inference may belong to different types under varied schemes of classification.

However, it may be questioned as to which scheme of classification brings out the fundamental difference among inferences belonging to different types. In this chapter, we shall consider only the schemes found in the Nyāya, Vaiśeṣika, Sāṁkhya, Mīmāṁsā and Vedānta systems, and shall try to find out whether any of these schemes of classification can be regarded as fundamental.

The first classification, which is found in almost all the systems, is the classification of *anumāna* into

1. *svārthānumāna* (inference for own self), and
2. *parārthānumāna* (inference for others).

This classification is based on the purpose (*prayojana*) to be served by an inference. There may be two purposes which may prompt a subject to make an inference – one is to gain knowledge about something and the other is to prove a thesis to someone in doubt regarding the truth of that thesis. When an inference is made for the first purpose, it is *svārthānumāna*; when it is made for the second purpose, it is *parārthānumāna*. The first can be a way of knowing and the second one a way of proving. In the language of Western logic, we may call the first one "inference" and the second one "argument". In *parārthānumāna*, language plays an important role. One who wants to prove a thesis to someone in doubt employs a compound sentence with five components (*pañcāvayava vākya*) and that sentence induces a process of inference in the mind of the hearer. This five-membered compound sentence has a definite form and in it the proposed thesis, the premises and the conclusion all are stated. So, this five-membered compound can be called an argument. The term *parārthānumāna* is applied to both the five-membered compound as well as the process of inferring which starts in the mind of the hearer.[1]

Now, irrespective of the purpose for which they are made, i.e. whether they are *svārthānumāna* or *parārthānumāna*, *anumāna*s are further classified on different principles in different systems of Indian philosophy.

In the *Nyāyasūtra* of Gautama,[2] *anumāna* has been divided into three kinds: (1) *pūrvavat*, (2) *śeṣavat*, and (3) *sāmānyataḥdṛṣṭa*. There have been speculations regarding the interpretation of these three types of inference. Vātsyāyana, the illustrious commentator

---

[1] Annaṁbhaṭṭa, 1963, *Tarkasaṁgraha* with his own commentary *Dīpikā* and Govardhana's commentary *Nyāyabodhinī*, ed. Y.V. Athalye and M.R. Bodas, pp. 37-38 and 251-54, Bombay: Sanskrit Series.

[2] Gautama, 1985, *Nyāyadarśanam*, *Nyāyasūtra* with Vātsyāyana's *Bhāṣya*, ed. Tārānātha Nyāyatarkatīrtha and Amarendramohan Tarkatīrtha, *sūtra* 1.1.5 with *Bhāṣya*, New Delhi: Munshiram Manoharlal.

of *Nyāyasūtra*, has explained them in two different ways. And Uddyotakara, in his *Nyāyavārttika*, has explored many more possible interpretations.

In the *Praśastapādabhāṣya*,[3] a text of the Vaiśeṣika system, we find the classification of inference into two types:

1. *dṛṣṭa*, and
2. *sāmānyataḥdṛṣṭa*.

The same classification is also found in the *Mānameyodaya*,[4] a text of the Bhāṭṭa school of Mīmāṁsā and in the *Nyāya-bhūṣaṇa*[5] of Bhāsarvajña, a Naiyāyika with deviant views (*nyāyaikadeśī*). In the *Śābarabhāṣya*[6] of Mīmāṁsā system also, it has been said that *anumānas* are of two types depending on *pratyakṣataḥdṛṣṭa sambandha* and *sāmānyataḥdṛṣṭa sambandha*, serving as the basis of inference. Regarding this classification also, there are different interpretations.

Mention of another way of classifying *anumāna* is found

---

[3] Praśastapāda, 1977, *Padārthadharmasaṁgraha*, with Śrīdhara Bhaṭṭa's *Nyāyakandalī*, ed. Sri Durgadhar Jha, pp. 507-10, Varanasi: Sampurnananda Sanskrit Visvavidyalaya.

[4] Nārāyaṇa Bhaṭṭa, 1933, *Mānameyodaya*, ed. C.K. Raja and S.S. Suryanarayana Shastri, pp. 60-61, Adyar, Madras: Theosophical Publishing House.

[5] Bhāsarvajña, 1968, *Nyāyabhūṣaṇam*, ed. Swami Yogindrananda, pp. 159-62, 229-30 and 300, Varanasi: Saddarsana Prakasana Pratisthanam.

[6] *tattu dvividhṁ pratyakṣataḥdṛṣṭasambandha sāmānyataḥdṛṣṭasambandham yathā dhumākṛtidarśanāt agnyākṛtivijñānam, sāmānyataḥdṛṣṭasambandham yathā devadattasya gatipūrvikāṁ deśāntaraprāpti upalambhāt āditye gatismaranam* – as quoted by Pārthasārathi Miśra, from the *Śābarabhāṣya* in his commentary *Nyāyaratnākara* on Kumārila's *Ślokavārttika*, ed. Swami Dvarikadas Shastri, Varanasi: Tara Publication, 1978.

in Sāṁkhya,[7] Mīmāṁsā and Nyāya texts. On this scheme of classification, there are two types of *anumāna*:

1. *Vīta*, and
2. *Avīta.*

Another well-known classification, discussed elaborately in the texts of Navya-Nyāya,[8] is of three kinds:

1. *Anvaya-vyatirekī,*
2. *Kevalānvayī*, and
3. *Kevala-vyatirekī.*

There are, however, different opinions regarding the exact principle on which this classification is done.

We shall consider each of the schemes of classification mentioned above, and compare them to see where they actually differ. We shall also try to find out which scheme of classification should be regarded as fundamental.

## I

We shall begin with the early Nyāya classification of inference into *pūrvavat, śeṣavat* and *sāmānyataḥdr̥ṣṭa.* It has already been mentioned that there are several interpretations of these three types of inference.

According to the first interpretation given by Vātsyāyana, *pūrvavat, śeṣavat* and *sāmānyataḥdr̥ṣṭa* respectively mean the following types of inference:

1. Inference of an effect from a cause,
2. inference of a cause from an effect, and
3. inference of an imperceptible entity (its being a cause or an

[7] Vācaspati Miśra, 1982, *Sāṁkhyatattvakaumudī*, ed. Sri Narayan Candra Goswami, Calcutta.

[8] Gaṅgeśa, 1996, *Tattvacintāmaṇi, Anumāna Khaṇḍa*, ed. Kamakhyanath Tarkavagish, p. 552, Delhi: Chowkhamba Sanskrit Pratisthan.

effect is not excluded) based on the inferential relation called *vyāpti* (pervasion), which the inferential ground has with an entity belonging to the same class to which the inferable entity belongs.

Let us discuss each of these in detail:

1. *Pūrvavat* (*Inference of an Effect from a Cause*): The etymological meaning of the term *pūrvavat* supports this interpretation. *Pūrva* means antecedent and *vat* is derived from the *matup*, means "having" (the compound expression thus means having an antecedent). Now, in causally related events, the cause is the antecedent. So, an inference which has an antecedent event or a cause as the *hetu* (inferential ground) is *pūrvavat anumāna*, where the effect of the cause is the *sādhya*. It is to be noted that *pūrvavat* may also mean the effect because the effect is the consequent which has an antecedent, i.e. a cause. However, *pūrvavat anumāna* on this analysis also would mean inference of an effect. Therefore, on the first analysis, *pūrvavat anumāna* means *pūrva* (*kāraṇa*) *hetuka anumāna*, i.e. an inference having a cause as the inferential ground and on the second analysis, it would mean *pūrvavat sādhyaka anumāna* (an inference of an effect).

   There is a third analysis. It says that the special causal condition (*karaṇa*) of an inferential cognition is technically termed as *anumāna* and that this is a cognition which has as its object the *hetu*; so when such a cognition has for its object an entity which is a cause (*pūrva*), it is to be called *pūrvavat anumāna*. So, it means *pūrva viṣayaka jñānam anumānam*, where *anumāna* stands for the means to inferential cognition and not *anumiti* (inferential cognition) itself. The term *anumāna*, due to the peculiarity of Sanskrit grammar, can be used to mean either the means to inferential cognition or the inferential cognition itself and sometimes it is used also to mean the entire inferential process (*anumāna prakriyā*) including the result, i.e. the inferential cognition. In the first analysis, *anumāna* is taken to mean the inferential ground, in the second, it is taken to mean the inferential cognition, and in the third, it stands for the means to inferential cognition. Nevertheless in all the analyses, they virtually involve reference to the same thing, i.e. an inference of an effect from a cause. Vātsyāyana's illustration of this type of inference is an inference of imminent rain on seeing an overcast sky. The cloud is the cause of rain and in this inference, cloud is used as the inferential ground, and rain is taken as the inferable thing. Hence, it is an inference of an effect from a cause.

2. *Śeṣavat* (*Inference of a Cause from an Effect*): The etymological meaning of *śeṣavat* too justifies its interpretation. *Śeṣa* means that which comes after, i.e. the consequent which is the same as effect and *vat* means "having" (this compound means having a consequent). And as in the case of *pūrvavat*, *śeṣavat* may also mean:

   i. an inferential argument having an effect as its *hetu*; or

   ii. an inferential cognition having as its object a cause (which is *śeṣavat*, because a cause has an effect or *śeṣa*); or

   iii. the cognition, which acts in the role of the special causal condition of *anumiti*, having as its object an effect.

   And in all the three analyses, *śeṣavat* involves reference to the same, i.e. inference of a cause from its effect. An instance of this type of inference, as given by Vātsyāyana, is the inference of previous rainfall on seeing flooded rivers with turbulent currents.

3. The third type of inference called *sāmānyataḥdr̥ṣṭa* which according to Vātsyāyana is an inference of an imperceptible entity based on a relation of *vyāpti* which the given *hetu* is known to have with a class of things which includes the imperceptible *sādhya.* Vātsyāyana does not actually explain in detail this type of inference but gives an example. However,

Vātsyāyana's understanding of this type of inference is most controversial and has been criticized severely by his successors in the Nyāya school. The example given by Vātsyāyana is the inference of the sun's motion. People at that time believed that the sun revolved around the earth. The inference is based on the fact of seeing the sun at different places in the sky (at different times). The sun's motion is imperceptible, so the inferential ground, i.e. being at different places cannot be seen to have *vyāpti* with the sun's motion. Even in the absence of the specific relation of *vyāpti*, the inference is possible because in respect of many other substances like a ball or a car we have seen that their being at different places is invariably related to their motion. Thus, on the basis of such generally ascertained relation of *vyāpti*, the inference of the sun's motion is drawn.

The point of criticism against Vātsyāyana is that after characterizing *pūrvavat* and *śeṣavat anumāna* as inference of an effect from its cause and inference of a cause from its effect respectively, for exhaustive classification of inference it would be natural to characterize the third type as an inference where the *sādhya* and the *hetu* are not causally related. Uddyotakara, the author of *Nyāyavārttika*,[9] in one of his interpretations characterizes *sāmānyataḥdr̥ṣṭa anumāna* in this way. His example is the inference of a water-body existing nearby, on seeing birds like storks. Since the inferential relation, i.e. *vyāpti* (pervasion), does hold not only in cases of causally related entities, this type of inference should include all such deductions where *hetu* and *sādhya* are not causally related. In addition to Uddyotakara's example, the inference that a given entity is a substance on knowing that it is earthen (*dravyam pr̥thivītvāt*) may be taken as an example of non-causal inference. But from Vātsyāyana's choice of examples it appears that he did not have in mind non-causal inferences only as *sāmānyataḥdr̥ṣṭa*

9 Uddyotakara, *Nyāyavārttika* on *Nyāyasūtra*. See *Nyāyadarśanam*, pp. 144-57.

*anumāna.* In the example given by him, the *hetu*, viz. being at different places, is an effect of the *sādhya*, i.e. the motion of the entity. So, it seems that he emphasizes the impreceptibility of the *sādhya* resulting in the imperceptibility of the relation of *vyāpti* as the characteristic of *sāmānyataḥdṛṣṭa anumāna.*

Let us now turn to Vātsyāyana's second interpretation of these three types of inference:

1. *Pūrvavat anumāna*: It is the type of inference, where on the basis of previous experience of an entity being concomitant with another, the inference is drawn. On seeing an entity of the first kind, a person infers that the entity is accompanied by the other. For example, from the previous experience of seeing smoke to be accompanied by fire, we infer the presence of fire in a place when we see smoke. This interpretation too can be justified by a grammatical analysis of the term *pūrvavat.* The term is constituted out of the word *pūrva* (before) and the suffix *vat* (like), thus the compound term means "like before" or "as before". In the *pūrvavat anumāna*, the cognition of the *hetu* is followed by the inferential cognition of the *sādhya*, as just in the previous experience, during the ascertainment of the relation of *vyāpti* in a particular instance, the cognition of the *hetu* was accompanied by the cognition of the *sādhya.* This is the most common type of inference.
2. *Śeṣavat anumāna*: It is also known as *pariśeṣa anumāna* and widely differs from the *pūrvavat* type of inference. Here, *śeṣa* or *pariśeṣa* means the residue or remainder. In this inference, through a process of elimination of different possibilities, the remaining or the uneliminated possibility is established as actual. As an example of this type of inference, Vātsyāyana presents an inference through which *śabda* (sound) is established as a *guṇa* (quality). Existence of *śabda* is known through preception and it is perceived to be a positive (*sat*) entity. *Śabda* is producible as well as a perishable entity, i.e.

*anitya*. These two properties namely, *sattā* and *anityatva* are present in substance, quality and motion alike, but are not present in universal, individual differentiation, inherence and absence. So, *śabda* is differentiated from the latter ones admiting the possibility of its being in any of the former three categories. To explain it further, sound as a real entity must belong to any of the seven categories admitted in the Nyāya-Vaiśeṣika system and its possibility is limited to the first three categories only because sound is known to be a positive (*sat*) and non-eternal entity. Of these three possibilities, the first one, i.e. being a substance is eliminated, because no substance, inheres in one single substance which sound does. Sound inheres in only one substance which is called *ākāśa*. The possibility of its being motion is also negated, because sound produces another sound but a motion never produces a thing of its own kind, i.e. another motion. So, the remaining possibility of its being a *guṇa* is asserted to be the case through this inference. Thus, *śeṣavat anumāna* actually turns out to be a series of inferences and not one single inference. In the given example, the knowledge that sound is a positive and non-eternal entity eliminates at the outset the possibility of sound being a universal or individual differentiation or inherence or absence. Thus, the possibility is restricted to three only, viz. being a substance, being a quality or being a motion. Then, by means of one inference the possibility of being a substance is denied and by another inference the possibility of being a motion is denied. Thus, the remaining possibility of sound being a quality is automatically established as the case. The scheme of *śeṣavat anumāna* would be like this:

i. *X*, by virtue of its properties *s* and *p*, is either *A*, *B* or *C* (any definite number of possibilities), there being no other possibility.

ii. *X* is not *A* because of *f*.

iii. *X* is not *B* because of *g*.

iv. *X* is *C*.

The entire argument may be summed up like this. *X* being neither *A* nor *B*, and there is no other possibility excepting *C*, *X* must be *C*.

Here we start with multiple information about *X*. We know that *X* has the properties *s*, *p*, *f* and *g*. Now based on this information, we first fix the possibilities as in (i) above. Then in (ii) and (iii) we make inferences with negative conclusions and finally, taking i, ii and iii as premises, we arrive at a positive conclusion about *X* in (iv). The entire inferential process is similar to disjunctive syllogism.

3. *Sāmānyataḥdr̥ṣṭa anumāna* in Vātsyāyana's second interpretation appears to be more or less the same as that in his first interpretation. The most common and important feature of *sāmānyataḥdr̥ṣṭa anumāna* in both interpretations is that the *sādhya* of the inference is an imperceptible thing, hence, no *hetu* can be ascertained to have a relation of *vyāpti* with it. So an imperceptible *sādhya* cannot be inferred directly based on a given *hetu* which has not been ascertained to have the relation of *vyāpti* with the proposed *sādhya*. The inference of the self from desire, etc. (desire/aversion/cognition/pleasure/pain/volition) has been cited by Vātsyāyana as an instance of *sāmānyataḥdr̥ṣṭa anumāna*. The self as an entity distinct from the body, sense organ, etc. is imperceptible. Desire as an internal state is perceptible, but its relation of *vyāpti* with the imperceptible self cannot be established. So the self cannot be inferred directly from desire. Still, the inference is possible because desire is known to be a quality[10]

---

[10] Though we are aware of the state of desire (*icchā*) in internal perception, that it is a quality (*guṇa*) can be proved with the help of a *pariśeṣa anumāna* (inference through elimination). Desire as a real entity should come under any of the seven categories, viz. →

and a quality is known to be invariably located in a substance, as seen in the cases of qualities like colour, taste and smell. Therefore, it is inferred that desire as a quality should also be located in a substance and that substance is called the self. The inference may be formulated as follows.

Desire is located in a substance because it is a quality. Here, it is to be noted that though desire has been regarded as the basis of the inference of the self, in the formulated inference neither does desire figure as the *hetu* nor does the self figure as the *sādhya*. The inference starts with the internally perceived state of desire from which we arrive at the knowledge that there is a self which is the locus of desire. For this reason, desire and the self are regarded as the *hetu* and the *sādhya* respectively. But, in the formal inference, desire is the *pakṣa*, being located in a substance is the *sādhya* and being a quality is the *hetu*. The inference is drawn on the basis of the following *vyāpti*.

> Whatever is a quality is located in a substance just as a colour (which is a quality) is located in a piece of cloth (which is a substance).

---

← *dravya, guṇa, karma, sāmānya, viśeṣa, samavāya* and *abhāva*. Now let us employ a *pariśeṣa anumāna:*

i. Desire cannot come under *sāmānya, viśeṣa* and *samavāya* (all of which are eternal) because it is transitory (non-eternal).

ii. Desire cannot be *abhāva* (which is a negative entity) because it is a positive state.

iii. Desire cannot be a *dravya* (substance) because it is partless (*niravayava*) while being non-eternal. (Explanation: all non-eternal substances are composite or *sāvayava* in nature.)

iv. Desire is not *karma* (motion) because it is not a non-inhering, i.e. *asamavāyī* cause of any effect. (Explanation: motion is always a non-inhering cause of some effect.)

Therefore, desire is a quality (which is the only remaining category).

Thus, a substance is inferred as a locus of desire and it is regarded as the self. That means, through this inference, the only knowledge that is obtained about the self is that it is the locus of desire. Later commentators of the Nyāya school pointed out that to establish the self as a substance other than the body, sense organs, etc. a *śeṣavat anumāna* would be necessary. By eliminating the possibility of any of the other known substances being the locus of desire, it can be proved that the locus of desire is a substance different from all other substances and that is the self.

Before concluding the discussion of Gautama's threefold classification of inference, we should mention another suggested interpretation of this classification. B.K. Matilal, in his *Logic, Language and Reality*,[11] points out that if *Nyāyasūtra* 1.1.5 is read along with *sūtra* 2.1.37, where Gautama considers some arguments put forward by the opponents to show the invalidity of the given examples of each of the three types of inference, a different interpretation will be suggested. The temporal characteristics of the *hetu* and the *sādhya* might have been Gautama's principle of classification. On this principle, *pūrvavat anumāna* would stand for an inference of a past (*pūrva*) event from present, and the inference of past rainfall from seeing overflooded river would be an instance of *pūrvavat anumāna. Śeṣavat anumāna* would be the inference of a future/later (*śeṣa*) event from a present event. To infer future rainfall is by seeing dark clouds or on seeing ants carrying eggs. It seems that on this interpretation, in *pūrvavat* as well as in *śeṣavat anumāna* the *hetu* and the *sādhya* may or may not be causally related. As we find in the second example of *śeṣavat anumāna* as mentioned in *Nyāyasūtra* 2.1.37 and *bhāṣya*, there is no causal connection between (future) raining and ants carrying eggs. However, there is a relation of temporal succession.

---

[11] B.K. Matilal, 1985, *Logic, Language and Reality*, chap. 1, pp. 33-39, Delhi: Motilal Banarsidass.

*Sāmānyataḥdṛṣṭa anumāna* in this interpretation is the one where the *hetu* and the *sādhya* are both present. Inferring the presence of a peacock on hearing a peacock's call is considered as an instance of this type of *anumāna.* It may be pointed out here that this example of *sāmānyataḥdṛṣṭa anumāna* taken by Vātsyāyana in his commentary on *sūtra* 2.1.37 is different from the two instances of the same type of *anumāna* cited by him in his commentary on *sūtra* 1.1.5. From his earlier examples, it was clear that the distinguishing characteristics of this type of inference is that it is about an imperceptible entity, i.e. its *sādhya* is imperceptible. But the example, given later in *Nyāyasūtra* 2.1.37, lacks this characteristic.

Now regarding the above-mentioned interpretation of Gautama's threefold division of inference, Matilal takes a clue from *sūtra* 2.1.37. In that *sūtra*, the opponents' positions were stated by Gautama. The first criticism was against the instance of the inference of a past event from a present one; then it was followed by the second criticism; this criticism is against the inference of a future event from a present event and lastly there was criticism against the inference of a present event from another event present at the same time. If this order is matched with the order in which Gautama mentions the three types of inference in *sūtra* 1.1.5, then the above interpretations seems plausible.

Matilal further argues that this interpretation can be taken to be supported by Vātsyāyana's comments in the *bhāṣya* on 1.1.5 that through *anumāna*, the present, past and future objects can be known. And the importance of the temporal character of the objects of *anumāna* is further shown by the fact that Gautama devotes a section on "time" in the context of justification of *anumāna* (*anumāna parīkṣā*).

Bhāsarvajña, a philosopher of the early Nyāya school, famous for his deviant views, has also given several interpretations of this classification in his book *Nyāyabhūṣaṇam.* The interpretation, which is argued for by Matilal, has been mentioned by Bhāsarvajña, among other interpretations. But Bhāsarvajña has not stated clearly which of the interpretations he prefers.

## II

The classification of the inferences into *dṛṣṭa* and *sāmānyataḥdṛṣṭa* is found in the Vaiśeṣika and Mīmāṁsā texts. Bhāsarvajña, a Naiyāyika, also makes this classification. But regarding the interpretation of these types also, there is a difference of opinion.

*Dṛṣṭānumāna*: There are two interpretations of this type of *anumāna*:

i. It is the inference of an entity belonging to a class, some other member of which was perceived at the time of ascertaining the relation of *vyāpti.* The inference of fire from smoke will be regarded as an example of *dṛṣṭānumāna* in this interpretation.
ii. It is the inference of a self-same entity which was perceived previously when the relation of *vyāpti* was ascertained. For example, on seeing the rising of the star named "Kṛttikā", it is inferred that the star named "Rohiṇī" would rise shortly. "Rohiṇī" is one single star which was perceived a number of times to follow the rise of "Kṛttikā", which is another particular star. So, the same Rohiṇī, which was preceived previously, is being inferred at a particular time.

Of these two interpretations, the Vaiśeṣikas accept the first one while the Mīmāṁsakas hold the second one, as we find in Nārāyaṇa Bhaṭṭa's *Mānameyodaya.* Bhāsarvajña, on the other hand, maintains that these are the two types of *dṛṣṭānumāna* and not two alternative interpretations.

Now both the meanings of *dṛṣṭānumāna* agree with the etymological meaning of the term *dṛṣṭānumāna.* Etymologically it means inference of the perceived (*dṛṣṭa-viṣayaka anumāna*). In the first case, though the particular object to be inferred was not perceived before, some other member of its class was perceived at the time of ascertainment of *vyāpti*. So, belonging to the same class as that of the perceived instance is also considered perceived or perceived-type (*dṛṣṭajātīya*). In the second case, the inferable entity itself was perceived previously during the perception of the relation of *vyāpti*.

In the *Śābarabhāṣya* on Jaimini's *Mīmāṁsāsūtra*, we find almost similar distinction between inferences based on *pratyakṣataḥdṛṣṭa sambandha* and those based on *sāmānyataḥdṛṣṭa sambandha*. The inference of fire on seeing smoke has been cited as an example of the first type of inference; and the inference of the sun's motion on the basis of the relation of *vyāpti* between motion and change of location, as ascertained in the case of an individual, who is seen to move and occupy different places is an instance of the second type. Though in both the cases, the relation of *vyāpti* is perceived, by *pratyakṣataḥdṛṣṭa sambandha*, Śabara means that relation of *vyāpti* which is perceived to hold between the particular *hetu* and the particular *sādhya* of a given inference, as between smoke and fire in the given example. But in the latter case, the relation of *vyāpti* with the particular *sādhya*, i.e. the sun's motion, has not been perceived, but the inference is drawn on the basis of the general *vyāpti* holding between motion as such and change of location ascertained through perception in some other instance, so this is called *sāmānyataḥdṛṣṭa sambandha*.

Śabara's view regarding inference based on *pratyakṣataḥdṛṣṭa sambandha* seems to cover both the interpretations of *dṛṣṭānumāna*.

*Sāmānyataḥdṛṣṭānumāna*: According to Praśastapāda, a Vaiśeṣika philosopher, and Bhāsarvajña, a Nyāya philosopher, a *sāmānyataḥ-dṛṣṭa anumāna* is an inference, which is drawn on the basis of a relation of *vyāpti* holding between two broader classes, one of which includes the class to which the *hetu* belongs, and the other is inclusive of the class to which the *sādhya* belongs. Thus, it is based on a general *vyāpti* rather than a specific *vyāpti* holding between the given *sādhya* and the given *hetu*. The example given by Praśastapāda is the inference of *svarga* (heaven) as the result of certain sacrificial rites performed by persons without the motive of some mundane gain. This inference is made on the basis of our experience that actions performed by a farmer, a trader or a king is followed by results like crops, money or kingdom. Thus, it is argued that just as the act of tilling, etc., have some result, like crops, etc. the sacrificial rite in question also has some otherworldly results, i.e. *svarga.* Actually, a relation of *vyāpti* is ascertained between action in general (*pravṛtti sāmānya*), which is the *hetu*, and having results in general (*phalavattva sāmānya*), which is a *sādhya* on the basis of the observation of the particular instances mentioned above. Another example of this inference is the inference of the visual sense organ from the occurrence of perception of colour. Here also, in the instance of felling a tree being performed with an axe, a relation of *vyāpti* is ascertained between the act and the instrument in general. And it is inferred that perceiving colour being an act is performed by means of some instrument, just as the act of felling a tree is done with an axe and that instrument is the visual sense organ.

We may point out here that this interpretation of *sāmānyataḥdṛṣṭa* is the same as Vātsyāyana's interpretation of this type of inference. In all the examples, the *sādhya* is an imperceptible entity, and the relation of pervasion holds between two broader classes including the class of entity which is the *sādhya* and the class of entity which is the *hetu.* This would be clear from Table 9.1.

**Table 9.1**

| *Sādhya* (*Inferable Entity*) | *Hetu* (*Inferential Ground*) |
|---|---|
| Example I: The self (Vātsyāyana's) | Desire, etc. |
| Example II: The *svarga* (Praśastapāda's) | Volition towards certain sacrificial rites |
| Example III: Sense organs (Visual, etc.) | Perceiving a colour, etc. |

The relation of *vyāpti* (pervasion) holds between:

| | |
|---|---|
| Example I: Being a quality under which comes<br>i. being a colour, etc.<br>ii. being a desire, etc. | Being located in a substance under which comes<br>i. being located in *tejas*, etc.<br>ii. being ......located in a substance which is the self |
| Example II: Being a volition (*pravṛtti*) under which comes<br>i. being the volition of a farmer, etc.<br>ii. being the volition of a member of the Vedic society towards certain sacrificial rites (*yajña*) | Having some result under which comes<br>i. having for its result, crop, etc.<br>ii. having *svarga* (heaven) as a result |
| Example III: Being an act which includes<br>i. being an act of felling a tree<br>ii. being an act of perceiving | Being performed through some instrument<br>i. being done with an axe<br>ii. being performed through an instrument which is a sense organ |

*Sāmānyataḥdṛṣṭa* inference in the second interpretation, as found in Mīmāṁsā text *Mānameyodaya*, is the inference of an individual entity belonging to a particular class from another entity belonging to another class, based on a relation of *vyāpti* holding between those two classes of entities. The inference of fire from smoke is an instance of this type of inference according to this interpretation. A relation of *vyāpti* holds between smoke as a class and fire as a class and on this *vyāpti* the inference of a particular fire on seeing a particular smoke is based.

So, we find that what is Praśastapāda's interpretation as an example of *dṛṣṭa anumāna*, has been regarded by Nārāyaṇa Bhaṭṭa, a Mīmāṁsā philosopher, as an instance of *sāmānyataḥdṛṣṭa anumāna.* He rejects Nyāya-Vaiśeṣika philosopher's view of *sāmānyataḥdṛṣṭa anumāna* on the ground that imperceptible entities are not inferable; they can be known by means of *arthāpatti pramāṇa* (postulation), so *sāmānyataḥdṛṣṭa* inference cannot be an inference about imperceptible *sādhya* as the Nyāya-Vaiśeṣika philosophers hold.

### III

In the *Tattvacintāmaṇi*, the pioneering work in Navya-Nyāya, Gaṅgeśa classified *anumāna* into three kinds:

i. *kevalānvayī,*

ii. *kevalavyatirekī,*

iii. *anvayavyatirekī.*

There is, however, no reason to believe that this classification is peculiar to Navya-Nyāya only. In early Nyāya, as well as in other philosophical systems, this classification was known. Uddyotakara and some other commentators on the *Nyāyasūtra* suggested that Gautama's division of *anumāna* into *pūrvavat, śeṣavat* and *sāmānyataḥdṛṣṭa* might correspond to *kevalānvayī, kevalavyatirekī* and *anvayavyatirekī.*

According to Gaṅgeśa's definition, a *kevalānvayī* inference is one where *vipakṣa*, i.e. a locus of the absence of the *sādhya*, is not available. The following is an example of this type of inference.

This is nameable because this is knowable just as a table is.

In this inference, "being nameable" is the *sādhya*, and no locus of the absence of nameability can be found because on Nyāya-Vaiśeṣika view every real thing is nameable.

*Kevalavyatirekī anumāna* is, on the other hand, an inference where *sapakṣa*, i.e. a known locus of *sādhya*, is unavailable. The following is an example of this type of inference.

A substance is different from things other than a substance because it has substancehood.

Here the *sādhya* is "being different from things other than substance", and this can be present in substances only. But, since all the substances are included in the *pakṣa*, no known locus of *sādhya* is available.

*Anvayavyatirekī anumāna* is an inference where both *sapakṣa* (known locus of *sādhya*) and *vipakṣa* (known locus of the absence of *sādhya*) are available. For example, the inference that the hill has fire because it has smoke. Here a known locus of fire (*sādhya*), such as a kitchen, and a known locus of the absence of fire, such as a lake, are both available.

There are different opinions among the Naiyāyikas regarding the principle on which this classification is done. The following views are found:

i. It is based on the form of the relation of *vyāpti*, admitting that there are different forms of *vyāpti*.

ii. It is based on the type of *sahacāra* (agreement) through the experience of which the relation of *vyāpti* is ascertained.

iii. It is based on the nature of the *sādhya*.

iv. It is based on the type of *dṛṣṭānta* (instance) available for substantiating the relation of *vyāpti*.

Gaṅgeśa holds that there are two forms of *vyāpti* known as *anvaya vyāpti* and *vyatireka vyāpti*, and a *hetu* can have either or both forms of *vyāpti* with the *sādhya*. By *anvaya vyāpti* means co-location of the *hetu* with the *sādhya*, which can be expressed as: wherever there is the *hetu*, there is the *sādhya*. We may call it a positive form of *vyāpti*. *Vyatireka vyāpti*, on the other hand, may be called the negative form of *vyāpti*, which means co-location of the absence of *sādhya* with the absence of the *hetu*. This type of *vyāpti* is expressed as: wherever there is absence of the *sādhya* there is the absence of the *hetu*. Now, in some cases of inference, due to the absence of the locus of the absence of *sādhya* (*vipakṣa*), no negative or *vyatireka vyāpti* is possible, but positive or *anvaya vyāpti* is available in such cases. In some other cases, due to the absence of a locus where *sādhya* is known to be present (*sapakṣa*), there cannot be *anvaya vyāpti*, but there is *vyatireka vyāpti.* In still other cases, both forms of *vyāpti* are possible.

While interpreting Gaṅgeśa's classification of inference, some Naiyāyikas hold that an inference which is drawn solely on *anvaya vyāpti* is *kevalānvayī anumāna*; an inference which is based on *vyatireka vyāpti* alone is *kevala-vyatirekī anumāna*; and an inference based on both forms of *vyāpti* is called *anvaya-vyatirekī anumāna.*

But some of Gaṅgeśa's predecessors in the Nyāya school[12] held that there can be only one form of *vyāpti*, i.e. *anvaya vyāpti.* According to them, an inference is always based on a *vyāpti* in the form of co-location of the *hetu* with the *sādhya.* But this *vyāpti* can be ascertained in two ways, either by observing the *hetu* being accompanied by the *sādhya*, i.e. *anvaya sahacāra* (argeement in presence), or by observing the absence of *sādhya* being accompanied by the absence of *hetu.* So, according to them, a *kevalānvayī anumāna* is that in which the *hetu* is ascertained to have the relation of *vyāpti* through the perception of agreement in the presence between the *hetu* and the *sādhya*; and a *kevalavyatirekī anumāna* is that in which the *hetu* is ascertained to have the relation of *vyāpti* by observing agreement in absence between the *sādhya* and the *hetu;* thus the inference where the relation of *vyāpti* is known in both the ways

[12] A widely held opinion among the modern scholars of Nyāya is that Udayanācārya was the upholder of this view. Pandit Badrināth Śukla in his Hindi commentary on Keśava Miśra's *Tarkabhāṣā* has mentioned Udayanācārya's name as the Naiyāyika who maintained this view. But I could not find any clear reference in Udayanācārya's writings to confirm this opinion. Jagadīśa, however, mentioned this view as one upheld by the Ācarya. Pandit Phaṇibhūṣaṇa Tarkabāgīśa mentioned that such a view was maintained by some philosophers of earlier period.

is called *anvayavyatirekī*. So, on this view, an inference with the same *sādhya* and the same *hetu* may be regarded as *kevalānvayī* or *kevala-vyatirekī* or *anvayavyatirekī*, depending on the way in which the relation of pervasion was actually ascertained.

The view that there is only one form of *vyāpti*, i.e. *anvaya vyāpti*, seems to be quite justified. The assertion that wherever there is the *hetu* there is the *sādhya* means the same as the assertion to the effect: wherever there is absence of the *sādhya*, there is absence of the *hetu*. Both assertions are about the relation of *vyāpti* which the *hetu* has with the *sādhya*; the second assertion reiterates the first assertion. The difference lies only in the way of apprehending the relation and in its expression. So, it is the *anvaya vyāpti* on which every inference is based. This is further shown by the admission that just as we can infer *vyāpaka* (*sādhya*) from *vyāpya* (*hetu*), we can also infer the absence of *vyāpya* from the absence of the *vyāpaka* and both the inference is based on the *vyāpti* which the *hetu* has with the *sādhya*. If it is argued that in the second case, there is a different *vyāpti* which the *vyāpakābhāva* has with *vyāpyābhāva*, then this would also be a case of *anvaya vyāpti* which *vyāpakābhāva*, the *hetu* of this inference has with *vyāpyābhāva*, i.e. the *sādhya* of this inference.

In the *Tarkabhāṣā*,[13] a manual of Navya-Nyāya, its author Keśava Miśra says that, an inference is called *kevalānvayī*, if no negative instance (*vyatireka dr̥ṣṭānta*) through which *vyatireka vyāpti* can be ascertained is available. Such an inference is based on *anvaya vyāpti* alone, which is ascertained through some positive instance (*anvaya dr̥ṣṭānta*). A *kevalavyatirekī anumāna* is that where no positive instance (*anvaya dr̥ṣṭānta*) is available, through which *anvaya vyāpti* can be substantiated. Here, the inference is based on the *vyatireka vyāpti* ascertained through a negative instance. And such cases of inference, where both positive and negative instances, through

[13] Keśava Miśra, 1968, *Tarkabhāṣā*, ed. with a commentary in Hindi by Badrināth Śukla, pp. 115-24, Varanasi: Motilal Banarsidass.

which positive and negative forms of *vyāpti* respectively can be substantiated are available, are called *anvayavyatirekī.*

Here though the difference between one type of inference and the another is shown in terms of availability or otherwise of positive and/or negative instance(s), the author actually accepts the view that the difference consists in the form of *vyāpti* on which the particular inference is based on. It may also be pointed out that this interpretation is in accord with Gaṅgeśa's definitions of these three types of inference.

Raghunātha in his *Dīdhiti,*[14] a commentary on Gaṅgeśa's *Tattvacintāmaṇi*, says that an inference is regarded as *kevalānvayī* if its *sādhya* is a *kevalānvayī* property, i.e. a property, the absolute absence of which cannot be found anywhere. Such a property is called a *kevalānvayī dharma.* For example, knowability (*jñeyatva*) is such one property according to the Naiyāyikas. They maintain that every real thing is knowable. So, nothing can be found where the property of knowability is absent, thus no *vipakṣa* or the locus known to have the absence of the *sādhya* is available. Such an inference is called *kevalānvayī.*

But most of the things in the world are *vyatirekī*, i.e. a property, the absolute absence of which is available in some thing or other. There are inferences with *vyatirekī* properties as *sādhya*, so the absence of *sādhya* is available in such cases. These inferences can again be of two types: *kevalavyatirekī* and *anvayavyatirekī.* When all the loci of a *vyatirekī* property are included in the *pakṣa* of the inference, no instance of the known co-location of a *hetu* with that *sādhya* (*sapakṣa*) is available and the inference is based on a negative *vyāpti* substantiated in a negative instance; this inference is called *kevalavyatirekī.* If, on the other hand, the *vyatireki sādhya* is known to have co-location with the given *hetu*, the inference is called *anvayavyatirekī.*

---

[14] Raghunātha Śiromaṇi, *Dīdhiti* on *Tattvacintāmaṇi*; see *Tattvacintāmaṇi*, Anumāna Khaṇḍa, *Kevalānvayīparakaraṇam.*

Now, this classification of inference has not been accepted in many philosophical systems. In Advaita Vedānta and Mīmāṁsā systems, *kevalānvayī* and *kevalavyatirekī* types of inferences have been rejected. There are however exceptions. In *Mānameyodaya*, this classification is accepted. Though it is known to be a text of Bhāṭṭa Mīmāṁsā, its author Nārāyaṇa Bhaṭṭa deviated from Kumārila's view in some cases. In Gāgā Bhaṭṭa's *Bhāṭṭacintāmaṇi* also, classification of inference into these three types is found.

In both Advaita Vedānta[15] and Mīmāṁsā systems, *kevala-vyatirekī anumāna* has been replaced by *arthāpatti pramāṇa*.[16] *Arthāpatti* (presumption) has been recognized as a distinct *pramāṇa*, and they say that the so-called *kevalavyatirekī anumāna* is only a case of *arthāpatti*. They argue that an inference can only be drawn on basis of the relation of *vyāpti* holding between the *hetu* and the *sādhya*, so the relation of *vyāpti* between the absence of *sādhya* and the absence of *hetu* cannot be relevant to an inference. In such cases, the cognition results from presumption or *arthāpatti*.

*Kevalānvayī anumāna* has been rejected by the Vedāntins[17] on the

---

15 Dharmarājādhvarīndra, 1970, *Vedāntaparibhāṣā*, ed. with the commentary *Paribhāṣāsaṁgraha* by Pandit Pañcānana Śastrī, p. 128, Calcutta.

16 *Arthāpatti* is recognized as a separate *pramāṇa* (means to knowledge) by a number of schools of Indian philosophy. In an application of *arthāpatti pramāṇa*, something is presumed in order to remove an apparent conflict between two facts. For example, Mr *X* is known to be alive but is not found to be present at his home; from this it is presumed that he is present elsewhere. Here, Mr *X*'s presence elsewhere is known through *arthāpatti pramāṇa*, which starts with two apparently confliciting facts and gets the conflict resolved through the presumption. In other words, the combination of two facts, which apparently seems inexplicable, is accounted for by the presumption of another thing. Thus, that which is presumed is proved to be true.

17 Dharmarājādhvarīndra, *Vedāntaparibhāṣā*, pp. 126-27.

ground that in their system no property is *kevalānvayī* or present everywhere, for, the absence of everything can be found in *Brahman* which is the only reality. So, they admit only *anvayī anumāna*, which is based on *anvaya vyāpti* alone. The Mīmāṁsakas also rejected *kevalānvayī anumāna*, but on a different ground. They argued that if the *sādhya* of an inference is a *kevalānvayī* property which is present everywhere, then there will be no doubt regarding the presence of the *sādhya* in the *pakṣa* under consideration. According to them, such a doubt (*sādhya-saṁśaya*), is said to constitute a precondition of inference, which is technically called *pakṣatā*. So, in the absence of *pakṣatā*, no inference can take place.

### Vīta and Avīta Anumāna

In the *Sāṁkhyatattvakaumudī*, Vācaspati Miśra says that *anumāna* is divided into two kinds - *vīta* and *avīta*. *Vīta anumāna* is that, where *sādhya* is established in a positive or an affirmative way. The form of such an inference is: the *hetu* is present in the *pakṣa*; wherever the *hetu is* present, the *sādhya* is present, therefore, the *sādhya* is present in the *pakṣa*. *Avīta anumāna*, on the other hand, establishes the *sādhya* in a negative way. A negative way of proving a position may either mean proving it by a process of negating other alternative positions or it may mean establishing a position based on the known agreement between the absence of *sādhya* and the absence of *hetu*. The first way of proving is the same as *pariśeṣa anumāna* and the second way is the same as *kevala-vyatirekī anumāna*. For Vācaspati Miśra, they are the same. He says that *pariśeṣa* and *vyatirekī*[18] are just different names of the same type of *anumāna*. He divides *vīta anumāna* into two kinds - *pūrvavat* and *sāmānyataḥdṛṣṭa*. But on his interpretation, *pūrvavat anumāna* is the same as *dṛṣṭānumāna* in the sense in which it is interpreted by the Vaiśeṣikas. Regarding *sāmānyataḥdṛṣṭa anumāna* also, he accepts the interpretation given by Vātsyāyana and Praśastapāda.

---

[18] Vācaspati Miśra, *Nyāyavārttika-tātparyaṭīkā*; see *Nyāyadarśanam*, pp. 144-57.

In this context, we may observe that the reason behind holding *pariśeṣa* and *kevalavyatirekī anumāna* to be the same, as done by Vācaspati Miśra, is not obvious. Though in both the cases, the inferential process is in some sense negative, there is a difference in two cases. In the case of *pariśeṣa anumāna*, the *sādhya* is established through a process of negating all but one of the possible alternative conclusions. Still, the final inference and intermediate inferences made in the process are not necessarily based on negative *vyāpti*. But, *kevalavyatirekī anumāna* is necessarily based on negative or *vyatireka vyāpti* only. So, it seems that bringing *śeṣavat* or *pariśeṣa anumāna* under *avīta anumāna* may not be justified if *avīta anumāna* is taken to mean an inference based on negative *vyāpti*.

## IV

Alter discussing different schemes of classification of *anumāna*, we may take up an inference and classify it under different schemes of classification. Take the stock example of *anumāna*, viz. *parvataḥ vahnimān dhūmāt* (The hill has fire because it has smoke). Table 9.2 will show how this inference will be classed according to different schemes of classification.

**Table 9.2**

| *Name of the Class* | *Scheme of Classification* |
|---|---|
| 1. *Śeṣavat* (i.e. inference of the cause from its effect) | Gautama's classification according to Vātsyāyana's first interpretation |
| 2. *Pūrvavat* | Gautama's classification according to Vātsyāyana's second interpretation |
| 3. *Dṛṣṭānumāna* | Praśastapāda's scheme |
| 4. *Sāmānyataḥdṛṣṭa* | Mīmāṁsā scheme as presented by Nārāyaṇa Bhaṭṭa in the *Mānameyodaya* |
| 5. *Anvaya-vyatirekī* | Navya-Nyāya scheme |

From this example, it is clear that one and the same *anumāna* may be described correctly as belonging to different types in relation to different schemes of classification.

We shall now try to find out which of the schemes considered above may be treated as basic, or, in other words, what should be the basic difference between two *anumānas* so that they are brought under two different types?

A close look into the different schemes would reveal that, in most of the cases, the classification is based on the nature of the *sādhya*. Let us have a look at Table 9.3.

**Table 9.3: Different Schemes of Classification of Anumāna**

I. Gautama's scheme according to Vātsyāyana's first interpretation:
   i. *Pūrvavat*: An effect as the *sādhya* or the inferable
   ii. *Śeṣavat*: A cause as the *sādhya* or the inferable
   iii. *Sāmānyataḥdr̥ṣṭa*: An imperceptible entity as the *sādhya* or the inferable

II. Mīmāṁsā scheme:
   i. *Dr̥ṣṭa*: The *sādhya* or the inferable is the same entity which was perceived before
   ii. *Samānyataḥdr̥ṣṭa*: The *sādhya* belongs to the same class, a member of which was perceived before

III. Vaiśeṣika scheme:
   i. *Dr̥ṣṭa*: The *sādhya* belongs to the same class, a member of which was perceived before
   ii. *Sāmānyataḥdr̥ṣṭa*: The *sādhya* is an imperceptible entity

IV. Gaṅgeśa's scheme of classification as interpreted by Raghunātha:
   i. *Kevalānvayi*: The *sādhya* is an unnegatable type of property
   ii. *Kevalavyatirekī*: The *sādhya* is a negatable type of property which is not known to have an agreement in presence with the *hetu*
   iii. *Anvayavyatirekī*: The *sādhya* is a negatable property which is known to have an agreement in presence with the *hetu*

So, according to Raghunātha's interpretation, *anumāna* is first divided into two types in respect of the difference in the type of *sādhya*, i.e. *kevalānvayī sādhyaka* and *vyatirekī sādhyaka*. The latter is again divided into two types: *kevalavyatirekī* and *anvayavyatirekī*.

But we think that difference in the nature of *sādhya* cannot be taken to constitute the basic principle of classification of *anumāna*. If *anumāna* is taken to be a way of knowing, then the basic difference between any two types of *anumāna* should be a difference in the way of knowing through them. Considering this point of view, Gautama's classification into *pūrvavat*, *śeṣavat* and *sāmānyataḥdṛṣṭa*, given Vātsyāyana's second interpretation and also the scheme of classification into *kevalānvayī*, *kevala-vyatirekī* and *anvaya-vyatirekī* as interpretated by Gaṅgeśa, may be regarded as basic schemes of classification of *anumāna*.

*Pūrvavat*, *śeṣavat* and *sāmānyataḥdṛṣṭa* may be regarded as three basic types of *anumāna* because each is a different way of inferring a *sādhya*. In *pūrvavat anumāna* a *sādhya* is inferred on the basis of a *hetu* which is known to be pervaded by the *sādhya*. It is a direct way of knowing a *sādhya* or establishing a conclusion. But *śeṣavat* and *sāmānyataḥdṛṣṭa* are indirect ways of concluding or knowing a *sādhya*. None of these two types of inference is based on a relation of *vyāpti* holding between the *sādhya* and the given *hetu*. *Śeṣavat*, as we have seen earlier, is an eliminative process comprising a series of inferences through which the *sādhya* or the conclusion is established. In *sāmānyataḥdṛṣṭa* too, *anumāna* is not based on the relation of *vyāpti* holding directly between two broader classes of entities, one of which includes under it the class of things presented as the *hetu* and the other includes under it the class of things presented as the *sādhya* (see Table 9.1).

Classification of *anumāna* into *kevalānvayī*, *kevalavyatirekī* and *anvayavyatirekī on* the basis of the different types of *vyāpti* used in different *anumāna* may also be said to reflect a difference in the way of knowing/establishing the *sādhya*. In *anvaya-vyatirekī*, both the forms of *vyāpti*, i.e. positive (*anvaya*) and negative (*vyatireka*), can be used, and so it can be taken to be the strongest and most convincing way of establishing a *sādhya* (conclusion). Here both the things, i.e. the *hetu* is accompanied by the *sādhya* and the absence of the *sādhya* is accompanied by the absence of the *hetu*, can be shown. Thus, the complete justification for the inference of the conclusion can be provided. In *kevalānvayī anumāna* only the positive form of *vyāpti*, i.e. *anvaya vyāpti*, can be used, and there is no way of showing that denial of the *sādhya* is not possible because there is no instance to substantiate the claim that the denial of the *sādhya* would lead to the denial of the *hetu*. In *kevalavyatirekī* on the other hand, only *vyatireka* form of *vyāpti* can be used and thus the *sādhya* is established negatively, by showing that denial of the *sādhya* is not possible, but there is no way of confirming that the *hetu* is accompanied by the *sādhya*.

However, in all the three types of inferences just mentioned, the *sādhya* is established by means of one single *hetu* having some form of *vyāpti* with the *sādhya*. So, all these types seem to come under *pūrvavat anumāna* in Gautama's classification (though we have seen that a different opinion is held by Vācaspati Miśra on this point). Therefore, compared to Gaṅgeśa's classification, Gautama's classification into *pūrvavat*, *śeṣavat* and *sāmānyataḥdr̥ṣṭa* may be shown to have more fundamental difference in the way of establishing the *sādhya*.

# 10

# Upamāna Pramāṇa
## Its Nature and Object

THE Sanskrit word *upamāna* is used in both literature and philosophy. The meanings of this word, as given in the dictionary, are similarity, resemblance, analogy and comparison. They all mean more or less the same. A sentence expressing similarity or comparison is called *upamāna vākya*; the knowledge of similarity is called *upamāna jñāna*. Most of the philosophical schools of India admit *upamāna* to be a *pramāṇa* (source of knowledge).

But, difference of opinion prevail among those philosophers on several points relating to *upamāna pramāṇa*. The points of disagreement can be put in the following questions:

1. Whether *upamāna* should be admitted as a separate (*svatantra*) *pramāṇa*? Or can it be subsumed under some or other of the accepted *pramāṇas*?
2. What is *upamāna pramāṇa*, i.e. the *karaṇa* (instrumental cause) of *upamiti*?
3. What is the object of *upamāna pramāṇa*?
4. What is the form of *upamiti*, i.e. the cognition resulting from *upamāna pramāṇa*?

Controversies among philosophical schools centre mainly around the above-mentioned questions. In this chapter, I shall cover these controversies with a critical exposition of each of the views regarding *upamāna pramāṇa.*

I shall begin with a brief outline of the discussion to follow. The Nyāya and both the Bhāṭṭa and Prābhākara schools of Mīmāṁsā admit *upamāna* to be a separate *pramāṇa*, and the Advaita Vedānta school, which shares the view of the Bhāṭṭa Mīmāṁsā school on many issues, also admits this. But the Vaiśeṣika, the sister system to the Nyāya, denies independent status to *upamāna pramāṇa* and holds that it is reducible to other *pramāṇas*. And Bhāsarvajña, who is a follower of the old Nyāya school, but is well known for his divergent views on certain issues, also holds that *upamāna* is not a separate *pramāṇa.*

The Naiyāyikas admit *upamāṇa* to be a means to the knowledge of the name-thing relation, i.e. the meaning relation; and according to them, the knowledge of similarity is the *kāraṇa* of *upamiti.*

The Mīmāṁsā school, on the other hand, holds *upamāna pramāṇa* to be a source of the knowledge of similarity that a remembered object is known to have with an object which is being perceived at that time. The *upamiti-jñāna*, according to them, is of the form "that thing is similar to this thing". This knowledge is obtained through the perceptual knowledge of similarity of the form "this thing is similar to that thing". So, according to the Mīmāṁsā philosophers, both *upamāna* and its result *upamiti* are the knowledge of similarity, but of two different forms.

In the texts of these philosophical schools, we find that a great deal of debate took place over *upamāna pramāṇa*. We shall see how the philosophers of different schools argued in favour of their respective positions and defended them from the objections raised by the opponents against their position.

## I

Let us start with the Nyāya theory of *upamāna pramāṇa*. In the *Nyāyadarśana*, we find that *sūtrakāra* Gautama says in 1.1.3:

"*pratyakṣa, anumāna, upamāna* and *śabda* are the *pramāṇas*". That means, according to the Nyāya school, perception, inference, comparison and verbal testimony are the four *pramāṇas* (sources of knowledge). In *sūtra* 6 of chapter 1, Gautama says that when something is known on the basis of similarity (*sādṛśya*) of a thing with a familiar thing, then the source of such knowledge is called *upamāna pramāṇa*. From this statement, it is clear that the knowledge of similarity of an unseen (unknown) object with a known or familiar object is the *upamāna pramāṇa*.[1] The next question is: what is the object that can be known by means of *upamāna pramāṇa*. The Naiyāyikas maintain that only a special kind of object is known through this *pramāṇa*; it is the meaning relation that holds between a word and a thing. According to them, there are many ways of knowing a meaning relation, of which *upamāna* is one. And they also say that a meaning relation is the most important, if not the only, object of *upamāna*.

The knowledge resulting from *upamāna* is called *upamiti*. The form of a *upamiti* is "the thing *x* is named by the word *A*". Now, *upamiti* is the *pramā* and *upamāna* is the *pramāṇa*; that means, *upamāna* is the *kāraṇa* of *upamiti*. Let us now consider the process of the causation of *upamiti* as held by the Naiyāyika. From this, we shall be able to know what exactly is the *kāraṇa* of *upamiti* and hence the *upamāna pramāṇa*.

We have already mentioned that *upamāna pramāṇa* has a special object, i.e. the meaning relation holding between a naming word and the thing named (*saṁjñā-saṁjñī sambandha*). The meaning relation is also known as *śakti*. It has also been said that a *śakti* can be known by several means, of which *upamāna* is one. Now, the application of *upamāna pramāṇa* is restricted to a special context. When a person hears a particular name but does not know what thing is named by that he/she may ask some knowledgeable person

---

1 Vātsyāyana, 1985, *Bhāṣya* on *Nyāyasūtra* 1.1.3 in *Nyāyadarśanam*, ed. Tārānātha Nyāyatarkatīrtha and Amarendramohan Tarkatīrtha, New Delhi: Munshiram Monoharlal.

about it. Suppose, the person hears the name *gavaya* (in English *gavaya* is translated as bison). This name denotes some type of animal, but which animal he does not know. He asks about it to a person who is a forester and knows a lot about animals. That person says that *gavaya* is an animal similar to the cow. From this, the enquirer gets an idea about the animal called *gavaya*. Later, somewhere he comes across an animal which is similar to the cow. Perceiving this similarity between that animal and the cow, he is reminded of the sentence, "*gavaya* is similar to *go* (cow)". After this, he comes to know that this kind of animal is called by the name *gavaya*. Thus, he knows the meaning relation between the naming word and the thing named (*saṁjñā-saṁjñī sambandha).* This knowledge is *upamiti*. Now we need to analyse the process of *upamāna pramāṇa* to identify the *kāraṇa* of *upamiti*. We have said in the beginning that *upamiti-jñāna* is based on similarity. And in the process described above, we find the mention of similarity (*sādṛśya*) three times. And it is obvious that *sādṛśya*, unless known, cannot be of any use in causing cognition. So we are to see how similarity is known so as to cause *upamiti jñāna*. First, a sentence about the similarity between the unseen thing, in this case, it is *gavaya* and a familiar or known thing, which is the cow in our example. The knowledgeable person uttered the sentence, "*gavaya* is similar to *go* (cow)". This sentence is called *atideśa vākya*. This is a statement of similarity between two things; on hearing this, the enquirer had a verbal or testimonial cognition about the similarity between the two. This is the first cognition of similarity. Next, he encounters an animal in, say, a forest that he perceives to be similar to the cow. So this perceptual cognition (*pratyakṣa-jñāna*) is the second cognition of similarity. After that, he remembers the sentence he had heard previously: "*gavaya* is similar to *go* (cow)". Here he has a recollection (*smṛti*) of the similarity between those two animals.[2]

Now the question is: of these three cognitions of similarity

[2] Viśvanātha, 1988, *Kārikāvalī-Muktāvalī*, ed. Śrī Śaṅkarrām Śāstrī, Delhi: Chowkhamba Sanskrit Pratisthan.

(*sādṛśya-jñāna*) preceding the occurrence of *upamiti*, which one is the *upamāna pramāṇa* or the *karaṇa*, i.e. the instrumental cause of *upamiti*? According to the Naiyāyikas like Uddyotakara and Vācaspati Miśra, the perception of similarity is the *kāraṇa* of *upamiti*. The matter as explained by them is that when the enquirer, who had heard that *gavaya* is similar (*sadṛśa*) to *go* (cow), encounters an animal looking like a cow, he perceives the similarity and then recollects the *atideśa vākya* stating the similarity between *go* and *gavaya*. After that, he has the cognition that the kind of animal he is seeing is called by the name *gavaya*. So, here, perceptual cognition of similarity aided by the memory cognition of similarity is the *kāraṇa* of *upamiti*, i.e. the *upamāna pramāṇa*. And *upamiti* is the cognition of the meaning relation holding between a word and the thing meant by it.

The next question is: what is the form of (*ākāra*) of *upamiti-jñāna*? According to the Nyāya, through *upamāna* we get the cognition of the meaning relation between a name and a thing in a particular context. In the example, we are considering the meaning relation between the name *gavaya* with some particular thing. Now, there can be three possible forms in which *upamiti-jñāna* may result.

i. *ayaṁ gavaya-padavācya* (this is called by the name *gavaya*);
ii. *go-sadṛśa gavaya-padavācya* (the animal which is similar to cow is called by the name *gavaya*); and
iii. *gavaya (gavayatva-viśiṣṭa) gavaya pada-vācya* (that the animal which possesses the universal property of *gavayatva* is called by the name *gavaya*).

The Nyāya philosophers' answer is that the third form mentioned above is the right form of *upamiti*.[3] When we are concerned with common names like man, cow, table and tree, the meaning relation must be a universal relation. Common names are class names, and a common or class name denotes all

[3] Viśvanātha, *Muktāvalī* with *Prabhā*, *Dinakarī* and *Rāmaruārī ṭīkā* on it, pp. 540-44.

particulars belonging to a class. So, we say the word "cow" denotes any individual cow possessing cowhood, or, in other words, any particular belonging to the class of cow.

Now, if we take the first form mentioned above, *ayaṁ gavayapada-vācya*, i.e. this animal is called *gavaya*, where a particular present before the knower is asserted to be the thing bearing the name *gavaya*, then the meaning relation is not established as a universal relation, only a particular as a particular is being known as meant by the word. So "this animal is called *gavaya*" cannot be the right form of *upamiti*. Here a particular animal possessing thisness (*idantā*) is known as the meaning of *gavaya*. "Thisness" is a property which belongs to a particular which is present before the knower at the time of making the assertion. This cannot be a class property present in all the members of a class at any time. So, a universal meaning relation cannot be known in this form.

Regarding the second form, i.e. *go-sadr̥śa gavaya pada-vācya*, the Naiyāyika's opinion is that this too cannot be the right form of *upamiti*. To accept this as the form of the knowledge of meaning relation, which the *upamiti* is, would amount to accepting similarity with the cow (*go-sadr̥śa*) as the reason for the application (*pravr̥tti nimitta*) of the word *gavaya*. But this cannot be accepted. Hence, the meaning relation between *gavaya* and the animal *gavaya* cannot be established. This point needs some elaboration. The Nyāya philosophers hold that a word or a name is applied to a thing on the basis of a property which must be owned by the thing to be named by it. For example, they would say the name "man" can be applied to someone possessing manhood. And the general rule as to what should be the basis or reason for the application of a name is that it should be a universal property (*jāti*).[4] If, for some reason, *jāti* is not available, then *upādhi* (a compound property) can be taken as

---

4 Gadādhara, 1995, *Śaktivāda*, Pariśiṣṭa Kāṇḍa III, pp. 270-72, 367, in *Gadādhara's Śaktivāda*, vol. II with English translation and notes by V.P. Bhatta, Delhi: Eastern Book Linkers.

the basis or reason for the application of a name. Now, according to the Naiyāyikas, *sādṛśya* (similarity) is not a universal property or *jāti* because a *jāti* has to be a unitary, unanalysable property. But *sādṛśya* (similarity) is a property which can be analysed into other properties; it is only an *upādhi*. Since the rule is that if a *jāti* is available, then an *upādhi* cannot be taken as *pravṛtti nimitta* or the reason or basis of the application of a word. So they hold that in the case of *gavaya*, *gavayatva jāti* is the basis of the application of the name *gavaya* and not *go-sādṛśya*. But if the knowledge of the meaning relation takes the form of *go-sadṛśa-gavaya-pada-vācya*, then *gavayatva*, is not known as the *pravṛtti nimitta*.

Therefore, the Naiyāyikas maintain that the third form, i.e. *gavaya gavaya-pada-vācya*, which is equivalent to *gavayatvaviśiṣṭa dharmī gavaya-pada-vacya*, is the form of *upamiti*. Thus, *upamiti* is the knowledge to the effect that a thing possessing the universal property (*jāti*) of *gavayatva* is named *gavaya*.

Another question needs to be addressed at this point. Regarding the property, which is the basis of or the reason for the application of a name (*pravṛtti nimitta*), it has already been said that the property must belong to the thing which is being named. But, for a knower to know that a particular thing, say X, bears the name *A*, he must know that the thing *x* possesses the property *p*, which is the basis of the application of the name. So in our example, the knower must know that the animal which is similar to a cow (*go-sadṛśa*) possesses the universal property of *gavayatva*; otherwise, he cannot know that the animal which is characterized by the property of *gavayatva* is the one that is named *gavaya*. The Naiyāyikas say that this condition is fulfilled here. In their theory, a *jāti* is perceptible if its locus, which is a particular, is perceptible. For example, if we can perceive a table, we can at the same time perceive the universal property of tableness which belongs to it. Hence, they say that when a person perceives a *gavaya*, just as he perceives its similarity with a cow, he also perceives its property of *gavayatva*. So, the person is in a position to know that the perceived animal, which is characterized by *gavayatva*, is called by the name *gavaya* (*gavayatva-viśiṣṭa-gavaya-pada-vācya*).

From what we have discussed so far, we have got an idea about the Nyāya view of *upamāna pramāṇa*. According to the Nyāya theory, knowledge of similarity of an unknown thing with a known thing is the *upamāna pramāṇa*; and the object of *upamāna pramāṇa*, or the thing known in *upamiti* is the name–thing relation.

## II

Now we shall consider some of the views which are opposed to the Nyāya position. First, we shall take up the view of Bhāsarvajña, who was a philosopher belonging to the old Nyāya school but maintained divergent opinions regarding some of the Nyāya theses. Bhāsarvajña maintained that the *upamāna vākya* (statement of similarity), as mentioned in Vātsyāyana's *Bhāṣya*, "*gavaya* is like *go*" is the *upamāna pramāṇa.* And this sentence which is uttered by an authoritative person (*āpta*) is nothing other than *śabda pramāṇa* (verbal testimony). Regarding the object of *upamāna pramāṇa*, he accepts the Nyāya view that the name–thing relation is the object of *upamāna*. According to him, it is by means of the *upamāna vākya* that the name–thing relation is known. He rejects the standard Nyāya view that perception of similarity aided by the recollection of *atideśa vākya* (*upamāna vakya*) is the *upamāna pramāṇa*. Bhāsarvajña argues that when a person wanting to know what the name *gavaya* means hears the sentence "*gavaya* is similar to *go*" uttered by an authoritative person (a person living in a forest and having direct knowledge of animals living there), he knows what thing is meant by the name *gavaya*. So the name–thing relation is known from the *upamāna vākya* itself. Later, when he sees a *gavaya* and perceives its similarity with the cow, he just remembers that it is a *gavaya* as he heard earlier. Bhāsarvajña argues that, that the name–thing relation is known in this case by means of the *upamāna vākya* is evident from the answer one gives when being asked, "how do you know that this is called *gavaya*?" the person answers: "I know it from the words of a forester". But he does not say that he knew it through *upamāna pramāṇa*, as is said in cases of the knowledge obtained through other three *pramāṇas*, viz. *pratyakṣa*, *anumāna* and *śabda*. If *upamāna* were a separate *pramāṇa*, one would have mentioned it as a means through which one knows some particular object like name-thing relation.

To sum up Bhāsarvajña's position on *upamāna pramāṇa*, we should note that he takes *upāmāna vākya* to be *upamāna pramāṇa*, hence he includes it under *śabda* or *āgama pramāna*. He interprets Gautama's *sūtra* on *upamāna* in that way and justifies his interpretation at the instance of common usage (*loka-vyavahāra*). So, according to Bhāsarvajña, the name-thing relation known through the sentence of an authoritative person stating the similarity which the name-bearer has with a familiar thing, in our example, the thing *gavaya* has some similarity with the cow. When we later come across a *gavaya*, we remember the already known relation between the name *gavaya* and the thing *gavaya*.[5]

The first objection that can be raised against Bhāsarvajña's position is that the *upamāna vākya* of the form "*gavaya*'s similar to the cow" can generate a verbal cognition of *gavaya*'s similarity with the cow, but it cannot generate a verbal cognition of the form "this is named *gavaya*" or "the name of this is *gavaya*". In order to have such knowledge of the name-thing relation a separate *pramāṇa* is required. The *upamāna vākya* by itself cannot produce this knowledge.

Bhāsarvajña considered this objection and replied to it. He said that the sentence, "*gavaya* is like the cow" does not only convey the similarity of *gavaya* with cow, but also means that what is similar to the cow is called by the name *gavaya*. So the intended meaning or import of *upamāna vākya* is that the thing which is similar to cow is called by the name *gavaya*. He justifies his argument by referring to

---

5 Bhāsarvajña, 1968, *Nyāyabhūṣaṇam*, ed. Swami Yogindrananda, pp. 417, 419-20, Varanasi: Ṣaḍdarśana Prakāśana Pratiṣṭhānam.

Gautama's *Nyāyasūtra* 1.1.10, where it is said *icchā* (desire), etc. are the inferential mark (*liṅga*) for proving *ātman* (self). Bhāsarvajña says that there also the import of the sentence is "what is proved through the inferential mark *icchā*, etc. is called *ātman*".[6] So, in both the cases, the given sentence produces the knowledge of name–thing relation.

Now the second objection. What Bhāsarvajña has said above indicates that the similarity with the cow (*go-sādṛśya*) has been taken as the basis of the application (*pravṛtti nimitta*) of the word *gavaya*. But according to the Nyāya school, the accepted principle in this regard is that if some universal property (*jāti*) is available, then that should be taken as the basis for the application of a word (*pravṛtti nimitta*) instead of an *upādhi* (a compound property). Similarity with the cow (*go-sādṛśya*) is a compound property, but *gavayatva* is a universal or class property which is simple and analysable. So *gavayatva* and not *go-sādṛśya* should be the reason for applying the name *gavaya*. Now, unless one sees a *gavaya*, one cannot know *gavayatva* because a universal or *jāti* can be perceived only when a particular exemplifying it is perceived. And if a thing is not known to have *gavayatva*, how can the name *gavaya* be applied to it? So, directly from the *upamāna vākya*, the name–thing relation cannot be known.

In reply to this, Bhāsarvajña says that *gavayatva* can be known from the *upamāna vākya* (similarity statement) itself. Just as showing a picture or giving a description, one can acquaint a person with some unseen thing; in that way, by similarity statement also this can be done. For example, by showing the picture of an elephant one may acquaint a child with the elephant by saying, "An elephant is like this", or, by describing a camel as "an animal having a long neck and a hump on the back is called camel" the camel is made known, thus elephanthood and camelhood are also made known to one who has not seen an elephant or camel.[7]

---

6 Bhāsarvajña, 1968, *Nyāyabhūṣaṇam*, 3.12, p. 421.

7 Ibid., p. 420.

He further says that if the *upamāna vākya* does not give the knowledge of the name–thing relation, then what is its use? The similarity between a known and an unknown thing can be known by perception even without hearing the *upamāna vākya*. So, for the knowledge of similarity, *upamāna vākya* is not needed. If one knows a cow and remembers its features, then seeing an animal, which happens to be a *gavaya*, the person can see its similarity with the cow. So *upamāna vākya* is not required for producing the knowledge of similarity.

Bhāsarvajña concludes that *upamāna* is not an additional *pramāṇa*. The so-called *upamāna pramāṇa* is the *upamāna vākya* and that being uttered by an authoritative person is *śābda-pramāṇa* only. By means of this type of *vākya*, the name–thing relation is known.

## III

The Vaiśeṣika philosophers also hold that *upamāna* is not an additional *pramāṇa*, it is *śābda-pramāṇa* only. But, according to them, *śābda-pramāṇa* also is not a separate *pramāṇa*, and it is included in *anumāna pramāṇa*. In their view, from *upamāna vākya* or the statement of similarity between a known and an unknown thing, the name–thing relation is known, not directly, but by means of an inference. They explain that on hearing the sentence *go sadṛśa gavaya* (*gavaya* is similar to the cow), the hearer constructs an inference by means of which he knows that an animal which is similar to a cow is named *gavaya*. Śrīdhara Bhaṭṭa in the *Nyāyakandatī*, his commentary on the *Praśastapādabhāṣya*, showed the form of the inference in the following way.[8] An animal which is similar to the cow is denoted by the name *gavaya*; because foresters, who are authoritative persons, unanimously apply the name *gavaya* to an animal which is similar to the cow. This is based on the *vyāpti sambandha* (relation of pervasion) to the effect "whichever word is used unanimously by

---

8 Śrīdhara Bhaṭṭa, 1963, *Nyāyakandalī*, a commentary on *Praśastapāda-bhāṣya*, ed. Durgadhar Jha, p. 533, Varanasi: Varanaseya Sanskrit Visvavidyalaya.

the authoritative persons to denote a particular thing, that thing is denoted by that name". So, according to the Vaiśeṣikas, from a sentence uttered by an authoritative person, with the help of inference, one can know the name-thing relation. Therefore, there is no need to admit a separate *pramāṇa* called *upamāna*.

The Naiyāyikas have raised objections against the Vaiśeṣika position. Many other formulations of the inference have been given by other Vaiśeṣika philosophers to replace *upamāna pramāṇa*, but the Naiyāyikas have argued against all of them. The one basic objection raised by them is the same one which has been raised against Bhāsarvajña. That is, when the word *gavaya* is said to denote *gavaya*, it denotes *gavaya* as characterized by the universal property of *gavayatva*. The universal property, i.e. *gavayatva jāti*, is the *pravṛtti nimitta* or the basis of the application of the word *gavaya*. Similarity with the cow (*go-sādṛśya*) cannot be the basis of the application of the word *gavaya* as it would violate the law of parsimony (*gaurava doṣa*). But in the *atideśa vākya* or *upamāna vākya*, similarity with the cow (*go-sādṛśya*) has only been mentioned. So, how can a person who hears this sentence know the universal property of *gavayatva* and can finally know that the animal which possesses *gavayatva* is denoted by the word *gavaya*? *Gavayatva* cannot be known by means *śabda* or *anumāna*; unless one sees a *gavaya*, one cannot know *gavayatva*, which is a universal property belonging to all the *gavayas*. Udayanācārya, a celebrated Naiyāyika, has raised this point in his book *Nyāyakusumāñjali*.

In reply to this objection, the Vaiśeṣikas say that though in *upamāna vākya* the word *go-sadṛśa* (similar to the cow) has been mentioned, this word through *lakṣaṇā* (metaphor) means *gavayatvavān*. So, by the *upamāna vākya* itself, *gavayatva* is known as the *pravṛtti nimitta*. Later, when the person who had heard the sentence sees a *gavaya*, he directly perceives the universal property of *gavayatva* possessed by a *gavaya*. And he then remembers, "this animal which is characterized by *gavayatva* is called *gavaya* as I knew earlier".[9]

The assertion that the word *go-sādṛśya* means *gavayatva* through metaphor (*lakṣaṇā*) has been discussed in detail by the Vaiśeṣika philosopher Śaṅkara Miśra in his commentary titled *Kaṇādarahasyam*. The Naiyāyikas are, however, not ready to accept this. They say that there is no scope for *laksaṇa* in the case of the *atideśa vākya* or *upamāna vākya* to the effect *gosadṛśagavaya* or *yaḥ gosadṛśa dharmi sa gavayapada-vācya*; because the word *gosadṛśa* (similar to the cow) taken in its primary meaning *mukhyārtha* can be related to the meaning of other words in the sentence to yield the sentence meaning. Had it failed to do so (*anvaya-anupapatti*), then the word could be taken in a metaphorical sense so that it can be related to the meanings of other words in the sentence and produce the cognition of sentence meaning. The reason for accepting a metaphorical or secondary meaning of a word is that the primary meaning of the word does not fit with the meanings of other words with which it is syntactically related in the given sentence; as a result, the sentence turns out to be meaningless. Instead of primary meaning, if the metaphorical meaning is taken, then the sentence becomes meaningful. But, this reason does not hold in the case of the word *gosādṛśya* occurring in the *atideśa vākya*. So, there is no need to take recourse to a metaphorical or secondary meaning.[10] Therefore, Vaiśeṣikas' assertion that through the similarity statement itself, the universal property of *gavayatva* is known as the *pravṛtti nimitta* or the reason for the application of the word *gavaya* cannot be justified.

---

9 Śaṅkara Miśra, *Kaṇādarahasyam*, in Praśastapāda *Bhāṣyaṭīkā Saṁgrahaḥ*, p. 107, Banaras: Chowkhamba Sanskrit Series.

Udayanācārya, *Nyāyakusumāñjali* with *ṭīkā* by Haridāsa Bhaṭṭācārya, *kārikā* 3.11, pp. 121-22, Varanasi: Chowkhamba Vidya Bhawan.

10 Udayanācārya, *Nyāyakusumāñjali*, *kārikā* 3.12.

## IV

Let us now take into account the Mīmāṁsaka philosophers' position regarding *upamāna pramāṇa*. The philosophers of both Mīmāṁsā and Advaita Vedānta schools admit *upamāna* as an additional *pramāṇa*. Like the Naiyāyikas, they also hold that the perceptual knowledge of the similarity of an object with another object is the *upamāna pramāṇa*. But they differ from the Naiyāyikas in their view regarding the object of *upamāna pramāṇa*. They admit *upamāna* to be a source of the knowledge of similarity which a remembered object has with an object which is being perceived at the moment. *Upamiti jñāna*, according to them, is of the form "that thing is similar to this thing". The adjective "that" refers to a thing which is not present before the knower at the moment but is only remembered. And the adjective "this" refers to a thing which is present before the knower and being perceived at the moment. In *upamiti*, the remembered object is known to be similar to the present perceived object. This knowledge is obtained by means of the perceptual knowledge of similarity which the present object has with the remembered object.[11] For example, a person sees a *gavaya* in a forest and perceives its similarity with the cow which he has in his home. So, he has the cognition of the form "this animal (*gavaya*) is similar to my cow". After that, he has another cognition to the effect, "my cow is similar to this animal (*gavaya*)". The first cognition of similarity, which is perceptual, yields the second cognition of similarity, which is the *upamiti*. The subjunct (*anuyogī*) and adjunct (*pratiyogī*) of similarity have changed their position in the two cognitions, one of which is the *upamāna pramāṇa* and the other is its result, the *upamiti*. In *upamāna*, the subjunct of similarity is being perceived, as is clear from its form "this is similar to that".[12] But in *upamiti*, the subjunct

---

11 Nārāyaṇa Bhaṭṭa, 1933, *Mānameyodaya*, ed. with English translation by C. Kunhan Raja, pp. 108-10, Madras: Theosophical Publishing House.

12 A relation holds between two things and we express it as *x* has a relation with *y*. Here *x* and *y* are the two terms of the relations, *x* →

is unperceived at the moment as the form shows "that is similar to this". The Mīmāṁsakas argue that this second cognition of similarity cannot be obtained by any other means of knowledge except *upamāna.*

The Mīmāṁsā view is criticized by philosophers of other schools who argued that *upamiti* as a form of the knowledge of similarity could be obtained by *pratyakṣa* or *anumāna pramāṇa*. It has been argued that when a person sees a *gavaya* and perceives its similarity with the cow known to him, he also perceives that cow to have similarity with the present *gavaya*. In the single act of perception, their mutual similarity is known, because the similarity between a cow and a *gavaya* consists in having some common features. So, when one perceives those common features in any of them, one perceives their mutual similarity. Hence, there is no need to admit a separate *pramāṇa* called *upamāna*. In reply, the Mīmāṁsakas say that to have perceptual knowledge of a cow having similarity with a *gavaya*, one should perceive the cow at that moment. But in this case, the cow is not present at the moment, it is remembered only. So, this knowledge of similarity cannot be perceptual. The present *gavaya*'s similarity with the remembered cow and the

← is called the *anuyogī* (subjunct of the relation) and *y* is called the *pratiyogī* (adjunct of the relation). There are different varieties of relation and in the case of some relation, the subjunct and adjunct positions are irreversible; for example, when we say the flower has colour, we mean there is a relation of inherence (*samavāya*) between the flower and the colour, where flower is the subjunct and colour is the adjunct, their position cannot be interchanged, we cannot say "colour has flower". But if we take the relation of contact or *saṁyoga*, it may be reversible in some cases, for example, when there is a contact between my index finger and thumb, we can say both that my index finger is in contact with my thumb and my thumb is in contact with my index finger. That means, in this case, each of the term can take the position of either a subjunct or an adjunct. Similarity is one such relation or relational property where subjunct and adjunct are interchangeable.

remembered cow's similarity with the present *gavaya* are different because the subjunct of similarity, which is the subject (*viśeṣya*) of the knowledge of similarity, is different in the two cases. So in one act of perception, the two forms of perceptual knowledge cannot be obtained. For a perceptual cognition, sense contact with the *viśeṣya* is necessary; therefore, perceptual cognition of a property in a remembered object is not possible.

The opponent philosophers also argue that if not by *pratyakṣa pramāṇa*, the cognition of similarity in the case in question can be obtained by inference (*anumāna*). We can infer that the remembered cow is similar to *gavaya* because *gavaya* is similar to it. This inference is based on the relation of *vyāpti* of the following form: "that with which some other thing is similar is itself similar to that other thing", just as the palm of each hand is similar to the other. On the basis of such general relation of pervasion, inference can be drawn in specific cases; the form of the inference would be: *y* is similar to *x*; therefore, *x* is similar to *y*.

In reply, the Mīmāṁsakas say that this cannot be a case of inference because, by inference, we can only know that the cow has some similarity with *gavaya*, but not the specific similarity which is there.[13] Just as and when we infer the existence of fire in a place on the basis of the inferential ground (*hetu*) that the place has smoke, we do not know what kind of fire is there. But when after perceiving a *gavaya* to be similar to a cow, we know that the cow which is not present before us is similar to the *gavaya*, we know clearly, as in perception, the real nature of the similarity. Since the cow is not being perceived at the moment, the cognition is not perceptual but being known by means of cognition of similarity, it is a case of *upamiti*. So, *upamāna pramāṇa* is to be admitted for this kind of knowledge.

The Mīmāṁsā philosophers' opinion regarding the Nyāya view of *upamāna pramāṇa* should also be mentioned here. They

---

[13] Nārāyaṇa Bhaṭṭa, *Mānameyodaya*, p. 111.

do not accept the Nyāya view that the name-thing relation in certain cases is the object of *upamāna pramāṇa*. About the case of the relation between the name *gavaya* and the thing *gavaya*, which the Naiyāyikas have shown to be the object of *upamāna*, the Mīmāṁsakas hold that the name-thing relation here is known by means of *śābda-pramāṇa* aided by *pratyakṣa*. The purpose of *atideśa vākya*, which states that *gavaya* is similar to the cow, is to show the name-thing relation. The purport of the *atideśa vākya* is that the name *gavaya* denotes a thing which happens to be characterized by its similarity with the cow (*gosādṛśyena-upalakṣitasya gavayaśabdaḥ saṁjñā-iti atideśavākyārtha*).[14] On hearing this sentence, a person knows only that, something having similarity with the cow is said to be named by the word *gavaya* until he sees a thing similar to the cow. Later, when he actually sees a thing similar to the cow, he remembers the *atideśa vākya* and knows the purport of the sentence; immediately after that, he knows that such a thing or animal is called *gavaya*. So, here, the remembered *atideśa vākya* actually produces this knowledge which, according to the Nyāya philosophers, is *upamiti*. Perception of the thing (animal) as having similarity with the cow is an aid to *śābda-pramāṇa* in this case. It is to be noted in this context that the Mīmāṁsā account of *upamāna* does not admit any role of *atideśa vākya* in generating *upamiti* as conceived by them.

## V

We started with the Nyāya view. Let us now sum up the Nyāya position regarding *upamāna*. According to them, *upamāna* is to be accepted as an additional *pramāṇa* as a means to the knowledge of name-thing relation in certain cases. They hold that a person who is willing to know what a particular word, say, *gavaya* means, first listens from a forester that a *gavaya* is similar to the cow. So, the

---

14 Pārthasārathi Miśra, 1978, *Nyāyaratnākara Vyākhyā* on Kumārila Bhaṭṭa's *Ślokavārttika*, ed. Dvārikādāsa Sastri, p. 310, Varanasi: Tara Publications.

process of knowing the name–thing relation, in this case, starts with the hearing of a sentence uttered by an authoritative person. From that sentence, the knower has a testimonial or verbal cognition about the unseen *gavaya*'s similarity with the cow. After that, when he sees an animal having similarity to a cow, he remembers the sentence "*gavaya* is similar to the cow", which he heard previously.[15] He then identifies it as a *gavaya,* and at the same time, perceives *gavayatva* which is a universal property present in all the members of the class of *gavaya.* And then he knows the name–thing relation to the effect, a thing which possesses *gavayatva* is the designate or the bearer of the name *gavaya.* The Nyāya philosophers argue that here neither from the *atideśa vākya* or *upamāna vākya* alone nor from the perception of *sādṛśya* can we know the name–thing relation. Here perception of similarity aided by the memory of the testimonial cognition of similarity leads to the knowledge of the name–thing relation of the form "*gavayatvavān gavaya-padavācya*",

---

[15] In the *Nyāyadarśana*, Gautama mentions a question which was raised by the opponents regarding the extent of similarity required in the case of *upamāna pramāṇa*. Should the similarity between two things be absolute, or, should it be profuse, or, should it be partial? And they argued that none of the alternatives will work in the case of *upamāna pramāṇa*. It cannot be absolute because absolute similarity between things amount to their identity. If it is profuse similarity then the sentence *go sadṛśa gavaya* may lead one to take an ox to be a *gavaya*, because an ox has most similarity with the cow. If, again, partial similarity in any respect is taken, then the sentence *go sadṛśa gavaya* can also mean a tiger to be a *gavaya* because a tiger has at least a similarity with *gavaya* in being a quadruped. So the opponents' point is that in the absence of a definite idea of similarity, *upamāna* or *sādṛśya-jñāna* cannot be a *pramāṇa*.

In reply, the Naiyāyikas say that there is no such strict rule as to the extent of similarity needed for *upamāna* to work as a *pramāṇa*. And that is not important even. The workability of the *upamāna vākya* depends on the context or situation (*prakaraṇa*). See *Nyāyasūtra* 2.1.44-45.

meaning thereby, a thing which possesses the universal property of *gavayatva* is denoted by the name *gavaya.* And this means of knowledge is *upamāna* which is other than *śabda*, *pratyakṣa* and *anumāna*. *Upamāna* is here the knowledge of similarity.

One thing should also be mentioned here that the Naiyāyikas admit, as Vātsyāyana says in his *bhāṣya*, that besides the name-thing relation, some other things can also be known by *upamāna pramāṇa*. The later Naiyāyikas have not elaborated on this point, and they do not even agree on the interpretation of the words of the *bhāṣyakāra* about other objects of *upamāna pramāṇa*. Some of the later commentators say that Vātsyāyana hinted at *upamāna* through *vaidharmya* (dissimilarity) when he said that other things could be known by means of *upamāna*. We are, however, not entering into this issue here.

After having discussed the views of the two major schools, the Nyāya and Mīmāṁsā, on *upamāna pramāṇa*, we have before us a brief account of important arguments in favour of and against the position held by each school. It is now left to the readers to form their own opinion on this issue.

# 11

# Meaning and Truth of a Sentence

## An Indian Point of View

### I

In this chapter, I shall deal with the question of the meaning and truth of a sentence from an Indian point of view. I shall concern myself, particularly, with the question regarding the status of sentences like the following:

i. Fire is cold.
ii. He is eating the moon.
iii. The bachelor's wife is beautiful.
iv. The round-square table is broken.
v. The present king of France is wise.

On hearing the above-mentioned sentences, the response one would naturally make is: "absurd", meaning thereby what is being said is absurd. Now, what is meant by "absurd" in this case? Is it meaningless or false? Are the sentences concerned meaningless or false? We shall approach the problem from the Nyāya point of view.

J.L. Shaw, in his paper entitled, "Professor Mohanty on Meaning and Transformation"[1] has dealt with this question and other issues

---

[1] J.L. Shaw, 1991, "Professor Mohanty on Meaning and Transformation", in *The Philosophy of J.N. Mohanty*, ed. Daya Krishna and →

with reference to the Nyāya view. According to his interpretation, all the sentences mentioned above are regarded as meaningful but false by the Nyāya philosophers. However, I hold a different opinion about the Nyāya position regarding the sentences (iii) and (iv). It seems that the Nyāya philosophers would normally regard the sentences containing contradictory expressions as meaningless rather than false. I shall argue here in favour of this position and also show why I hesitate to accept Shaw's interpretation.

I shall first briefly state Shaw's arguments in favour of his position. He argues that even though a sentence containing contradictory expressions like "a son of a barren woman", "a bachelor's wife" or "a round-square" cannot generate a cognition, it can be meaningful because it has a truth-value which can be ascertained. Shaw explains that the sentence "a son of a barren woman" is false because the relation of a barren woman to a son is unreal. He writes:

> We come to know the falsity of this sentence when we know the truth of a sentence about a son. When we know someone as a son, we know him as someone who is related to a woman by the relation of motherhood, and thereby we know the absence of a barren woman by the relation of motherhood in him. ... Since we know that a son has an absence of a barren woman by the relation of motherhood, we know the falsity of the sentence "a son of a barren woman".

Shaw says that if there is syntactic expectancy among different parts of an expression, there is a relation among the referents of the parts and this relation constitutes the meaning of the sentence, over and above the meanings of different constituent parts of the sentence. But if the sentence lacks semantic competency (*yogyatā*), it fails to generate cognition in the hearer. Now, if the relation among the referents of the constituent words in a sentence turns

← K.L. Sharma, New Delhi: Indian Council of Philosophical Research, and Munshiram Manoharlal.

out to be unreal, then the sentence would be false, but it can never be meaningless. So, according to Shaw's interpretation, every sentence having syntactic expectancy among its constituent parts is meaningful, even if it lacks semantic competency. Contradictory expressions certainly lack semantic competency, but, according to Shaw, that does not stand in its way of being meaningful; it only makes the sentence false. Furthermore, he maintains that inability to generate a cognition does not rob it of its meaning. He says that there is a difference between the "meaning of a sentence" and "understanding the meaning of a sentence", and holds that the former is independent of the latter. Understanding the meaning of a sentence means having a cognition of the relation among the referents of the parts of a sentence, and that is possible only with semantic competency, but if there is syntactic expectancy, the sentence would be meaningful.

However, I hesitate to accept this interpretation because the Nyāya philosophers would not regard the meaning of a sentence to be independent of the understanding of a sentence. By the meaning of a sentence, they mean the relation among the referents of the constituent words of the sentence, which forms the content of the cognition generated by the sentence. So, a sentence to be meaningful, it must be capable of producing a cognition in the hearer. Therefore, it would not be possible to talk about the meaning of a sentence which cannot generate cognition. Shaw has admitted that sentences containing contradictory expressions cannot generate cognition in the hearer; how can they then be meaningful?

Jagadīśa, a Navya-Naiyāyika, has said that a semantically incompetent (*ayogya*) sentence can be admitted to produce a testimonial cognition in the form of counterfactual supposition (*āhārya śābdabodha*). But, there is a rule that no mediate (*parokṣa*) cognition can be *āhārya*, i.e. of the nature of supposition; if this rule is accepted, semantically incompetent sentences cannot be regarded as meaningful.[2]

---

2 *vahninā seka ityādyapi vākyameva, parantu bādhitārthakatvāt* →

I will now elaborate on my position regarding this issue and argue for it. To address this question, we must start with the notion of a sentence, its meaningfulness, its truth or falsehood.

To be clear about the notion of a sentence we shall consider two alternative definitions of a sentence as found in the Nyāya texts:[3]

I. A sentence is a collection of words which expresses a complete meaning.

II. A sentence is a collection of words, characterized by the property of *ākāṅkṣā* (expectancy), where *ākāṅkṣā* means a sequential order among the words.

The first definition denies the very possibility of a meaningless sentence, whereas, the second one seems to leave that possibility open. So, if the first definition is accepted, then the sentences we are considering should either be denied the status of a sentence or be regarded as false. Acceptance of the second definition, however, would bestow sentencehood upon them because each of them is characterized by *ākāṅkṣā*,[4] which is a syntactic property that makes them grammatically correct or well-formed. (We cannot go into the details of the property of *ākāṅkṣā* because we are not using Sanskrit language here, which was the language of classical India

← *ayogyam* । *śābdamaterāhāryatvopagame "nirvahni vahnimān"* । *"pacan na pacati" ityādikamapi vākyameva, na cedapārthakameva* ॥ – Jagadīśa, 1981, *Śabdaśaktiprakāśikā* (*Sārthakaśabda Prakaraṇam*, p. 145), ed. Madhusūdana Nyāyācārya, with Bengali translation, Calcutta: Sanskrit College Research Series

3 **Def. I:** *padasamūho vākyamarthasamāptau*, Vātsyāyana's *Nyāyabhāṣya* on *sūtra* 2.1.55 in *Nyāyadarśanam*, ed. Tārānātha Nyāyatarkatīrtha and Anandamohan Tarkatīrtha, 1985, New Delhi: Munshiram Manoharlal.

**Def. II:** *mithaḥ sākāṅkṣa śabdasya vyūha vākyaṁ* – Jagadīśa's *Śabdaśaktiprakāśikā*, v. 13.

4 *yena padena vinā yat padasya anvaya ananubhābakatva tena padena saha tasya ākāṅkṣā* । – Viśvanātha, *Kārikāvalī-Muktāvalī*, *kārikā* 84 and its explanation.

and Indian theories of language were for Sanskrit language.) Since, in the definition, there is no reference to the meaningfulness of a sentence, it would allow the possibility of a meaningless sentence. So, a sentence like "Fire is cold" may be either meaningless or false.

However, the position will only be clear once we consider the notion of meaningfulness of a sentence. The Nyāya maintains a referential theory of meaning so far as word meaning is concerned, but as regards sentence meaning, their position is different. According to them, a sentence is meaningful if it can produce a belief in the mind of the competent hearer, and the content of that belief would be the meaning of the sentence. Take, for example, the sentence "A table is brown". Each of the constituent words, e.g. "table", "is" and "brown" are meaningful, they stand respectively for a particular substance, a particular relation and a particular shade of colour. On hearing these words uttered in a sequence, one who knows the language is reminded of these meanings and after that grasps the connected meanings of these words. To put it more clearly, what is cognized on hearing a sentence is a relational complex comprising meanings of the constituent words and their mutual relations,[5] and that is the meaning of the sentence.

Now, it is admitted by all that a sentence cannot be meaningful unless it is grammatically correct. For example, a mere collection of words like "cow, horse, man and elephant" will not produce in the mind of the hearer any belief with specific content, because such a collection does not follow syntactic rules. That means such a collection lacks *ākāṅkṣā*. To form a sentence, each word must be related to an appropriate word, without which it cannot contribute to the meaning of a sentence.

## II

Now, the question is: is grammatical correctness a sufficient condition for meaningfulness? Or, in other words, are all

---

[5] *sākāṅkṣaśabdairyo bodhastadarthānvayagocaraḥ* । – Jagadīśa, *Śabdaśaktiprakāśikā*, v. 3.

grammatically correct sentences meaningful? Regarding this question, the opinion of some of the Naiyāyikas is that in order to be regarded as a sentence, a grammatically correct sequence of words should also possess another property called *yogyatā*[6] (semantical fitness or competency). This *yogyatā*, though mentioned as a property of words which constitute a sentence, is actually a property of the things meant by the words. The words in a sentence can be said to have *yogyatā* if the things meant by them can be related to one another in the way the grammatical form of the sentence shows. It is to be noted that *yogyatā* is a modal concept. It does not mean that things meant by the words are actually related in the manner revealed by the sentence; they may or may not be thus related, but what is required is that it should not be impossible for them to be related in that manner. If it meant the actuality of such a relationship, then every *yogya* sentence would have been true, and there could be no meaningful but false sentences. However, we shall come to this point later. At this moment, let us be clear about the notions of a *yogya* sentence and an *ayogya* (semantically unfit) sentence. Consider the following two sentences.

i. The man is eating a slice of cake.
ii. The man is eating the moon.

Both sentences have grammatically correct form. A subject term, a verb and an object term are arranged in an appropriate order in both sentences. Nevertheless, the first one is regarded as a *yogya* sentence, whereas the second is not. The reason is that while a slice of cake is a fit object related to the act of eating, the moon is not a fit object of the same act. So what is being said in the second sentence is impossible – it is not possible for a man

6 *padārthe tatra tadvattā yogyatā parikīrtitā* । – Viśvanātha, *kārikā* 83, p. 638.

*eka padārthe aparapadārtha sambandha yogyatā* । Viśvanātha, 1988, *Kārikāvalī-Muktāvalī*, ed. Shankararam Shastri, p. 632, Delhi: Chowkhamba Sanskrit Pratisthan.

to eat the moon. Therefore, it is an *ayogya* sentence and hence meaningless.

A question may, however, be raised regarding the type of possibility, which is being discussed here. Is it the logical or the empirical possibility of connecting the meanings of the words? For example, let us take the sentence "Fire is cold". It is logically possible to connect fire with cold, which means it would not be self-contradictory to assert that fire is identical to a thing characterized by coldness. But if we take the sentence "The bachelor's wife is beautiful", then it is logically impossible to connect bachelor with the property of having a wife, for such an assertion leads to self-contradiction. So, the question is: are both the sentences *ayogya* or semantically unfit or only the latter is so and not the former? A section of Naiyāyikas would hold that both are *ayogya* and hence meaningless. Therefore, on this view, all the sentences, except the last one listed at the beginning, would be meaningless because they all lack the property of *yogyatā*. We have already considered three of these sentences and have found that they fail to satisfy the *yogyatā* condition. Let us now turn to the other two:

a. The round-square table is broken.
b. The present king of France is wise.

In both the sentences, descriptive phrases occur in the subject position. Based on the Nyāya theory, descriptive phrases are treated as sentences, not names. Since they are not names, they do not refer to any entity, but can mean something, i.e. the relation among the things meant by the constituent words if the conditions for meaningfulness are satisfied. In the given sentences, the descriptive phrases, e.g. "the round-square table" and "the present king of France" are to be regarded as sub-sentences. Now the intended meaning of the sub-sentence "the round-square table" is a relational complex comprising a particular table as the qualificand and both the round shape and the square shape as qualifiers at the same time. But such a relational complex is logically impossible: one cannot even think of connecting at the same time both the round and the square shape of a table or any substance whatsoever. So the entire sentence "The round-square table is broken" fails to fulfil the condition of *yogyatā* and hence would be regarded as meaningless.

Of the five sentences, only the last one, e.g. "The present king of France is wise" will pass the test of *yogyatā* on this theory and should be regarded as meaningful. The intended meaning of the sub-sentence "the present king of France" is "the relation" of France to the present king. This is indeed a logically as well as a factually possible combination though, actually, such a relational complex is not available. So, the sentence "The present king of France is wise" cannot be discarded as a meaningless sentence. It could be the case that there is monarchy in France even at the present time and there is someone who rules France and is wise. Therefore, on the Nyāya analysis, it is a meaningful sentence.

## III

At this point, the question about the truth and falsity of a sentence arises. According to the Nyāya school, truth and falsehood are properties of cognitions or beliefs. A belief is true if it corresponds to the fact, and it is false if it does not do so. A sentence can be said to be true if it generates a true belief. That means, if a sentence produces a true belief in the mind of the competent hearer, then it is to be regarded as true. And the Naiyāyikas hold that a sentence can produce a true belief if

i. it is a meaningful sentence, and
ii. it is uttered by an authoritative person (*āpta puruṣa*).

For the time being, we shall concentrate only on the first condition, i.e. the condition of meaningfulness, which is a necessary but not a sufficient condition for the truth of a sentence.

The Nyāya view, which we have considered so far, regards *yogyatā* to be a condition for meaningfulness. But this view is rejected by some later Naiyāyikas.[7] According to them, *yogyatā* is not a condition for meaningfulness, but it is a condition for truth. They hold that a sentence, even if *ayogya*, can produce a belief in the hearer if the hearer does not feel the combination to be semantically incompatible or if he somehow has a false sense that the given combination of word-meanings is semantically compatible. Therefore, in the Nyāya view, if a sentence produces a belief, it is meaningful. So, on this view, even the *ayogya* sentences can be meaningful.

Some philosophers of the Grammarian school[8] have argued in favour of this point. They said that if an *ayogya* sentence like "Fire is cold" were meaningless, then it would not have evoked any response whatsoever. The fact that one responds to such sentences shows that they are meaningful. So, when one reacts to hearing such sentences and says that they are absurd, what one means is that they are not true.

So *yogyatā* is to be regarded as a condition for truth. But that again is only a necessary condition and not a sufficient condition for truth, because even *yogya* sentences sometimes produce beliefs, which are false. For example, the sentence. "There are lions in the forests of the Sundarban" is semantically fit (*yogya*), but the belief it produces would be false. So both *ayogya* and *yogya* sentences may fall within the class of false sentences, but *ayogya* sentences are necessarily false, and *yogya* sentences are sometimes false. A *yogya* sentence says something, which is capable of being actual, whereas an *ayogya* sentence says something which is not capable of being actual. If we turn to our examples, "Fire is cold" and "There are lions in the forests of Sundarban", both sentences are false but what the former sentence says could never be true in this world, whereas, what the latter one says could be the case. But both are false due

---

[7] See Note 2.

[8] Nāgeśa, 1989, *Vaiyākaraṇasiddhāntalaghumañjūṣā*, p. 507, Varanasi: Chowkhamba Sanskrit Series.

to the same reason that the beliefs they produce, respectively, do not correspond to the actual state of affairs. In other words, the relational complex, which constitutes the content of the belief produced by each of them, is not available in the objective world, so what they mean is not true.

In conclusion, we may say that since the Naiyāyikas define the meaning of a sentence in terms of the cognitive state of the hearer, i.e. the meaning of a sentence is that which is grasped in the act of understanding the sentence, they cannot discard a sentence as meaningless if it is somehow understood by a hearer. So, even though the intended relation among the meanings of the words in a sentence is impossible, the sentence can be meaningful, but it would necessarily be false.

It may be questioned here whether a self-contradictory phrase like "The round-square table" or a self-contradictory sentence like "A bachelor is a married man" can produce a belief in the mind of the hearer. The hearer would be unable to connect in thought the meanings of the words constituting the self-contradictory phrases or sentences because in such cases, the hearer cannot but feel the absurdity of such connections. According to the Naiyāyikas, the hearer cannot have a believe on hearing a sentence if he is aware that the intended connection between the meanings of the words is impossible. So normally, self-contradictory sentences cannot produce any belief and hence should be regarded as meaningless rather than false. The philosophers of the Grammarian school, however, differ on this point and hold that even a self-contradictory sentence can be understood and, therefore, should be regarded as meaningful, but false. However, it seems that they have overlooked the distinction between understanding a sentence and understanding the meanings of constituent words of a sentence. Understanding the meaning of a word means nothing but having a memory image of the thing, which may be a substance or a relation or any other property, for which the word stands. In the case of a self-contradictory sentence, we may understand the meanings of individual words constituting the sentence. However, an attempt to understand the meaning of the sentence, which means grasping the connection of the meanings of individual words, would be thwarted. So the view of the Grammarians standing on this point is unacceptable.

12

# The Self and Self-Knowledge in Indian Tradition

In India, philosophy has never been considered to be a purely theoretical discipline. It has a practical goal, viz. *mokṣa* (freedom from suffering) as well. And at the centre of all philosophical discussion is the self (*ātman*). For, it is the self that suffers pain and wants to get freedom from suffering. This freedom again is possible through self-knowledge, because ignorance or misconception regarding the real nature of the self is the root cause of suffering or bondage (*saṁsāra*). Philosophy is the means of self-knowledge. So, the self philosophizes and acquires self-knowledge which liberates it from suffering for ever. This outlook of Indian philosophers shows the importance of the concepts of the self and self-knowledge in Indian tradition.

We shall start our discussion with the concept of the self (*ātman/puruṣa*). The notion of "I" is present in every individual and is therefore undeniable. So, every Indian philosophical system admits the existence of something corresponding to this I notion, or, in other words, they admit something as the referent of the pronoun word *aham* (I) and that is called the self. Basically, two conceptions of the self are found in Indian philosophy:

i. the self is a substance endowed with consciousness, and
ii. the self is consciousness itself.

The first view is held by the philosophers of the Nyāya, the Vaiśeṣika, the Mīmāṁsā and the Cārvāka schools, and the second view is found in the Sāṁkhya, Vedānta, Yogācāra, Bauddha and Jaina systems. As regards the first conception, there is again a difference of opinion as to what thing it is that possesses consciousness and is called the self.

In this chapter, I shall confine myself to the discussion on the self and self-knowledge as developed in the orthodox systems of Indian philosophy.

## I

We may start with the commonly accepted notion that the self is the thing denoted by the pronoun word "I" (*aham padārtha*). For determining the nature of the thing, meant by the word "I", we may be guided by the prevalent verbal usages involving the pronoun "I". We find verbal usages like "I know", "I am happy" and "I do", and also the usages "I am thin", "I am dark", etc. In the above usages,[1] knowledge, happiness, etc. are ascribed to the thing denoted by "I", whereas in the latter usages, the properties like thinness and dark complexion are ascribed to the thing for which the pronoun "I" stands. Thus, these verbal usages show the self to be the substratum of both physical and mental properties. The ascription of physical properties to the self led some philosophers like the materialist Cārvākas to hold the position that the body is the self. They argue that the body which is perceived to be the substratum of physical properties must also be owner of the properties like consciousness, because in both the cases, the owner is referred to as "I". But the philosophers of the Nyāya–Vaiśeṣika and Mīmāṁsā schools would say that verbal usages ascribing physical properties to the self are erroneous and result from confusion between the self and the

[1] Vīrarāghvācārya, *Rasāyana Ṭīkā* on *Vaiśeṣikasūtra* 3.2.17 in Kaṇāda's *Vaiśeṣikadarśanam*, p. 129, Madras, 1958.

Madhvācārya, 1986, *Sarvadarśanasaṁgraha*, p. 3, Calcutta: Asiatic Society.

body. According to them, the self is different from the body and they prove this by means of arguments. So, they hold that what is meant by "I" is a thing distinct from the body, sense organs, etc. and is the substratum of consciousness, happiness and other internally perceivable qualities.

The Advaita Vedāntins on the other hand hold that "I" (*aham*) does not stand for the real self which, according to them, is pure consciousness. "I" always means consciousness falsely identified with *antaḥkaraṇa* (inner organ) (*antaḥkaraṇa-tādātmyāpanna caitanya*).[2] This complex, according to them, is *jīva* (individual self) or the empirical self (*vyāvahārika jīva*). And this *aham* is the locus of such properties as *pramātṛtva* (knowerhood) and *kartṛtva* (agenthood). According to them, all the properties that are ascribed to the self belong really to *antaḥkaraṇa*. There being superimposition (*adhyāsa*) of *antaḥkaraṇa* on the self due to ignorance (*avidyā*), these properties are falsely attributed to the self. Thus, the complex of consciousness and inner organ, which is referred to by *aham* (I), is said to possess knowledge, happiness, etc.

Likewise, there being superimposition of the body and sense organs along with *antaḥkaraṇa* on the self, the physical properties are also attributed to the self. So, according to the Advaita philosophers, both the usages, viz. those ascribing physical properties and those ascribing mental properties to the self are erroneous. The real self, which is pure consciousness, is devoid of all properties. So, all the usages are only results of superimposition.

The Nyāya-Vaiśeṣika and Mīmāṁsā philosophers, on the other hand, do not deny that mental properties like knowledge and happiness belong really to the self. So usages like "I am happy" are true. But they add that these properties are contingent, for, they occur in the self as long as the self is attached to a body, sense organs and an inner organ. But when liberated, the self is not attached

---

2 Dharmarājādhvarīndra, 1960, *Vedāntaparibhāṣā*, ed. Panchanana Sastri, pp. 25-26, Calcutta.

to any of these and therefore does not possess those contingent properties. Thus, these realist philosophers also draw a distinction between empirical self and self in its essence (*svarūpataḥ ātmā*). But this distinction merely points to different states of the real self. The empirical self is the self in bondage and the liberated self is the self in its essence and is devoid of all specific qualities like consciousness, happiness and pain. The self as such is unconscious according to these philosophers because consciousness is not regarded as an essential property of the self. This position is opposed to the idealist position of Advaita Vedānta, i.e. the self is pure consciousness. The Bhāṭṭa Mīmāṁsakas, however, hold that the self as such is endowed with potential consciousness. So, they describe the self as *cid-acidrūpa* or *jaḍabodhātmaka* (conscious-unconscious).

We may now enquire about the definition of the self. Indian philosophers are very keen on having a definition for each kind of real entity, for, they hold that the reality of a thing is to be established by both *pramāṇa* (proof) and *lakṣaṇā* (definition). Then, how do the Indian philosophers define *ātman*? The definition that is commonly found in the Nyāya and Mīmāṁsā texts is that the self is the substratum of consciousness (*jñānāśraya* or *jñānādhikaraṇa*).[3] But we have just seen that these philosophers do not consider consciousness to be an essential property of the self and they hold that the liberated self does not possess it. So, this definition would fail to apply to the liberated souls. To cover the liberated self some other definition is to be found out. We may try to formulate a universally acceptable definition of the self. The self may be defined as an entity which is subject to bondage (*bandhana*) and liberation (*mokṣa*) (they express it as *bandha-mokṣa-bhāgitva*).[4] It has been accepted by all that every individual self is subject to both of these states. The state of bondage is beginningless and liberation

---

3 Annaṁbhaṭṭa, 1969, *Tarkasaṁgraha* with *Dīpikā*, ed. Satkariram Bangiya, p. 19, Varanasi.

4 Nārāyaṇa, 1933, *Mānameyodayaḥ*, ed. C. Kunhan Raja, p. 196, Madras.

is an attainable end. Therefore, this definition would be applicable to both the selves, one who is in bondage and one who is liberated.

But the Naiyāyikas would hesitate to accept this definition because they admit the existence of a supreme soul (*paramātmā*), who is God (*Īśvara*). And God is beyond bondage and liberation. So the Nyāya-Vaiśeṣika philosophers give another universally applicable definition of *ātman* in terms of *ātmatva jāti* (universal selfhood).[5] They say that all the things that are called by the same name *ātman* have some common as well as exclusive property in them which serves as the reason for the use of that name to them and them alone. And that property is *ātmatva* (selfhood) by virtue of which the self can be differentiated from everything that is non-self.

The Advaita Vedāntins would have no objection in accepting the definition of the self as one who is subject to bondage and liberation so far as *jīvātmā* is concerned. But *jīva* for them is not the real self. They define the self in a different way, not in terms of properties but by stating its *svarūpa* (nature). They say that the self is identical to existence, consciousness and bliss (*saccidānanda svarūpa*).[6]

Regarding other characteristics of the self, the orthodox philosophers hold that the self is eternal (*nitya*) and all-pervasive (*vibhu*). Excepting the Advaita philosophers, they believe in the plurality of selves. The Advaita Vedāntins hold that the real self is only one but individual selves are many. The individual self, according to them, is consciousness falsely identified with *antaḥkaraṇa* and as there can be multiple *antaḥkaraṇa*, consciousness identified with different *antaḥkaraṇas* can be regarded as different individual selves (*jīvas*).

As for the argument in favour of admitting the multiplicity of selves, the Indian philosophers say that the application of the law of *karma* and difference in respect of *bhoga* (experience of pleasure and pain) among different persons cannot be accounted for unless

---

5 Viśvanātha, 1988, *Kārikāvalī-Muktāvalī*, p. 381, Delhi.

6 Sadānanda, 1979, *Vedāntasāraḥ*, pp. 4-5, Varanasi.

a different self in every individual is admitted. Each self would enjoy and suffer the results of his/her good and bad deeds and their experience would vary accordingly.

To avoid the violation of the law of *karma* (principle of cosmic justice), the self should also be regarded as eternal (*nitya*). If the individual self did not exist beyond one particular life, it would not be able to experience the results of all its deeds, which means, some good or bad deeds would remain unrequited. This is a violation of the law of *karma*. So the Indian philosophers admit the self to be eternal or ever-present.

The Nyāya-Vaiśeṣika and Mīmāṁsā philosophers maintain that the self is *vibhu*. To be all-pervasive means to have an infinitely large size. They hold that every substance has a size.[7] Some substances like a *paramāṇu* (atom) have an infinitely small size or atomic size; some substances like tables, chairs, a grain of rice and a mountain have middle size (*madhyama mahat parimāṇa*) and some substances have infinitely large size (*parama mahat parimāṇa*) and the self is one of the substances having an infinitely large size. They argue that the self cannot be of an infinitely small or atomic size because in that case, the self could not experience pleasure or pain all over the body simultaneously. But we do have such feelings, so the self must be in conjunction with all parts of the body at a time which could not have been possible for a substance of atomic size. It cannot even be admitted that the self has a medium size like that of the body to which it is attached. For medium-sized substances are all made of parts and hence destructible. But the self has been proven to be eternal, so it cannot have a medium size. Therefore, the only possible size the self can have is an infinitely large size.

To conclude the discussion on Indian philosophers' conception of the self, it should be mentioned that the Nyāya-Vaiśeṣika philosophers hold the self to be the knower (*jñātā*), the agent (*kartā*) and the experiencing subject (*bhoktā*). This will be evident if we take

---

7 Viśvanātha, 1988, *Kārikāvalī-Muktāvalī, Kārikās* 109-10, pp. 706-07.

note of the specific qualities of the self. Knowledge, desire, aversion, volition, pleasure, pain, merits and demerits (*dharmādharma*), and impressions called *bhāvanās* are the specific qualities of the self. The qualities of knowledge and impression show the self to be the knower. Desire, aversion and volition make the self an agent and the qualities of pleasure, pain, merits and demerits show the self to be the experiencing subject. However, the characterization of the self as the knower or *jñātā* is primary, because without knowledge neither *karma* (action) nor *bhoga* (affective experience) would be possible.

The Mīmāṁsā philosophers too agree with the Nyāya–Vaiśeṣika philosophers in holding the self to be the knower, the agent and the experiencing subject. But the Sāṁkhya and Vedānta philosophers do not accept this. The Sāṁkhya philosophers hold *buddhi*, the first evolutes of *prakṛti*, to be the knower of the qualities of knowledge, pleasure, pain, etc. but the *puruṣa* (self) being in an unreal relation with *prakṛti* is regarded as the experiencing subject. As regards the Vedānta position, we have seen that they hold that these properties belong to *antaḥkaraṇa* and, due to its superimposition on the self, the properties are falsely ascribed to the self. The Sāṁkhya and the Vedāntin views of the self are very similar.

## II

Let us now pass on to the other part of our subject, i.e. self-knowledge. In Indian tradition, self-knowledge may mean three things:

1. self-consciousness,
2. theoretical knowledge regarding the real nature of the self, and
3. self-realization, i.e. the immediate awareness of the real nature of the self within oneself.

Self-knowledge of all three types is possible according to the Indian philosophers. Every individual self does actually have the first type of self-knowledge, i.e. self-consciousness. The other two types of self-knowledge are required for the attainment of liberation.

In the context of self-knowledge, a number of questions are raised by Indian philosophers, such as, by which *pramāṇa* do we get self-knowledge? Is the self an object of knowledge? The nature of self-knowledge and different questions regarding it have been discussed in all the systems of Indian philosophy. I shall now give a brief account of Indian theories of self-knowledge.

We shall begin with self-consciousness as a form of self-knowledge. Every individual has self-consciousness or I-consciousness (*ahaṁ pratyaya*). Regarding self-consciousness, there are at least three different views held by different schools. These are:

I. The self is self-luminous (*svaprakāśa*), which means it reveals itself.

II. The self is revealed by the self-luminous consciousness as the subject of consciousness.

III. The self is known by the internal perception of the form *ahaṁ sukhī, ahaṁ duḥkhī*, etc.

The first view is held by the Advaita Vedāntins. We have already seen that the self, according to them, is not the owner of consciousness, but it is identical to consciousness. Now, consciousness reveals everything else as well as itself. If it could not reveal itself and waited for some other thing to get itself revealed, then it could not reveal other things either. So the self is not the object of consciousness, nor does it need to be proved by any *pramāṇa*. It is self-proved (*svataḥsiddha*). It is presupposed by all *pramāṇas*. The function of a *pramāṇa* is to relate other objects to consciousness.

The second view is maintained by the Prābhākara Mīmāṁsakas. They say that the self who is the owner or subject of consciousness is revealed by every state of consciousness. According to them, consciousness is self-revealing (*svaprakāśa*) and in every state of consciousness the object, the subject and the consciousness itself, these three are revealed simultaneously. This is called by them as *tripuṭī pratyakṣa*.[8] They, however, assert that the self is not the object of consciousness but is regarded as the subject or knower. According to them, all kinds of knowledge take the form of "I know this".

The Bhāṭṭa Mīmāṁsakas and the Naiyāyikas hold the third view. They hold that in the internal perception of different specific qualities of the self, the self is aware of itself as the owner of those qualities. Those qualities alone are not perceived, that is, we do not have such awareness as "this is pleasure", "this is desire", etc. but we perceive those qualities as owned by ourselves. So, we have the perception "I am happy", "I desire", etc. Of this perception, the self is also an object. Thus, whenever we have such a perception, we have self-consciousness.

None of the realist schools admits the self to be self-luminous as the Vedāntins hold. But among them, the Prābhākara Mīmāṁsakas say that though not self-luminous, the self is not an object of knowledge either. The self is the subject (*jñātā*) and is revealed as the subject in every state of consciousness. So, both the Vedāntins and Prābhākaras deny that the self is an object of knowledge. Against the Bhāṭṭa and the Naiyāyika philosophers, they argue that to say that the self knows itself in an act of knowledge is to say that one and the same thing can be both the subject and the object of the same act.[9] But this is not possible because there is an incompatibility between *kartṛtva* (agency/subjectness) and *viṣayatva* (objectness). An act of the subject is directed towards something else, which means that the result of the act done by the agent is produced in another thing which is called the object. For example, when somebody cooks rice, the result of the act of cooking, viz. softening is produced in the rice. So, the agent who cooks and the thing that is cooked are different. Therefore, the self who is the knower knows something else. It itself cannot be the object of its own act.

---

8 Śalikanātha, 1961, *Prakaraṇa Pañcikā*, pp. 167-69.

9 Nārāyaṇa, 1933, *Manameyodayaḥ*, pp. 195-96.

The Bhāṭṭa Mīmāṁsakas defend their position by giving some counterarguments. Pārthasārathi Miśra in his *Śāstradīpikā* strongly argues against the Prābhākaras. He questions how can it be said that the act of knowing does not produce its result in the subject or the knower. The purpose of an act of knowledge is manifestation or revelation and is not self-revealed. How else is it revealed if not by its own act of knowing? The Prābhākaras too admit that the self is revealed when it knows an object.

To this, the Prābhākaras might argue that though there is a manifestation of the self by the knowledge, neither the definition of *karma* is satisfied by the self nor does the inflexion for objective case apply to the self, because the object is defined as *parasamavetakriyā-phala-bhāgitva* (an object is that which possesses the result of an act that belongs to someone else). Since the self is not revealed by an act of knowledge belonging to some other, the definition of *karma* does not apply to it. And in a sentence in Sanskrit expressing an act along with its subject and object, the objective inflexion is applied to the object only; for example, in a sentence expressing the knowledge *aham ghaṭam jānāmi*, the objective inflexion *am* is applied to *ghaṭa* and not to the pronoun *aham* (I) which stands for the self. This shows that the self is not the object. The Bhāṭṭa Mīmāṁsakas say in reply that there are usages where the self has been used in the objective case with respect to its own act of knowing. There are such usages as *svasaṁvedya sa bhavati*, *ātmānaṁ veda* and *ātmā jñātavya*. So, the self should be regarded as the object of its act of knowing. But that does not mean that the subject is always the object of its own act. The self is regarded as an object of its own act only when usages justify this. There is such a Vedic sentence as *sa mānasina ātma janānām*, which means that the self is known by people through *manas*. The Bhāṭṭas claim that the above-mentioned usages justify their position that the self is internally perceived as the object of "I-consciousness" (*mānasa ahaṁpratyayagamya ātmā*).[10] Pārthasārathi Miśra further argues that the fact of recognition cannot be explained if the self

10 Parthasarathi Miśra, 2008, *Śāstradīpikā* (*Tarkapāda*), pp. 565-71.

is not admitted to be an object of knowledge. In recognition of the form, "I am seeing something which I saw before" the self, which is revealed as the seer of the thing in the past, cannot be the subject of the present recognitive awareness. So, it is to be admitted that the self as related to the past seeing is revealed as an object only in the present act of recognitive awareness.

As regards the Vedānta position that the self is self-luminous, the Bhāṭṭas deny the self-luminosity of the self. They argue that if the self were self-luminous, self-consciousness should be there always, but during *suṣupti* there is the absence of self-consciousness. Besides, this position is in contradiction with the above-mentioned Vedic sentence.

Now we may ask how would the Naiyāyikas tackle this problem of *karma-kartṛ virodha* which their position regarding self-knowledge would also face. For, they also hold that in our internal perceptions of knowledge, pleasure, etc. the self is also perceived as the owner of these states. We always have internal perception in the form of *aham duḥkhī, aham sukhī* and so on. Here, the self is known as qualified by knowledge and other internal properties, or, in other words, knowledge, etc. are known as belonging to the self. So, this is also a case where the self, knowing itself along with other objects, hence the objection of *karma–kartṛ virodha* may be raised here.

Jayanta Bhaṭṭa defends the Nyāya position in this way.[11] He says that if we accept the principle of incompatibility between the subject and the object of an act, then self-knowledge would not be possible at all whether through perception or through inference, because the self is to be known by itself. In the case of any knowledge of the self, the self is both the knower and the known. Since we do actually have perceptual as well as inferential knowledge of the self, it is to be admitted that in these cases at least there is no *karma–kartṛ virodha*. However, it is to be added that though the self

[11] Jayanta Bhaṭṭa, 1982, *Nyāyamañjarī*, Dvitīya Bhāga, pp. 207-09.

can be both the subject and the object of knowledge, its relation to knowledge when it is the subject and when it is the object are different. The self as a knower or subject is related to knowledge by the relation of inherence (*samavāya*) and, as an object, it is related by the relation of objectness or *viṣayatā*. The self can be related to knowledge in both the relations at the same time.

From the above discussion, we may conclude that all Indian philosophical systems admit that we have a direct awareness of ourselves which we term "self-consciousness", though different systems give different interpretations of self-consciousness.

Let us now come to the second form of self-knowledge. This form of self-knowledge is philosophically very important, because the real nature of the self, or what thing the self is, is not known by the state of self-consciousness. What this I (*aham*) is, of which we are aware when we have self-consciousness? We can at most know that it is the subject (the knower) or the owner of the states of pleasure, pain, etc. But, there may be doubt regarding the nature of the *I*: is it the body or the sense organ or the inner organ or states of consciousness or an aggregate of all these? And each of these alternatives has been accepted by different heterodox systems of philosophy. Orthodox schools of philosophy hold that the self is something other than the body, sense organs, etc. To identify the self with the body, etc. is a misconception and such a misconception is the root cause of all suffering. So, these philosophical systems have advanced several arguments to prove the real nature of the self as distinct from the body, etc. Through these philosophical arguments, we have mediate (*parokṣa*) knowledge of the truth about the self.

I shall present here very briefly a few arguments commonly used by the realist philosophers belonging to the orthodox tradition to prove that the self is different from the body, sense organs, inner organ and states of consciousness.

At the level of self-consciousness, an individual is aware of himself/herself as the owner of knowledge, desire, pleasure, etc. Now since an individual has a body, a sense organ and an inner organ (*manas*), it may be possible that one of these three is the owner of these states and that is the self, referred to as "I". One important argument used by the Nyāya philosophers to discard these possibilities is that the remembrance and recognitive awareness that an individual experiences throughout his/her life could not be accounted for if the knowledge belonged to the body/ or sense organ or inner organ.[12] They argue that remembrance and recognitive awareness require the unity of the knower. One and the same knower who has experiences of different types and of different objects throughout his/her life can remember those experiences at any time and can synthesize his/her past and present experiences. This condition of the unity of the knower is not satisfied by the body because the body undergoes changes due the growth and decay of its parts. So, the body does not remain the same throughout one's life. This would make it impossible for a young or old body to remember the experiences which the child body had. For, the impressions (*saṁskāras*) of childhood experiences are stored in the child body which gets destroyed when the child body is changed into adult body and so due to the absence of impressions, which is the cause of remembrance, there would be no remembrance of those experiences.

Sense organs even cannot be the knower, because each sense organ has a specific object which alone can be known by it and that object too can be known by that specific sense organ alone. So, if these sense organs are the knower, there will be numerous knowers. This would make a synthesis of different experiences by different sense organs impossible. But we do have such recognitive awareness as "I am touching the thing which I saw", where a visual and a tactual experience are synthesized by one and the same knower. So sense organs cannot be the knower or the self.

---

[12] Gautama, 1985, *Nyāyadarśanam*, *sūtras* 3.1.1-17 with *Bhāṣya*.

These problems would not however arise if *manas* is taken to be the knower, because it has been admitted that *manas* is an eternal entity and only one *manas* is present in an individual. So, the fact of memory and recognition could be well accounted for in terms of one eternal *manas*. But this would not really be possible because *manas* is imperceptible due to its atomic size, and thus *manas* cannot be perceived as one who experiences, remembers and recognizes. *Manas* cannot be the I, when one says "I know", "I remember", or "I recognize this to be that". So *manas* is not the self.

The same argument from memory and recognition has been advanced against the Yogācāra Buddhists' position that the self is nothing but a series of momentary consciousness. Since the Buddhists would not admit the series to be a continuing entity over and above its members, the self according to them would be identical to a state of consciousness which is transient. We have seen that if the knower is transient, memory and recognition would not be possible. None of the members will be able to remember its own or others' experiences.

Besides this argument from memory and recognition, the Nyāya–Vaiśeṣika and Mīmāṁsā philosophers advance many more arguments to prove each of the conclusions, viz. that the self is different from the body, it is different from sense organs, it is different from the inner organ and also different from the states of consciousness.

To sum up, the way in which the second type of self-knowledge is obtained, we can say that the inferential process employed here is a *śeṣavat* or *pariśeṣa anumāna*.[13] We start with the cases of internally perceived qualities like knowledge, desire and pleasure, and conclude that these qualities must be located in a substance as all other qualities like colour are. Then by means of a series of arguments, the possibility of the substances like body, sense organ and *manas* to be the substratum of these qualities is eliminated. The only possible substratum of these qualities which remains is the

[13] Gautama, 1985, *Nyāyadarśanam*, *sūtras* 1.1.5 and 3.2.39.

self as distinct from the body, etc. Thus, the conclusion that the self who is the knower and the experience of pleasure, pain, etc. is the self as distinct from the body, sense organ, etc. is proved.

The third type of self-knowledge is the most important for Indian philosophers because that is the means for the attainment of the supreme goal, i.e. *mokṣa* (liberation). In the Vedic texts it has been said that the self is to be known through *śravaṇa* (learning the Vedic texts), *manana* (inferences and arguments) and *nididhyāsana* (meditating upon the truth learnt through *śravaṇa* and *manana*).[14]

*Śravaṇa* means learning the truth about the self from the Vedic texts under the instruction of a preceptor. After this, the truth learnt from *śruti* is to be reaffirmed by means of inferences and arguments. This is the stage of *manana*, when one has intellectual conviction through analytical means.

The second type of self-knowledge that we have just discussed is obtained through *manana*. Finally, the truth about the self is to be realized by the individual within his own self. This is a form of immediate awareness like "I am not the body, etc.". The deep-rooted confusion between the self and the body is immediate (*aparokṣa bhrama*) in nature and it can be removed only by immediate awareness of the self as distinct from the body, etc. *Nididhyāsana* (constant meditation) as advised in Yogaśāstra on the real nature of the self is a prerequisite for the immediate awareness of the real nature of the self. Through the above-mentioned three-step process this final self-knowledge is attained and the self becomes free from bondage.

This immediate awareness of the real nature of the self is the third type of self-knowledge which is called self-realization.[15] It is a kind of extraordinary perception which a *yogī* can have by the power of mediation, i.e. yogic power; hence it is called *yogaja* (caused by *yoga*) *pratyakṣa*.

---

[14] Sadānanda, 1979, *Vedāntasārah*, pp. 72-73.

[15] Viśvanātha, 1988, *Kārikāvalī-Muktāvalī*, *kārikā* 63, 64, pp. 458-69.

# 13

# The Concept of Caitanya in the Nyāya System

## A Different Interpretation

In this chapter I shall critically analyse the concept of *caitanya* as used in the Nyāya system of philosophy, with an attempt to clarify the concept from the Nyāya point of view.

The English word, which is generally used for *caitanya*, is consciousness. The concept of consciousness and the distinction between conscious and unconscious are found in philosophy, science and common speech. In this chapter, however, I shall confine the discussion to Indian philosophy only. *Caitanya* (consciousness) is the pivotal concept of the Vedānta philosophy and it is also a central concept in the Sāṁkhya philosophy. But in other schools of Indian philosophy, of which the Nyāya is one, it has been regarded as an important though not a central concept. They treated *caitanya* as equivalent to *jñāna* (cognition). The Nyāya philosophers do not usually use the term *caitanya* in their writings. In the *Nyāyasūtra* with *Bhāṣya* and other texts like the *Nyāyakusumāñjali*, we find the use of this term only when they dealt with the opponents' position relating to *caitanya*, once, while refuting the Sāṁkhya position, which says that *jñāna*, *buddhi* and *caitanya* are not the same. The other occasion was the refutation of the Cārvāka view that material bodies are the substrate of *caitanya* (*bhūtacaitanyavāda*). There they used the term *caitanya* for *jñāna*, obviously for the sake of using common terminology.[1]

Now, there are two ways of conceiving *caitanya* in Indian philosophical systems. According to one, it is an eternal, self-luminous entity which is identical with the soul (*ātman/Brahman/puruṣa*).[2] For the other, *caitanya* is an occurrent property/quality which is located in the soul. The Nyāya school holds the second view. In both the views, *ātman* (soul) is *cetana*, but according to the former view, *cetana* means being identical with *caitanya*, i.e. *caitanya svarūpa*. Going by the latter view, *ātman* is *cetana* as being qualified by the property of *caitanya*, i.e. *caitanyāśraya*. Since the Nyāya affirms the identity between *caitanya* and *jñāna*, for them to be *jñāta* is to be *cetana*.

Before we consider the Nyāya view regarding *caitanya*, I must mention that we shall be talking about *jīvātmā* (finite soul) and its *caitanya* only. The Nyāya school admits *Paramātmā* (supreme soul), which is *Īśvara*, as omniscient (*sarvajñāna*); hence they admit *Īśvara* to be *cetana*; but *caitanya* or *jñāna*, which *Īśvara* possesses is eternal (*nitya*). We shall exclude *Īśvara*'s *nitya-jñāna* from the purview of our discussion because the problem we shall be facing concerns *janya-jñāna* of *jīvātmā* only.

Now regarding the identity between *caitanya* and *jñāna* as held by the Nyāya, a doubt can be raised as to whether this position can be maintained consistently with some of the relevant metaphysical

---

1 Gautama, 1985, *Nyāyasūtra with Vātsyāyanabhāṣya*, *Nyāyadarśanam*, ed. Tārānāth Nyāyatarkatīrtha and Amarendramohan Tarkatīrtha, *Bhāṣya* on 1.1.15, 3.2.3 and 3.2.46, New Delhi: Munshiram Monoharlal.

2 Sadānanda, 1979, *Vedāntasāra with Vidyatmanorañjanī ṭīkā* with Hindi tr. Badrināth Śukla, pp. 1-4, Varanasi: Motilal Banarsidass.

Kapila, 1954, *Sāṁkhyadarśanam with Pravacanabhāṣya* by Vijñānabhikṣu with Bengali commentary by Kalivarā Vedāntavāgīśa, ed. Durgacarana Sankhya Vedāntatīrtha, pp. 342-43, 145-46, Calcutta: Central Book Agency.

and epistemological tenets of the Nyāya system. Let us begin with those tenets. To the Nyāya system:

1. The soul (*ātmā*) is the locus of *jñāna*.
2. *Jñāna* is not an essential (*svābhābika*) but an adventitious (*āgantuka*) quality of the soul because it is not present in the liberated soul, if it were an essential property, then it would always be present in the soul.
3. *Jñāna* arises in *jīvātmā* (finite soul) only when it goes through the state of life (*jīvana*). This point needs an explanation. Though the soul is beyond birth and death, we still talk about an individual's life. An Individual soul is a soul attached to a body which is created to reap the results of his/her past deed (*karmaphala bhoga*). And an individual soul's *jīvana* means the soul's conjunction with the *manas*, which is attached to the body created for the purpose of *bhoga* (which the soul has begun to enjoy).[3]
4. But even during the lifetime of an individual soul, there are some exceptional conditions when *jñāna* is not produced. These are the state of *suṣupti* (dreamless sleep) that everyone goes through regularly; and the state of *mūrchā* (swoon), which some undergo on certain occasions.[4] The Naiyāyikas explain *suṣupti* as a state which occurs when *manas* enters inside an organ called *puritat nāḍī* which is within the body and is known as *nidrā nāḍī*, i.e. the organ for sleep. This *puritat nāḍī* has no skin (*tvak*) inside it and hence does not contain the tactile sense organ (*tvagindriya*), as skin is the locus of that sense organ. So when *manas* enters inside this organ of sleep, it loses contact with the tactile sense organ. And the

---

3 Gautama, *Nyāyadarśanam*, 3.2.26 with *Bhāṣya* on it.

4 Dinesh Candra Bhattacharya Shastri, 1972, *Prācīna Bhāratīya*, Manovidya, pp. 305-13, Kolkata.

Dharmarājādhvarīndra, 1960, *Vedāntaparibhāṣā*, ed. Pancanan Bhattacharya Shastri, pp. 281-82, Calcutta: Sanskrit Pustak Bhandar.

Naiyāyikas hold that this absence of contact between *manas* and the tactile sense organ (*tvagindriya*) is the reason for the absence of cognition during dreamless sleep (*suṣupti*). Based on this cognitionless state of *suṣupti*, the Naiyāyikas concluded that the contact between *manas* and the tactile sense organ is a general causal condition for the production of cognition (*jñāna-sāmānya kāraṇa*). The absence of cognition in *suṣupti* can be explained only by showing the absence of this general causal condition of cognition.[5]

The state of *mūrchā* is more or less similar to *suṣupti*, though caused by some other factor. In the absence of any discussion on it in Nyāya texts, we may assume a similar explanation for the absence of *jñāna* at that state. Therefore, it is to be admitted that the soul is *acetana*/unconscious during these states due to the absence of cognition (*jñāna*).

What we have said so far about the Nyāya position shows that the soul can have cognition only in the waking state and in dreams, meaning, the living soul is conscious during these states. But the problem starts here. Let us question whether the soul continues to have uninterrupted cognitive states throughout the waking condition. If not, then at the time when no cognition occurs, the soul should be regarded as *acetana*/unconscious. And we shall see that the Naiyāyikas must admit that we do not have cognition at every moment of waking state. Let us see why. According to the Nyāya school, *jñāna* is an event; it is a *janya guṇa* which arises in the soul. It occurs when certain causal conditions are present. It is produced at a particular moment. And according to the Nyāya, a *janya-jñāna* (cognition) is transient; it gets destroyed at the third moment of its occurrence (*tṛtīya-kṣaṇa-vināśī*).[6] So, it stays for two moments only. And it is not necessarily the case that at the third

[5] Viśvanātha, 1988, *Kārikāvalī-Muktāvalī*, ed. Sankarram Shastri, *kārikā* 58 with *Muktāvalī*, Delhi: Chowkhamba Sanskit Pratisthan.

[6] Ibid., *kārikā 27* with *Muktāvalī*.

moment another piece of cognition is produced. We know that the soul possesses six perceptible specific qualities, viz. *jñāna*, *sukha*, *duḥkha*, *icchā*, *dveṣa* and *prayatna*. After a cognition, some or other of these qualities may be produced instead of a cognition. We know that after having the cognition of a thing, we may have the desire to obtain it or feel aversed to it. So after a cognition, a *icchā* or *dveṣa* may be produced. After a cognition, a state of pleasure or pain can also arise; for example, after hearing a song, we may feel pleasure.

Here it may be asked, whether it be possible that a cognition, a desire or pleasure, etc. arise at the same moment. The Nyāya answer is negative. They hold that perceptible specific qualities of infinite substances (*vibhu dravya*) do not occur simultaneously. That means, the six perceptible specific qualities of the self mentioned above, and *śabda*, the perceptible specific quality of *ākāśa* can be produced only in succession.[7] So, it is not possible that both a cognition and a desire or any other of those qualities arise in the soul simultaneously, nor is it possible that there goes only a series of cognitive states in the soul at any time. Thus, there are moments when the soul is devoid of cognition, but has a desire, aversion, will, pleasure or pain. Will then the soul be regarded as *acetana* at such moments? This would be the consequence if the identity between *jñāna* and *caitanya* is maintained, which goes against common sense. This is the problem. So, we should think over the Nyāya position and find out some solution. A distinction needs to be drawn between *jñāna* and *caitanya*, because when one is having a mental state or quality other *jñāna*, there is nothing odd in saying or admitting the person is not having a cognitive state (*jñāna*) at that moment. But it seems absurd to say that the person does not have consciousness or is unconscious when he is desiring or willing to do something. To say this is definitely going against common sense.

For a solution, I think, we can modify the Nyāya position

7 Viśvanātha, 1988, *Kārikāvalī-Muktāvalī*, *kārikā 26* with *Muktāvalī*, *Muktāvalī* on *Pakṣatā*, p. 498.

and say that *caitanya* is not identical with *jñāna*, but it consists in having any of the perceptible specific qualities of the soul. That is to say, to be *cetana* is to have any of the qualities, viz. *jñāna*, *icchā*, *dveṣa*, *prayatna*, *sukha* and *duḥkha*. In Western philosophy too, we find that in one of the senses in which the term "consciousness" is used stands for the states of consciousness, which include all the mental states. If a similar interpretation is given to the Nyāya view, then we can say that when the soul has a desire or will, then it is definitely *cetana*. So, throughout the waking state the soul is *cetana*, as it has some specific quality or other at that state. But though the soul (*ātmā*) is both *cetana* and *jñātā*, it is not *jñātā* throughout the waking state. That means, we have to draw a distinction between *jñātā* and *cetana*. *Cetana* is not always *jñātā*.

There is another interpretation of the Nyāya position held by Paṇḍit Badrināth Śukla.[8] According to him, *cetana* has the awareness to the effect "I know", which means to be conscious is to be aware of oneself as the owner of *jñāna*. So, in this interpretation, *caitanya* would mean not *jñāna* as such but *anuvyavasāya* (internal perception) (*mānasa pratyakṣa*) of one's *jñāna*.

This interpretation also is similar to a view we find in Western philosophy. John Locke defined consciousness as "the perception of what passes in a man's own mind". This is what is later called introspection. Introspection is the perception of different states of the mind. So consciousness is being aware of the different states of mind as they occur, according to that view.

On Badrināth Śukla's interpretation of the Nyāya view, i.e. *caitanya* consists in having *anuvyavasāya* of awareness. There is some difference between introspection and *anuvyavasāya*, for, introspection is the perception of any mental state, whereas *anuvyavsāya* is the perception of a state of cognition only.

---

[8] Paṇḍit Badrināth Śukla while visiting the Department of Philosophy at Jadavpur University, delivered a lecture on the Nyāya philosophy where he mentioned this position.

But this interpretation of *caitanya* as *anuvyavasāya* does not seem to solve the problem relating to the identity between *jñāna* and *caitanya*. According to the Nyāya, *anuvyavasāya* does not necessarily occur whenever a cognition is produced.[9] They do not admit that a cognition must be known to its owner (*avaśyavedyatva* of *jñāna* is denied) because to admit this would lead to an infinite regress. Suppose I have a cognition $c_1$ about a thing, say, a table and it has to be cognized, so it is followed by a cognition $c_2$ of which $c_1$ is the object. This $c_2$ being itself a cognition, must also be followed by its cognition, i.e. $c_3$; in this way the process will go on infinitely. As a result, there cannot be cognitions about other objects and there cannot even arise other mental states like desire, pleasure, etc. because we have already seen that mental states are produced successively, not simultaneously. So, to avoid this unacceptable situation, the Naiyāyikas hold that every cognition does not need to be cognized subsequently. From this conclusion, it follows that the self is not always aware of itself as the owner of its awareness. But, will the self then be regarded as *acetana* when there is absence of such awareness? Thus, we are back to the same problem, i.e. going against common sense.

Let us then return to the solution suggested before. The modification of the Nyāya position, as shown above, is a plausible solution. We have said already that if we define *caitanya* as having the qualities of cognition, desire, aversion, will, pleasure and pain disjunctively, then throughout the waking state the soul can be said to have *caitanya*. As long as a person is awake, he continues to have some or other of these mental states, so he is conscious even when having desire, will or pleasure, etc. Therefore, there is no conflict with common sense.

To accept this interpretation does not mean total rejection of the original position of the Nyāya, i.e. consciousness means cognition. This interpretation extends the concept of *caitanya*, by

---

9 Vardhamānopādhyāya, 1911, *Nyāyanibandhaprakāśa*, a commentary on Udayana's *Tātparyapariśuddhi*, Asiatic Society, p. 49.

including other mental qualities like desire, aversion, volition, pleasure and pain, along with cognition. So, identity between consciousness and cognition is denied in the sense that some other mental qualities are also accepted to come under consciousness or *caitanya*. It is true indeed that cognition enjoys a primacy among the other mental qualities, because, desire, aversion and will or volition are caused by cognition. Pleasure and pain also are necessarily accompanied by their awareness (*avaśyavedya*). It never happens that we have pain or pleasure but are not aware that we are happy or suffering. Because of this intimate connection of these mental qualities with *jñāna*, each of these qualities implies the presence of cognition before or after their occurrence, so, they can be grouped into one and called *caitanya*.

In favour of this interpretation, I can refer to a text which seems to give a hint regarding the plausibility of this interpretation. While presenting the opponent Cārvākas' view that the body (*śarīra*) is *ātman* (self) as it is the locus of *caitanya*, Viśvanātha says in *Muktāvalī nanu caitanyam jñānādikam eva* (*Caitanya* is *jñāna* etc.). It is to be noted that Viśvanātha adds the word *ādi* to *jñāna*. What does *ādi* mean? It means similar other things. In the commentary, titled *Prabhā* on *Muktāvalī*, the commentator says, *ādina icchadeḥ parigraha*, which means, *icchā*, etc. are to be taken by the word *ādi*.[10] *Ādi* (etc.) means other specific attributes of self, such as, *sukha*, *duḥkha* and others. So, it is clear that the commentator includes all the specific attributes of the self under the meaning of *caitanya*.

So, according to the proposed modified version of the Nyāya view, *caitanya* would mean any of the six perceptible internal qualities beginning with *jñāna* as enumerated in the *Nyāyasūtra*. Now, whether this interpretation is acceptable or not is to be decided by the scholars.

---

[10] Viśvanātha, 1988, *Kārikāvalī-Muktāvalī*, *Prabhā Ṭīkā* (by Nṛsiṁha Śāstri) on it, p. 386.

# 14

# The Nyāya-Vaiśeṣika Concept of Manas

The concept of *manas* (mind) is of immense importance in Indian philosophy because according to them, the entire cognitive life of an individual self depends on *manas* (mind). It should be mentioned here that even though we translate *manas* as mind, this mind is not the same as it is conceived in Western philosophy. In their philosophy, mind is another name for the soul or the self. So to the mind and the self are identical. But according to Indian philosophers *manas* is entirely different from the self (*ātman*). Orthodox schools of Indian philosophy hold that for every individual soul (*jīvātmā*) there is a *manas* with which it is attached as long as the soul is in the state of bondage. Both the *ātman* and the *manas* are eternal (*nitya*) entities, according to them. At every birth of an individual (*jīva*), along with the soul, the mind also gets attached to a body which is perishable (*anitya*). It is within such a body that the *manas* performs all its functions for the *ātman*. Another name for *manas* is *antaḥkaraṇa*, because it is situated inside the body and it functions as an instrument (*karaṇa*). Several functions of *manas* have been admitted by Indian philosophers.

*Manas* has a place in the list of categories (*padārthas*) provided by the Nyāya-Vaiśeṣika schools. In *Vaiśeṣikasūtra* 1.1.5, Kaṇāda mentions *manas* in the list of substances (*dravya*) admitted in his system. *Manas* is the ninth substance, the other eight being *pṛhivī* (earth), *āp* (water), *tejas* (fire), *vāyu* (air), *ākāśa*, *dik* (space), *kāla* (time) and *ātman*. So, *manas*, according to the Vaiśeṣika, is a substance which is distinct from the *ātman*.

In *Nyāyasūtra* 1.1.9, Gautama mentions *manas* in the list of *prameyas* (knowables), the knowledge of which is the means to the attainment of *mokṣa* (liberation). He enumerates twelve *prameyas*, viz. *ātman*, *śarīra* (body), *indriya* (sense organs), *artha* (sensible qualities), *buddhi* (cognition), *manas*, *pravṛtti* (volition), *doṣa* (defects), *pretyabhāva* (rebirth), *phala* (results of good and evil actions), *duḥkha* (suffering) and *apavarga* (liberation). *Manas* here figures as the sixth *prameya*, and it is mentioned separately from *ātman*.

Besides the Nyāya-Vaiśeṣika systems, other orthodox and heterodox philosophical systems also include *manas* in their list of categories and it has been accepted by almost all the Indian philosophers that *manas* is not perceptible. We cannot perceive *manas* by means of our sense organs. So the main task of the philosophers is to prove its existence. And to do this they have to show how and by which *pramāṇa* the existence of *manas* can be known.

In this chapter we shall discuss the arguments put forward by the Nyāya-Vaiśeṣika philosophers to prove the existence of *manas*.

We know that besides *pratyakṣa* (sense perception) the Indian philosophers admit *anumāna* (inference) and *śabda* (verbal testimony) as two important *pramāṇas* by means of which the existence of things can be known and proved. The Nyāya-Vaiśeṣika philosophers prefer to use *anumāna pramāṇa* to prove their thesis. So, here too, they apply *anumāna pramāṇa* to prove the existence of *manas*.

As shown in the text of *Nyāyadarśana* we get more than one formulation of inference by means of which they prove the existence of *manas*. From these inferences, we can also know the nature (*svarūpa*) and properties (*dharma*) of *manas*.

Let us consider a line from Vātsyayana's *bhāṣya*, just preceding the *lakṣana-sūtra* of *manas* (1.1.16):

*smṛti-anumāna-āgama-saṁśaya-pratibhā-svapnajñāna-uhāḥ sukhādipratyakṣam-icchādayāśca manaso liṅgāni teṣu satsuiyamapi –*
*yugapaj-jñānānutpattirmanaso liṅgam* ।

– *Nyāyasūtra* 1.1.16

Here, he mentions many kinds of cognitive states (*jñāna*) and many specific qualities of the self (*ātma-viśeṣaguṇāḥ*) as the ground (*hetu* or *liṅga*) for inferring the existence of *manas*. Then he says that in addition to these *hetus* there is another one which is stated in *Nyāyasūtra* 1.1.16.

Now, if we analyse Vātsyāyana's statement quoted above, we can construct as many as three different arguments advanced as the proof for the existence of *manas*. And the fourth one is stated in Gautama's *sūtra* 1.1.16, quoted above.

By means of these four inferences the Naiyāyikas claim to have proved the existence of *manas* as having four different functions. These are as follows:

i. *Manas* as a causal condition (*kāraṇa*) of all kinds of non-perceptual cognition (*pratyakṣa-bhinnam-jñānam*).
ii. *Manas* as the instrumental cause (*karaṇa*) of the perception of internal attributes (*āntarguṇāḥ*) of the self.
iii. *Manas* as one of the causal condition (*kāraṇa*) for the origin of all the specific attributes (*viśeṣa gunāḥ*) of the self.
iv. *Manas* as an auxiliary cause (*sahakārī-kāraṇa*) of external sense perception (*bāhya pratyakṣa*) of colour, sound, taste, smell, etc.

Here, we shall consider the full form of each of these arguments and assess them critically.

## I

*First Argument*: Here all non-perceptual (*pratyakṣa-bhinna*) cognitive states like recollection and inferences are taken as the ground (*hetu*) for inferring the existence of *manas*. The inference can be formulated as follows:

i. *Smṛti* (recollection), *anumiti* (inferential cognition), *śābda-jñāna* (verbal cognition), *saṁśaya* (doubtful cognition), *pratibhā* (premonition), *svapna* (dream) and *uhāḥ* (indirect argument) are occurrent cognitive states.

ii. Every occurrent cognitive state is produced by some instrumental cause (*karaṇa*) just as the perceptual cognition (*pratyakṣa-jñāna*) is.

iii. The *karaṇa* in this case cannot be external sense organs because these cognitions are non-perceptual. There must be some other *kāraṇa* of this cognition and that is designated as *manas*.

By this inference, they proposed to prove the existence of *manas* as the *kāraṇa* of all non-perceptual cognitions (*pratyakṣa-bhinna-jñāna*).

Against this inference, it can be argued that for each of the cognitions which is non-perceptual, there is some accepted instrumental cause, like knowledge of pervasion (*vyāpti-jñāna*) for *anumiti*, *saṁskāra* (impressions left by past experience) for *smṛti* and similarly in other cases too. So why should there be an additional instrumental cause for those cognitive states? An answer to this question can be found in Vācaspati Miśra's *Tātparyaṭīkā* and Udayanācārya's *Tātparyapariśuddhi*, both of which are explanatory notes on the *Nyāyasūtra* and *Bhāṣya*.[1] They have explained there that what Vātsyāyana meant when he said that all non-perceptual cognitions like *smṛti* and *anumiti* require a *karaṇa* for their production is that like perceptual cognition they also need a sense organ as their instrumental cause. Udayanācārya further explained that here by a sense organ is meant a substance which is

---

1 Udayana, *Tātparyapariśuddhi*, p. 259 on *sūtra* 1.1.16, ed. Anantalal Thakur, New Delhi: Indian Council of Philosophical Research, 1996.

Vācaspati Miśra, *Tātparyaṭīkā* p. 216 in Gautama's *Nyāyadarśanam*, ed. Tārānātha Nyāyatarkatīrtha and Amarendramohan Tarkatīrtha, New Delhi, Munshiram Manoharlal, 1985.

attached to the body of the knower and acts to produce cognitions (*śarīrasaṁyukta dravyarūpa karaṇa*). Vācaspati Miśra said that in addition to their respective *karaṇa* like *saṁskāra* and *vyāpti-jñāna*, they need some *indriya* as their cause and that is to be taken as the *kāraṇa* of all these cognitions, though that sense organ does not function in these cases as the cause of sense perception (*pratyakṣa*).

The Naiyāyikas' argument here is like this. Perceptual cognitions of external objects like colour, taste and smell are produced by means of sense organs. By this analogy, it is to be admitted that all other types of cognition are also produced by some instrument like a sense organ. This instrumental cause which is similar to the sense organ is what is called *manas*. Its similarity with sense organs consists in its being a substance which is attached to the body and in its ability to cause cognition. But they maintain that *manas*, though a sense organ, functions here only as a general causal condition for all other types of cognition.

In Vātsyāyana's commentary on *Nyāyasūtra* 3.1.16, where an argument is given to establish that *ātmā* (self) is different from *manas*, we find a similar argument. There, Vātsyāyana explains that the self or the knower requires some organs as instruments of knowledge (*jñānasādhana*), for example, by means of *cakṣu* or visual sense organ the knower sees; and there are altogether five external sense organs which are instrumental causes of perceptual cognitions (*pratyakṣa-jñāna*). Similarly, the knower needs another organ as an instrument by means of which he can have all other types of cognition. He termed this as *matisādhana*, because he uses the term *mati* to mean all types of cognition other than *pratyakṣa*. This *matisādhana* is the inner organ or *antaḥkaraṇa*. And he argued that if one denies the need of an instrumental cause, i.e. *antaḥakaraṇa* for non-perceptual cognition then one should also deny the need for external sense organs (*indriyas*) to perceive external objects.

## II

Let us now take the second argument. Here the awareness or cognition of different internal properties of the self like *sukha* (pleasure) and *duḥkha* (pain) are taken as the ground for inferring the existence of *manas*. In the Nyāya–Vaiśeṣika systems, the self has been admitted to have nine specific attributes (*viśeṣa guṇas*) of which six are perceptible.[2] These are *jñāna* (cognition), *sukha* (pleasure), *duḥkha* (pain), *icchā* (desire), *dveṣa* (aversion) and *pravṛtti* (volition). For the perception of these internal attributes, a separate sense organ is needed, and that sense organ is to be admitted and designated as *manas*.

This argument can be formulated in this way.

i. Our awareness of pleasure (or any other perceptible internal attribute of the self, like pain and desire) is direct awareness (*sākṣāt-pratīti*).

ii. Every direct awareness is produced by some sense organ just as the direct awareness of colour is produced by the visual sense organ.

iii. External sense organs like visual sense organ (*cakṣu*), which produce a perception of external things like colour and smell cannot produce a perception of internal objects because they, being external, cannot have required specific relation *indriyārtha-sannikarṣa* with the internal objects.

iv. Therefore, some internal sense organ must be there which produces direct awareness of pleasure and other internal attributes. For the sake of economy, only one internal sense organ (*antaḥkaraṇa*) is to be admitted which can produce a perception of all the internal attributes.

This argument is simple and must be acceptable to all because we all have direct awareness of both external things and internal

---

2 Praśastapāda, *Praśastapādabhāṣya* with *Vyomavatī*, by Vyomaśivācārya, part II, p. 6, ed. Gaurinath Sastri, Varanasi, 1983.

states, and that an external perception is produced by an external sense organ is proved by agreement in the presence and absence (*anvaya-vyatireka*) between a sense organ and a sense perception, for example, one who does not have visual sense organ (*cakṣu*) cannot see colour, and one who has that sense organ can see colour. For giving a uniform explanation of the causation of both external and internal perceptions, sense organs of both kinds, i.e. external and internal are to be admitted. So *manas* has been admitted as the *antaḥkaraṇa*.

## III

Now the third argument. We have already seen that the self has a number of specific internal attributes like *jñāna*, *icchā*, *sukha* and *duḥkha*. All these attributes are occurrent states. They are produced, stay for some moments and then get destroyed. Since they are occurrent events, there must be some causal conditions for their production. On the Nyāya-Vaiśeṣika theory of causation, every positive event (*bhāva kārya*) depends on three types causal conditions for their origin.[3] These are:

a. *Samavāyī kāraṇa*, which may be called the material cause, it actually is the substratum of a positive product;

b. *asamavāyī kāraṇa,* which means a cause, which through its relation with substratum, i.e. the *samavāyī kāraṇa*, causes the effect; and

---

3 Among the seven categories admitted by the Nyāya-Vaiśeṣikas, one named *abhāva* is negative and the rest are positive. Of the *bhāva padārthas*, *sāmānya* (universal), *viśeṣa* (differentiator), *samavāya* (inherence) are *nitya* (eternal). Among the other four categories, *dravya* (substance) and *guṇa* (quality) include both eternal and non-eternal varieties. Non-eternal are the products or effects. *Karma* (motion) is always non-eternal, i.e. an effect only. These three kinds of effects are *bhāvas*. The seventh category *abhāva* is of four varieties of which one is *dvamsābhava* (annihilative absence) that is an effect. *Dvaṁsābhāva* of a thing is produced when the thing is destroyed. Destruction of a thing is caused by an efficient cause only. *Bhāva* effect needs three types of causes for its production.

c. *nimitta kāraṇa* (efficient cause), which may be more than one, like the agent, instruments and many other general causal conditions like time (*kāla*), etc. which are accepted by the Naiyāyikas.

So, in the case of these attributes of the self, all these causal conditions must be present for their production. These attributes originate in the self and are located there in the relation to *samavāya*. Therefore, the self is the *samavāyī kāraṇa* or the substratum where the attributes inhere. But, what is the *asamavāyī kāraṇa* of these attributes? Here the Nyāya–Vaiśeṣika philosophers argue that there must be a substance which is an inner organ and which has conjunction (*saṁyoga*) with the self; that conjunction would be the *asamavāyī kāraṇa* of these attributes. That substance, which is located inside the body and is in conjunction with the self and produces these attributes, is named *manas*. Here, they conceived *manas* as a relatum (*sambandhī*) of the relation of conjunction (*saṁyoga*) with the self (*ātman*), which functions as the *asamavāyī kāraṇa* of the specific attributes of the self.

A question can be raised against this argument. According to Nyāya–Vaiśeṣika philosophers, these specific attributes of the self can arise in the self only when the self is conjoined with a body (*śarīra*). So *śarīra–ātmā-saṁyoga* (self–body conjunction) has to be admitted as a cause of these attributes. In that case, why can it not be regarded as the *asamavāyī kāraṇa*? Why is *ātma–manaḥ-saṁyoga* needed as the *asamavāyī kāraṇa* of the self's specific attributes?

In reply, they say that the self is an all-pervasive (*vibhu*) substance and regarding the production of specific attributes of all-pervasive substances, a special rule holds.[4] The rule is that a specific attribute is produced in an all-pervasive substance only

---

4 Viśvanātha, *Kārikāvalī-Muktāvalī, kārika* 27.

Padmanābha Miśra, 1929, *Setu*, a commentary on *Praśastapādabhāṣya*, ed. Gopinath Kaviraja and Dhundhiraja Sastri, pp. 416-23, Benaras: Chowkhamba Sanskrit Series.

in the location where the *asamavāyī kāraṇa* is present. This rule excludes the possibility of self-body conjunction being regarded as the *asamavāyī kāraṇa* of specific attributes of the self. This is because the self, being all-pervasive, is related to the whole body by the relation of conjunction. So, at anytime the self is conjoined with the whole body. If the self-body conjunction were the *asamavāyī kāraṇa* of all the specific attributes like pleasure and pain which the self has, then these attributes would have been produced all over the body, as the whole body is conjoined with the self. But that does not always happen. If we take pain as an obvious example, pain is localized in some parts of the body. We find that one may have or feel pain in different parts of the body at different times. In the Nyāya terminology it is said that specific attributes like pain are produced in the self, as limited by some particular part of the body (*śarīravayava-avacchedena ātmani viśeṣa guṇotpatti*). Though the self, which is all-pervasive, is in conjunction with the whole body which is of medium size (*madhyama parimāṇa dravya*),[5] specific attributes are not produced in the self pervading the whole body. Therefore, the self-body conjunction, in spite of being a cause of the specific attributes of the self, cannot be regarded as the *asamavāyī kāraṇa* of them. They argued that in this case, the *asamavāyī kāraṇa* would be the self's conjunction with some other substance, which resides inside the body, is of minute size (*aṇu parimāṇa*) and is also capable of movement (*kriyā*).[6] This substance, which is a relatum of the

5 According to the Nyāya-Vaiśeṣika philosophers, all substance products, except *dvyaṇuka* (dyad), which is the first product of atoms, have medium size. *Dvyaṇuka*, which is a product of two *paramāṇus*, has a small size, the same as the size of its component atoms. But beginning with *trasareṇu* (triad) which is a product of three dyads, all other substance products are of medium size (*madhyama parimāṇa*) though varying in largeness. The human body is also a product of the earth and has a medium-large size.

6 On the Nyāya-Vaiśeṣika theory, all substances having limited size (*paricchinnaparimāṇavat*) are capable of movement (*kriyā*). By finite size is meant either *aṇu* or *madhyama parimāṇa*. Substances having →

conjunction with the self is designated as *manas*. If this self-mind conjunction (*ātmā-manaḥ-saṁyoga*) is accepted as the *asamavāyī kāraṇa* of the specific attributes of the self then it can account for the production of a specific attribute in the self as limited by only a part of the body and not as limited by the whole body. Let us explain this point. The *manas* being a substance of minute size (*aṇu parimāṇa*) can be in conjunction with only a part of a medium size (*madhyama parimāṇa*) substance, in this case, the body. And being capable of movement (*kriyā/gati*), it can be related to different parts of the body at different times. So, it is possible for specific attributes like pain to be produced in the self as limited by some particular part of the body at different times.

This was the third argument advanced by the Nyāya-Vaiśeṣika philosophers to prove the existence of *manas* as a component of the *asamavāyī kāraṇa* of the specific attributes of the self (*ātma-viśeṣaguṇāḥ*).

## IV

Now we shall consider the fourth argument, which has been given great importance by the Nyāya philosophers. We have already mentioned that Gautama, the founder of the Nyāya system, presented this argument in his *Nyāyasūtra* 1.1.16. There he said that the fact of the non-production of different perceptual cognitions by different sense organs simultaneously (*yugapad*) proves the existence of *manas* as an auxiliary cause of external perception (*bāhya pratyakṣa*). This argument needs some elaboration. We have five different external sense organs, viz. *cakṣu* (visual sense organ), *śrotra* (auditory sense organ), *ghrāṇa* (olfactory sense organs), *rasana* (gustatory sense organ) and *tvak* (tactile sense organ). Each of them has a particular class of objects knowable by them respectively, these are colour (*rūpa*), sound (*śabda*), smell (*gandha*), taste (*rasa*) and touch

← such size are called *mārta* and they all have *kriyā*. *Manas* being a substance of the smallest or infinitesimal size is also capable of *kriyā*.

(*sparśa*). So, there being five sense organs and their respective five objects, it is quite possible that more than one sense organ can be in perception-causing relation with their respective objects at the same time; as a result, there should be perception of more than one object by different sense organs at the same time. But the Nyāya-Vaiśeṣika philosophers say that this does not happen. We do not have perception of different objects by means of different sense organs simultaneously. They hold this to be a fact and argue that this fact can be explained by admitting that the external sense organs need an auxiliary cause, in the absence of which they cannot produce the perception; and this auxiliary cause must be such that it cannot assist more than one sense organ at a time. So in the absence of simultaneous assistance by the auxiliary cause external sense organs cannot produce perceptual cognition of their respective objects simultaneously, even though they are appropriately connected to their respective objects. This auxiliary cause is a substance of infinitesimal size and partless (*niravayava*),[7] which can be in contact with only one external sense organ at a time and that contact is necessary for the production of external perception by an external sense organ. If it had parts (*sāvayava*), it could be in contact with many sense organs through different parts. One and the same thing can be in contact with different things if it is a composite substance made of different parts. So, the auxiliary cause, which is to be admitted, must be a partless substance. This substance is *manas*, which assists the external sense organs in producing perceptual cognition by being in contact with them successively.

Let us explain the matter with the help of an example. Suppose,

---

[7] The Nyāya-Vaiśeṣika philosophers hold that every substance product (*janya dravya*) is composite. They are made of parts, i.e. *sāvayava*. The parts are called *avayava*. Eternal substances on the other hand are partless (*niravayava*). *Ākāśa, dik, kāla* and *ātman* are infinitely large eternal substances which have no part. Similarly *paramāṇu* and *manas* are infinitely small eternal substances which have no parts.

I am visiting a flower garden; I am seeing flowers and someone accompanying me is telling me the name of those flowers. Here, I am having two kinds of perception, i.e. visual perception of flowers and auditory perception of the names of the flowers. The Nyāya–Vaiśeṣika philosophers would say that I am having these two kinds of perception successively and not at the same time. Though my visual sense organ and auditory sense organ are connected to their respective objects, viz. the flower and the naming word at the same time, I am not having the perception of both objects simultaneously; either I am seeing the flower first, then hearing the name; or, I am hearing the name first and then seeing the flower. There may be a seeming simultaneity but in reality, there is successiveness. And these philosophers say that this absence of simultaneous perception of different objects by different sense organs can be explained by admitting *manas* (mind) as an auxiliary cause of the external perception of things. *Manas* is a very small partless substance which is located in our body. It is capable of quick movement and so it can move towards different sense organs and can be in contact with them in quick succession. And thus we can have different perceptions by different sense organs in quick succession which one may mistakenly think as simultaneous perceptions.

The above argument of the Nyāya–Vaiśeṣika philosophers is not a really strong argument, it has some shortcomings. And the main shortcoming is that the basic premise on which their argument is formulated is not accepted by philosophers of several other schools.[8] They formulate their argument with the premise that simultaneous perceptions by different sense organs do not occur. They take this to be a statement of fact, but many other philosophers of different schools deny this. According to them, we do have perceptions by more than one sense organ, even by all the five sense organs simultaneously. A reference has been made by Gaṅgeśa and other

[8] Gaṅgeśa, *Tattvacintāmaṇi*, Pratyakṣa Khaṇḍa, pp. 770, 779-81, ed. Pandit Kāmākhyānāth Tarkavāgīśa, Delhi: Motilal Banarasidass, 1974.

philosophers to a view held by some philosophical schools, that simultaneous perception of different sensible qualities is possible in many cases. They give a suitable example where all the five sensible qualities are perceived simultaneously. When a person munches a large crispy wafer (*śaṣkulī* in Sanskrit) he perceives its taste, smell, its touch, hears the sound of munching and can also see the large wafer held in his hand while having a bite. The Mīmāṁsā school which admits *manas* to be infinitely large (*vibhu*) and the Sāṁkhya, as well as the Vedānta schools, that admit *manas* to be made of component parts (*sāvayava*), admit the possibility of simultaneous perception. So what the Nyāya-Vaiśeṣika philosophers use as a premise is only an assumption, and is not accepted as true by many philosophers. They themselves were aware of the weakness of the argument and so they put forward other arguments to prove the existence of *manas*, as we have seen earlier.

But the Naiyāyikas have given much importance to this argument because they have derived all the characteristics of *manas* on the basis of this argument. As explained above, we have seen that to account for the absence of simultaneous perception by means of different external sense organs, *manas* has been admitted as a partless substance, which is one in each body and has infinitesimal size; it has movements and can come in contact with different sense organs. The contact of *manas* with an external sense organ is one of the casual conditions for the production of external perception. So, from this argument, they have inferred the existence of *manas* along with many of its characteristic properties. That is the reason why they have given so much importance to this argument.

## V

Of the four arguments that we have considered so far, the second one is the strongest one. By that argument *manas* has been inferred as the instrumental cause of perception of internal qualities of the self. The same argument can be found in many of the Nyāya-Vaiśeṣika texts like the *Kārikāvalī* by Viśvanātha, *Tarkasaṁgrahaḥ* by

Annambhaṭṭa and *Nyāyalīlāvatī* by Vallabhācārya, as proof for the existence of *manas*. This indicates the greater acceptability of that argument. That we perceive our internal states like pleasure and pain cannot be doubted; and the argument that we need an internal sense organ for the perception of internal states is quite reasonable, because external sense organs cannot cause the perception of those states. A uniform account of external and internal perception can be given by admitting *manas* as an internal sense organ.

We have already discussed the fourth argument and have shown how from that argument different properties of *manas* have been derived. From the other arguments also, we get some other properties of *manas* and compiling all the properties we get the Nyāya–Vaiśeṣika concept of *manas*.

We find that *manas* has been inferred as an instrument of knowledge and to function as an instrument of knowledge it has to come in contact with the soul and also with the external sense organs in some cases. So *manas* must be a substance, because only a substance can come in contact with another substance. The self or *ātman*, external sense organs and *manas* – they all belong to the class of substances.

*Manas* has been regarded as an internal sense organ because it has been admitted as the instrumental cause of the perception of pleasure, pain, cognition, etc. which are internal properties of the self. It should be mentioned here that neither in the *Vaiśeṣikasūtra* nor in the *Nyāyasūtra* where sense organs were enumerated, *manas* has been mentioned. But Vātsyāyana, in his *Bhāṣya* on *Nyāyasūtra* 1.1.4, explained that Gautama undoubtedly admitted *manas* to be a sense organ as held by the Sāṁkhya school and also mentioned in scriptures. Had he not accepted this position, he would have refuted it. According to a principle of interpreting texts, called *anumata*, if an author does not try to refute a position held by others, then it is to be understood that he agrees with them and accepts that position. Therefore, it is to be understood that the Nyāya and its sister system Vaiśeṣika also admit *manas* as an internal sense organ. Though a sense organ, *manas* is different from external sense organs in many respects and that is the reason why Gautama did not mention it along with external sense organs in the same list. Our external sense organs are either products of elements (*bhautika*) or an element by themselves. Of the five sense organs, the visual sense organ is a product of the element fire (*tejas*), the olfactory (*ghrāṇa*) sense is a product of earth (*kṣiti*), the gustatory sense organ (*rasana*) is a product of water (*ap*) and the tactile sense organ (*tvak*) is a product of the element air (*vāyu*). The auditory sense organ (*śrotra*), according to them, is *ākāśa* as delimited by the auditory organ present in our body. So, all of them are *bhautika* in nature. But *manas* is a separate substance.[9] Being a partless substance, it is not a product and hence it is eternal, i.e. it is ever present; it is neither produced nor destroyed. Both the *ātman* and the *manas* are eternal. For every self, there is a *manas*, and they are connected till the attainment of *mokṣa*.[10] Besides functioning as the internal sense organ, it plays an important role in producing different types of cognition about different objects, internal or external, as we have already seen.

In the end, it should be mentioned that the Nyāya-Vaiśeṣika concept of the *manas* as has been constructed here was not accepted

[9] Raghunātha Śiromaṇi, 1976, *Padārtha-tattvanirūpaṇam*, ed. Madhusūdana Bhaṭṭācārya Nyāyācārya, p. 8, Sanskrit College, Calcutta. Raghunātha, a renowned Navya-Naiyāyika, made a critical assessment of the metaphysical categories admitted by the Nyāya-Vaiśeṣika schools in his book *Padārtha-tattvanirūpaṇam*. There, he has given a modified list of categories which are accepted by some other systems but are rejected by old Nyāya-Vaiśeṣika schools and he also reduced the number of categories accepted by orthodox Nyāya philosophers by showing that some of those categories can be included in the basic categories. He did not admit *manas* to be an additional substance and held that it is included in the four basic elements, i.e. earth, water, fire and air. According to him, *manas* is an uncaused form of these elements (*asamavetabhūtaviśeṣa*).

[10] Jayanta Bhaṭṭa, *Nyāyamañjarī, dvitīya bhāga*, ed. Gaurinath Sastri, pp. 300-301, Śivakumar Śāstrī-granthamālā, Varanasi, 1983.

by all schools of Indian philosophy, even though they all have admitted *manas* as an entity. Each of the characteristics of *manas* as conceived by the Nyāya-Vaiśeṣika systems has been disputed by some school or other. To mention briefly,

i. that *manas* is eternal (*nitya*) is denied by Advaita Vedāntins;
ii. that *manas* is of infinitesimal size (*aṇu parimāṇa*) is denied by Advaita Vedānta, Bhāṭṭa Mīmāṁsā and the Yoga schools;
iii. that *manas* is not a product of elements (*abhautika*) is disputed by the Advaita Vedāntins; and
iv. that *manas* is a sense organ has been disputed by the Jaina school and Vivaraṇa branch of Advaita Vedānta. In appropriate contexts, the issues have been debated by the opposing schools.

Here we can make an observation about the arguments put forward by the Nyāya-Vaiśeṣika schools for proving the existence of *manas*. If we critically consider the arguments we have discussed above, it appears that the Nyāya-Vaiśeṣika philosophers have assumed the existence of *manas* and conceived its nature in a way that fits into their system of epistemological and metaphysical beliefs. We have seen that they based their arguments on certain beliefs such as:

a. simultaneous perceptions by different sense organs do not occur,
b. all non-perceptual cognitions should also have some instrumental cause similar to the external sense organs,
c. their casual theory of *samavāyī kāraṇa* and *asamavāyī kāraṇa*, and
d. perception of internal states like pleasure and pain should also be caused by some sense organ.

But these beliefs are not shared by all other philosophical schools. Only as long as we are confined to the Nyāya-Vaiśeṣika systems, these arguments are found to be effective.

# 15

# Udayana's Doctrine of Jāti-bādhaka

## A Defence

### I

ALTHOUGH there is no doubt that the doctrine of *jāti-bādhaka* is an integral part of the Vaiśeṣika theory of *jāti* (universal), there seems to be some confusion regarding the role this doctrine plays. Udayanācārya was the first philosopher to discuss the *jāti-bādhakas*. In his *Kiraṇāvalī* he mentioned six *jāti-bādhakas*: *vyakterabheda*, *tulyatva*, *sāṅkarya*, *anavasthā*, *rūpahāni* and *asambandha.*[1]

Now the important question is: what is the purpose that these *jāti-bādhakas* are supposed to serve? Or, in other words, what use did the Vaiśeṣika philosophers make of them? The answer is that these *jāti-bādhakas* play a role in establishing the *jātitva* of a property. According to the Vaiśeṣikas, property is regarded as *jāti*, if and only if it satisfies any one of a number of positive conditions, which we shall mention shortly and a negative condition, viz. having no *jāti-bādhaka* (reason for cancelling its claim to be regarded as a *jāti*). To identify a *jāti*, besides other things, it is necessary to see whether or not any of the *jāti-bādhakas* is present. If a *jāti-bādhaka* is present, the property under consideration cannot be regarded as a *jāti*, even though it fulfils some positive conditions.

---

1 Udayanācārya, *Kiraṇāvalī* with *Prakāśa* by Vardhamana Upadhyaya and *Prakāśa-Vivṛtti* by Rucidatta, 1989, p. 161.

Let us explain the point a little. The primary reason for admitting a *jāti* according to the Vaiśeṣikas is to account for the fact of *anugata pratīti*, i.e. perception of a number of different individual entities in the same form. Assumption of a property shared in common by each, individual entity can explain this sort of perception.[2] For example, we have perception in the form "This is a pot" with regard to a number of pots. Now, though each pot individually differs from the other pots, each is perceived as a pot because they have in common the property called "potness". Even where such perception does not occur, the existence of a *jāti* is inferred as the *avacchedaka dharma* of *kāraṇatā* or *kāryatā*, i.e. the property which determines the property of causeness or effectness.[3] What it means is that the causeness/effectness with respect to a particular effect/cause does not reside in everything in the world, but only in a specific class of things; and it is so because there is a property determining the causeness/effectness with respect to a particular effect/cause; and all those things and only those things have the causeness/effectness with respect to a specific effect/cause which has that determining property.

There is yet another reason for admitting a *jāti*. Corresponding to every meaningful term that stands for some object or objects, there is a *pravṛtti nimitta*, i.e. the reason for the application of that term to the object or objects. Usually, for the sake of the economy, a *jāti*, if available, is regarded as *pravṛtti nimitta* by the Nyāya-Vaiśeṣika philosophers. For example, the term "pot" applies to a number of pots because all of them possess the property of potness which is a *jāti* as well as the *pravṛtti nimitta* (which is also called *śakyātavaccheda dharma*) in this case. Wherever potness is present, the term "pot" applies. So we may infer a *jāti* as the *pravṛtti nimitta* of a particular term.

---

2 Nṛsiṁha Śāstri, *Prabhā Ṭīkā* on Viśvanātha's *Kārikāvalī-Muktāvalī*, 1988, p. 101.
Mahadeva, *Dīnakarīya Ṭīkā* on *Kārikāvalī-Muktāvalī*, 1988, p. 101.

3 Śaṅkāra Miśra, *Kaṇādarahasyam*, 1917, p. 159.

These three constitute the positive conditions, at least one of which must be satisfied by a property if it is to be regarded as a *jāti*. And any property fulfilling either of these three conditions has a prima facie claim to be regarded as a *jāti*.

Each of these positive conditions implies that a *jāti* is an *anugata dharma*, i.e. a property which functions as the principle of classification of a number of individual objects. Now a property, in order to be a common property, must be one; and if it is one, it must be *nitya* (eternal). Because if all the members - past, present and future - are to possess one and the same property, the property must be eternal; and if they do not possess one and the same property, they cannot be brought under one and the same class. A *jāti* is also an *akhaṇḍa dharma*, i.e. a simple and indefinable property. A property that is not simple, cannot unify different individuals. That *jāti* is a simple property is proved by the fact that it is presented in our thought in an unqualified way (*svarūpataḥ bhāna*), i.e. by itself and not as qualified by some property (*viśeṣaṇa*). So, we find that a *jāti* has the following characteristics:[4]

i. It is the object of *anugata pratīti.*
ii. It is the *avacchedaka dharma* (determining property) of *kāraṇatā* (causeness), etc.
iii. It is the *pravṛtti nimitta* (reason for applying a name).
iv. It is *akhaṇḍa* (simple).
v. It is one.
vi. It is eternal.

Now we should note that though every *jāti* has all these characteristics (in some cases, the first characteristic is absent), it cannot be said that whatever possesses any of these characteristics is a *jāti*. A property may be the object of *anugata pratīti* (uniform perception), but still not a *jāti*, e.g. *bhūtatva* or *jātitva.* Again, a property may be the property determining causeness, but still not

[4] Udayanācārya, *Kiraṇāvalī*, 1989, pp. 119-23.

a *jāti*, e.g. *indriyatva.* A property again may be a *pravṛtti nimitta*, yet, may not be a *jāti*, such as *ākāśatva* and *viśeṣatva.* A property may be *akhaṇḍa*, but not a *jāti*, e.g. *abhāvatva.*

But in each of these cases, there is a scope of doubt as to whether the property under consideration is a *jāti*. Because each having at least one of the characteristics, which belongs to the *jāti*s, has a claim to be regarded as a *jāti*. So, we must have some way to remove this doubt and decide what these properties are. *Jāti-bādhaka*s are the means of removing this doubt and ascertaining whether a proposed *jāti* is really so.

Different *jāti-bādhaka*s admitted by the Vaiśeṣikas demonstrate that the properties mentioned above and also certain other properties cannot be regarded as *jāti*, either because some of them cannot serve the function of unifying several individuals, as is the case with *ākāśatva*, or they do so with the help of some other *jāti*, as in the case of *mūrtatva*; or the purpose is served by some other simple property, as in the case of *kambugrīvādimatva*, or because the admission of some properties as *jāti* leads to some absurd or unacceptable consequences, which is the case with *jātitva* and *viśeṣatva*; or if the proposed *jāti*, like *abhāvatva*, cannot be related to its loci in relation to *samavāya*, which a *jāti* can appropriately have with its loci.

We see that the *jāti-bādhaka*s constitute certain conditions preventing the admission of *jāti.* At this point, we should mention that a *jāti-bādhaka* is either the condition preventing the admission of *jātitva* of a property, or the condition preventing the admission of any *jāti* in certain kind of things. In the first case, a *jāti-bādhaka* is *jātitva bādhaka* and in the latter case it is *jātimattva-bādhaka.*[5] The Vaiśeṣikas admit *jāti* in *dravya*, *guṇa* and *karma* only and not in the rest of the categories recognized by them, viz. *sāmānya*, *viśeṣa*, *samavāya* and *abhāva.* The reason for not admitting any *jāti* in the last four categories is also provided by the *jāti-bādhaka*s. It is shown

---

[5] Nṛsiṁha Śāstri, *Prabhā Ṭīkā*, 1988, p. 102.

that the presence of some *jāti-bādhaka*s disallows the possibility of their being the loci of any *jāti.*

Again, while admitting *dravya, guṇa* and *karma* can possess and do possess some *jāti*, they deny that any property which they possess is a *jāti*, even though it fulfils some of the positive conditions. Some of the *jāti-bādhaka*s negate the claim of such properties to be regarded as *jāti.* So we see that the absence of all the *jāti-bādhaka*s is a necessary condition that a property must satisfy to be a *jāti*, and a thing must satisfy it in order to be the locus of some *jāti.*

Now, with the help of the two sets of positive and negative conditions mentioned above, the Vaiśeṣikas identify the class of *jāti*s. After this, they formulate the definition of *jāti* by picking out those characteristics of *jāti*s, in terms of which it can be differentiated from non-*jāti*s. So, they formulated a definition of *jāti*, which does not apply to any properties that are non-*jāti*s with the help of *jāti-bādhaka*s. We shall come to this point presently.

There is another point which we should consider while discussing the need for the *jāti-bādhaka*s. The context in which Udayana first introduced the *jāti-bādhaka*s in the *Kiraṇāvalī* is the division of *jāti*s into two kinds: *parā* and *aparā*. There he mentions that this division holds good only in the cases where two *jāti*s reside in the same locus. Immediately after this, he mentions the *jāti-bādhaka*s. It seems that he anticipated some objections against this division, and to answer that objection, he mentions the *jāti-bādhaka*s. We may try to construct the objection in the following way. One may object that this division of *jāti*s, residing in the same locus, into *parā* and *aparā* cannot be possible under three circumstances:

1. if two *jāti*s reside in one and one individual only;
2. if two *jāti*s have exactly the same extension while residing in more than one thing;
3. if there is partial overlapping between the extension of the two *jāti*s.

Because *parā* means having wider extension and *aparā* means having narrower extension; and in the cases mentioned above, none of the two *jātis* can be said to have wider or narrower extension compared to the other.

Udayanācārya seems to answer this charge by saying that no *jāti* is admitted in the above-mentioned cases, but those cases necessitate the formulation of the preventing condition or *jāti-bādhakas*. First three *jāti-bādhakas*, viz. *vyakterabheda*, *tulyatva* and *sāṅskarya*, are relevant in this context. But though the other three *jāti-bādhakas* are not relevant to that context; he mentions them in order to make the enumeration of the *jāti-bādhakas* complete.

So we can say that both the definition and division of *jāti* can be defended with reference to the *jāti-bādhakas*. Because, the identification of *jātis* is not possible without the help of *jāti-bādhakas*. Unless we have a clear idea regarding the class which is being defined and divided, there remains the possibility of making errors while defining or dividing a class. Once we know for certain which things are members of the class and which are not, we can formulate the correct definition and divide it correctly.

## II

*Jāti* has been defined by the Vaśeṣikas as the *nitya* and *aneka samaveta dharma*, i.e. a property which is eternal and resides in many in the relation of inherence.[6] Now, all these characteristics which constitute the definition of *jāti*, is necessitated by the function which a *jāti* is to serve.

We have already seen that a *jāti* has been admitted to explain *anugata pratīti*, i.e. the same form of perception about different individuals; or, in other words, to function as a principle of classification of several individuals. To do this, the property must be *aneka-anugata* or *anekavṛtti*, i.e. it must reside in many individuals and must also be *nityā* (eternal).

[6] Annaṁbhaṭṭa, *Tarkasaṁgrahaḥ*, 1969, p. 75, Viśvanātha, *Kārikāvalī-Muktāvalī*, 1988, p. 98.

It can also be shown with the help of the law of parsimony (*lāghava nyāya*) that to be the *avacchedaka dharma* of *kāraṇatā*, etc. the property determining the causeness, etc. should be *anugata*, i.e. residing in many.

Now regarding the relation between a *jāti* and the individuals in which it resides, the Vaiśeṣikas argue, with the help of the principle of elimination (*itarabādha*) and the law of parsimony (*lāghava nyāya*) that the relation can be nothing but inherence (*samavāya*) which is already established as a relation between a substance (*dravya*) on the one hand, and *guṇa* and *karma* on the other. Therefore, a *jāti* is *aneka samaveta*, i.e. related to many in the relation of inherence.

A *jāti* is to be eternal also, as otherwise, it could not have brought under one class, several individuals, including those who existed in the past and which will come into existence in future.

Now, those characteristics of a thing are regarded as the defining characteristics with respect to which it is differentiated from the rest of the things. In the case of *jāti*, the properties of being eternal and being related to many in the relation of inherence happen to be such characteristics though they were initially required for serving the purpose of explaining *anugata pratīti* and to ensure the simplicity of the hypothesis.

Here, we should consider the doubt raised by some that we do not need *vyakterabheda* and *asambandha* as *jāti-bādhaka*, since they are not independent of the definition of *jāti*. These *jāti-bādhakas* are said to be formulated in terms of some of the defining characteristics of *jāti*. But, then, the purpose that those *jāti-bādhakas* serve can be served by the definition of *jāti* itself, so, there is no need to admit those *jāti-bādhakas*. Because, it can then be said that a particular property cannot be regarded as a *jāti* as it does not satisfy the definition of *jāti*.

At this point, one may argue that, the fact that the definition of *jāti* does not apply to certain properties cannot prove that those properties are not *jātis*; on the contrary, one may raise the charge that the definition is too narrow because it does not apply to a number of properties which should be regarded as *jāti*. So, we need to settle as to whether those properties are *jāti* or not, independently of the definition. The two *jāti-bādhaka*s under consideration become useless for this purpose as they are not independent of the definition.

Let us now consider how far the objection is tenable. It is said that *vyakterabheda* cancels the claim of *jātitva* of a property like *ākāśatva* by showing that a part of the defining property is absent in it. *Anekavṛttitva* (common to many entities) is a part of the definition of *jāti*, which is absent in *ākāśatva*. Similar is the case with *asambandha*. It denies the claim of such property as *abhāvatva* to be regarded as *jāti* because the said property does not have a part of the defining property, i.e. *samavetatva* or being related to its loci in the relation of inherence.

We may try to answer this objection and try to prove the necessity and adequacy of those *jāti-bādhaka*s, from the Vaiśeṣika point of view.

Now the first *jāti-bādhaka*, viz. *vyakterabheda*, denies the claim of *ākāśatva* to be regarded as a *jāti* on the ground that only one individual is the locus of this property. We have seen that the primary purpose of admitting a *jāti* is to bring several individuals under a class and thus explains *anugata pratīti* about them. But, such properties as *ākāśatva* cannot serve the purpose only because it resides in one individual object. So, this *jāti-bādhaka*, viz. *vyakterabheda*, shows that the property under consideration cannot perform the function that a *jāti* must do. Its claim to be regarded as a *jāti* is therefore denied. Actually, the need for admitting a *jāti* is not felt in this case, because there is no question of forming a class consisting of a number of similar individuals. But, what then is the necessity of admitting a *jāti-bādhaka* to deny *jātitva* of such property? The reason is that since a property which is a *jāti* is also the *pravṛtti nimitta* or the reason for applying a term, one may mistakenly think that whatever property functions as the reason for the application of a term is a *jāti*. So, one may think that *ākāśatva* being the reason for the application of the term, *ākāśa* is also a *jāti*. This confusion is removed by the first *jāti-bādhaka*.

*Asambandha* denies the claim of *abhāvatva* to be regarded as *jāti* on the ground that it cannot be related to its loci in the relation of *samavāya*, which is the appropriate relation between a *jāti* and its loci.

But, it will be wrong to suppose that these *jāti-bādhakas* are not independent of the definition of *jāti*, which includes the properties of *aneka vṛttitva* and *samavetatva*. We have already seen that on independent ground, it has been proved that a *jāti* must have the feature of being related to many individuals and that the relation which it has with its instances can be nothing other than the relation of inherence. These features were then chosen to be the defining characteristics of *jāti*.

We can further say that since it has been proved that *ākāśatva*, *abhāvatva* and certain other properties cannot be *jāti*, the definition of *jāti* should be formulated in such a way as to exclude those properties, from the scope of the definition and thus be able to distinguish *jāti* from those properties. That is why those features, which a *jāti* possesses as a matter of necessity and non-*jātis* do not possess, have been included in the definition. Thus, we arrive at the notion of *jāti* as *nityatve sati aneka samavetatva*, i.e. a property which is eternal and is present in many individuals in the relation of inherence.

## III

We may now take up another problem regarding *asambandha*. The problem is: what should be the correct interpretation of *asambandha*? According to some, if *asambandha* is interpreted in a particular way, which seems to be a quite justified interpretation too, then it can replace two other *jāti-bādhakas*, viz. *anavasthā* and *rūpahāni*. And it will be in conformity with the law of parsimony if only one *jāti-bādhaka* can serve the purpose of all the three.

The proposed interpretation is as follows: *asambandha* means not being the locus of anything in the relation of inherence (*samavāya*). This *jāti-bādhaka* stands in the way of admitting any *jāti* in a thing if it cannot be the locus of anything in the relation of *samavāya.* Now, this interpretation is not unjustified for the following reason. *Asambandha* means the absence of the relation, which in this context is the relation *samavāya*; and a thing can have absence of the relation in two ways:

i. if it is not the locus of anything in that relation, and

ii. if it is not located in anything in that relation.

Now, it is the first way which is relevant for preventing the admission of any *jāti* in an individual because if an individual is to possess a *jāti*, it must be the locus of it in the relation of *samavāya.* So, by showing that a thing cannot be the locus of anything in the relation of *samavāya*, it can be shown that it cannot have any *jāti.* And this being the case with *sāmānya* and *viśeṣa* also, in addition to *samavāya* and *abhāva*, the presence of any *jāti* is denied in each case. So, *anavasthā* and *rūpahāni* can be eliminated.

Though this view seems justifiable, there is a stronger reason for retaining the original interpretation. According to the original interpretation, *asambandha* or having the absence of the relation of *samavāya* means being neither the locus of anything in the relation of *samavāya* nor a thing located in another thing in the relation of *samavāya* (*anuyogītva pratiyogitva etad anyatara sambandhena samavāyābhāva*).[7]

*Asambandha* has to be interpreted in this way because this *jāti-bādhaka* is to serve the triple purpose of showing that

1. *abhāvatva* and *samavāyatva* cannot be *jātis*;
2. *samavāya* and *abhāva* cannot possess any *jāti* whatsoever; and
3. *abhāva* and *samavāya* themselves cannot be *jātis.*

[7] Nṛsiṁha Śāstri, *Prabhā Ṭīkā* on *Muktāvalī*, 1988, pp. 102, 112-13. Paṭṭābhīrām Śāstrī, *Mañjuṣā Ṭīkā* on *Muktāvalī*, 1988, pp. 112-13.

Now, not being the locus of anything in the relation of *samavāya*, which is a part of the meaning of *asambandha*, is relevant for the first and second purpose; and, not being located in another thing, the relation of *samavāya* is relevant for the third purpose. So, *asambandha* is a *jāti-bādhaka* in both senses, i.e. as being *jātimattva-bādhaka* and *jati-bādhaka*. Therefore, we are not free to interpret *asambandha* simply as not being the locus of anything in the relation of *samavāya*: because, then, we will need another *jāti-bādhaka* to serve the third purpose. It cannot even be said that there is no need to show that *abhāva* and *samavāya* cannot be *jātis*.

That *samavāya* and *atyantābhāva* have the claim to be regarded as *jātis* cannot be denied, because each of them is one and is related to many. So, we have *anugata pratīti* or uniform experience with regard to them. The Vaiśeṣikas will have to show why *jātitva* is denied of them.

Now it is evident that *asambandha*, interpreted in this way, cannot serve the purposes which *anavasthā* and *rūpahāni* serve. *Anavasthā* shows that *sāmānyas* cannot have any *jāti* in them; and *rūpahāni* shows that *viśeṣas* cannot have any *jāti* in them. *Asambandha* cannot serve these purposes because both *sāmānya* and *viśeṣa* are properties located in certain things in relation of *samavāya*; so *asambandha*, in its original interpretation, cannot be present in their case. Therefore, we need *anavasthā* and *rūpahāni* as *jāti-bādhakas*.

These two *jāti-bādhakas* show that admission of *jāti* in *jātis* and *viśeṣas* leads to unacceptable consequences. *Anavasthā* (infinite regress) is a general fallacy and it has been used as a *jāti-bādhaka* because it clearly shows the absurdity which results in assuming any *jāti* in *jātis*. *Rūpahāni* also brings out the absurdity of assuming a *jāti* in *viśeṣa* by pointing out that it defeats the purpose of admitting *viśeṣas*. Thus, the assumption of *jāti* will ultimately lead to the denial of *viśeṣas*, or will reduce *viśeṣas* to *guṇas*, because if *viśeṣas* which inhere in substances only, possess a *jāti* in them, then they become indistinguishable from *guṇas*.

Let us go back again to the problem regarding the interpretation of *asambandha*. We have seen that the original interpretation should be preferred as it serves more than one purpose simultaneously. That interpretation of *asambandha* does not lead to the elimination of *anavasthā*s and *rūpahāni*. Furthermore, we can say that even if *asambandha* is interpreted as not being the locus of anything in the relation of *samavāya* (*anuyogitā sambandhena samavāyābhāva*), it cannot replace *anavasthā* and *rūpahāni*. Because, we cannot be certain that *sāmānyas* and *viśeṣas* do not have anything in them in the relation of *samavāya* unless we already know that there cannot be any *jāti* in them. As both of them are *pratiyogī*s of *samavāya*, i.e. each is related to something in the relation of *samavāya*, it may be quite possible that they may also figure as the *anuyogī* of *samavāya*, if there were some *jāti*s to be related with each of them. They are not in principle incapable of being a relatum to the relation of *samavāya* in the sense of being the *anuyogī* of it. So, the denial of having a *jāti* by *sāmānya* and *viśeṣa* on the ground that they are not *anuyogī* of *samavāya* would seem to have presupposed the absence of *jātitva* of the relevant properties like *sāmānyatva*, *viśeṣatva* and thus to involve the fallacy of *petitio principii*.

The same problem may arise in the case of *samavāya* and *abhāva* also. In the case of *samavāya* it can be said that *samavāya* being one, it is impossible for *samavāya* to be a term of the relation of *samavāya*, at least in the primary sense of the term. But, the case with *abhāva* remains undecided. So, it may be questioned whether *asambandha* can really be regarded as the condition preventing the admission of *jāti* in *abhāva*.

## IV

Our study of the Vaiśeṣika doctrine of *jāti-bādhaka* will remain incomplete unless we show the need for admitting two other *jāti-bādhakas*, viz. *tulyatva* and *sāṅkarya*. Hence, let us see why we need these *jāti-bādhakas*. Supposing that there are more than one generic properties, what sorts of relation may hold between any two such properties? There seem to be the following possibilities:

1. The two properties are incompatible or mutually exclusive.
2. The two properties are compatible and the extension of one of them includes the whole of the extension of the other, not conversely.
3. The two properties are coextensive.
4. One part of the extension of each overlaps while the other part of the extension of each remains outside the extension of the other.

Now among these four possibilities, the first two types of relation may hold between two *jātis*. But, where the third and the fourth types of relation hold, the properties concerned are not usually regarded as *jātis*. If the third sort of relation is admitted to hold between two *jātis*, then it would amount to the acceptance of two principles for forming the same class, and that is unnecessary. Again, if the fourth type of relation were admitted to obtain between two *jātis*, then none of the *jātis* would be able to form a class distinct from the class formed by the other. All the *jātis* excepting *sattā*, which has the widest extension, function as unifying and differentiating factors. But in the cases where the fourth type of relation holds, the supposed generic properties would fail to serve the function of differentiation.

In the cases 3 and 4 mentioned above, *jātitva* is denied of the properties concerned, with the help of the *jāti-bādhakas*, viz. *tulyatva* and *sāṅkarya*. The argument at the basis of *tulyatva* is that to form a class, we need only one and, if available, a simple property; now, if a property, e.g. *kambugrīvādimatta*, i.e. having a neck like that of a conch shell, is found to be coextensive with another property, say, *ghaṭatva*, i.e. jarness, and the latter property is a simpler one as is the case with our example, then the latter one will be regarded as a *jāti*, but not the former one. If both properties under consideration are simple in the case of *kalaśatva* and *ghaṭatva*, then they will be regarded as the same *jāti*.

The argument on which the use of *sāṅkarya* as a *jāti-bādhaka* is based seems to be this. In some cases, for the sake of convenience or serving some other purpose, we group several things based on some similarity. But these groups do not constitute classes over and above the existing classes of things. For example, we call the first five substances admitted by the Vaiśeṣikas by the name *bhūta*, so here we form a group consisting of a number of substances, but that cannot be said to form a separate class of things. We group them, based on their similarity in respect of having some externally perceivable specific quality. Again, we form a group of *indriyas* (sense organs), members of which comprise different types of substances. We form another group of *mūrta dravyas* (substances) as having finite dimensions. In this way, based on some similarities, we form different groups.

Now, this practice of grouping leads one to think that corresponding to every such group, there is a *jāti*. Because, in these cases too, we use general words just as we do in the cases where a classification is made on the basis of a *jāti*. So, the use of general words suggests that there is some *jāti* which unifies a number of individuals. But, there is a great difference between the two cases. Where a class is formed on the basis of some *jāti*, all the members of the class possess one identical property; but where groups are made, the members possess not the same property, but similar or the same kind of property. These groups do not stand for separate and independent classes; on the contrary, it is found that some of the members of a particular group come under another group also. This happens because these groups depend on the fundamental classes of things and often two such groups include members of the same class. On the other hand, a real class cannot have any member, which is a member of another real class, unless the other class is a subclass of it, or it itself is a subclass of that class. This can be treated as a criterion by which a real class can be distinguished from a mere group. *Sāṅkarya* points out that in some cases, a property, which is proposed as a *jāti*, includes in its extension some other group which is not a subgroup or a supergroup of it. In such cases, the property cannot be regarded as a *jāti* which is taken to form a real class. But, what would be the status of the other property, that is the basis of the second group, whose extension is shared by the first group? Because, in the case of that property also, the situation is the same. It includes in its extension some members of another group which is not its subgroup or supergroup. In most cases, the answer is that even the second property cannot be regarded as a *jāti*, in some cases, the other property is viewed as a *jāti* for some supporting reason. For example, in the case of properties, viz. *indriyatva* (the property of being a sense organ) and *pr̥thivītva* (the property of being earth), though there is partial overlapping of extension between them, *indriyatva* is not regarded a *jāti* (universal), but *pr̥thivītva* is. The Vaiśeṣikas claim that there is some reason for regarding it as a *jāti*.

We may formulate the supporting argument in the following way. If of the two properties between which *sāṅkarya* obtains, one property forms a group which is presupposed by the other group formed by the other property, then the first property will be regarded as a *jāti*. For example, there is *sāṅkarya* between *pr̥thivītva*, *jalatva*, etc. on the one hand and *indriyatva* on the other. Now the class of *indriyas* presupposes the classes of *pr̥thivī*, *jala*, etc. because a thing to be *indriya* must first be a *pr̥thivī* or *jala*, etc. So, these latter groups are to be regarded as real classes, and the properties which form these classes are to be regarded as *jāti*.

But, in the cases where none of the properties involved in *Sāṅkarya* forms a group, which is presupposed by the other group formed by the other property, none of the properties will be regarded as *jāti*, e.g. *bhūtatva* and *mūrtatva*. Since a thing can be a *bhūta* without being *mūrta* and, again, a thing can be *mūrta* without being a *bhūta*, none of the groups presupposes the other. So, there is no reason to regard any of them as a *jāti*.

## V

In conclusion, we may sum up the outcome of our study of the Vaiśeṣika doctrine of *jāti-bādhakas*. We have found that:

1. *Jāti-bādhakas* have their use in identifying the *jātis*.
2. *Jāti-bādhakas* are independent of the definition of *jāti*.
3. They are not needed to supplement the definition of *jāti*.
4. All six *jāti-bādhakas* are needed; it is not possible to eliminate any of them. Each of them functions as a *jāti-bādhaka* in the proper sense of the term.

16

# Concept of Sattā in the Nyāya-Vaiśeṣika System

THE concept of *sattā* is used in different systems of Indian philosophy either to justify the application of the word *sat* to different entities (*sat vyavahāra*) or to account for the cognition of different entities as *sat* (*sat-buddhi*). But, though the use is common, the notion of *sattā* varies from system to system.

The concept of *sattā* as found in different systems can be brought under the following three heads:

i. *Sattā* is the property of being real, i.e. *vastutva*.

ii. *Sattā* is the property of being a positive entity, i.e. *bhāvatva*.

iii. *Sattā* is a universal (*jāti*).

Of these, the first position is held by the Advaita Vedāntins, Prābhākara Mīmāṁsakas and the Buddhists.[1] The second one is

---

[1] The Advaita Vedāntins define *sattā* as *kālatrayābādhyatva*, which means, that the existence of which cannot be denied at any segment of time, viz. past, present and future is real. The Buddhists define *sattā* as *arthakriyākāritva* meaning thereby that, only that which is causally efficacious is real. The Prābhākara Mīmāṁsakas define *sattā* as *pramāṇagamyatva* or *pramāṇasambandhayogyatva*, i.e. to be real is to be knowable by some *pramāṇa*. Bhāṭṭa Mīmāṁsakas, like the Vaiśeṣikas, admit *sattā* as a *jāti*.

held by the Navya-Naiyāyika Raghunātha Śiromaṇi and the third position is held by the Nyāya–Vaiśeṣika school.

We may try to find out the reason for such variation in the concept of *sattā*. If we start with a grammatical analysis of the word *sattā*, we find that the word is constructed by using the nominal suffix *tal* in the sense of *bhāva* (essence/nature) to the word *sat* (*sat* + *tal* = *sattā*). So, it means etymologically the essence or nature of *sat*. In philosophy, *bhāva* is used to mean *pravṛtti nimitta* or the reason for applying a term to a thing which stands for the property by virtue of possessing which a thing becomes the referent of that term. Therefore, *sattā* would mean a property by virtue of possessing that, a thing is called *sat*. But, what is this property? To identify this property, we need to know the meaning of the term *sat*. We can get an idea about the meaning of *sat* by contrasting it with its opposite term *asat*. The term *asat* is used in two senses:

1. *alīka*, which means unreal or fictitious; and
2. *abhāva*, meaning absence or negation.

So, its opposite *sat* would mean either not-fictitious, i.e. real (*vastu*), or *not-abhāva*, i.e. positive (*bhāva*).

If we take the first sense of *sat* then *sattā* would be the property of being real (*vasutva*), that is, the property by means of which real entity can be distinguished from unreal or fictitious entities. And in this sense, the term *sattā* would be a property of all the real entities, positive (*bhāva*) and negative (*abhāva*). If, on the other hand, the second sense of *sat is* taken, then *sattā* would be the property of being a positive entity, i.e. *bhāvatva* and it would be a property of all the positive entities only. We have said that both these ways of conceiving *sattā* are present in Indian philosophical systems. But, according to the orthodox Nyāya–Vaiśeṣika philosophers, *sattā* is neither *vastutva* nor *bhāvatva*, it is a universal (*jāti*) which is possessed by *dravya* (substance), *guṇa* (quality) and *karma* (motion) only. The term *sat* means primarily the locus or the seat of *sattā jāti*.

In this chapter, I shall concentrate on the Nyāya-Vaiśeṣika position and consider some of the problems that arise due to their position regarding *sattā* and evaluate the offered solutions to those problems.

Let us start with a summary of the Nyāya-Vaiśeṣika position regarding *sattā*. The Nyāya-Vaiśeṣika school maintains that a universal called *sattā* should be admitted to account for the common form of awareness to the effect "this is *sat*" which we have with respect to substances (*dravya*), qualities (*guṇa*) and motions (*karma*).[2] For, different pieces of cognition can have the same form only if they have a common object. So, when we have the same form of cognition concerning different individual entities, they are all cognized as characterized by a common property, and this common property is the object as well as the cause of such uniform cognition. By this argument, the Nyāya-Vaiśeṣika philosophers prove the existence of the universal *sattā* as the cause and object of the uniform awareness of substance, quality and motion as *sat*. *Sattā*, according to them, is a *jāti*, because it is an eternal property existing in every individual substance, quality and motion in the relation of inherence. By having recourse to the law of parsimony they admit only one *sattā*, which accounts for the awareness of the form "this is *sat*" with respect to a number of individual entities. And if it is one, it has to be eternal as otherwise, it could not exist in many individuals who existed in the past or would come into existence in the future and were or would be cognized as *sat*. *Sattā* is considered as the highest or the most extensive among all the universals.[3] For *sattā* exists in the locus of every *jāti*. Substance, quality and motion are the three categories that, according to the Nyāya-Vaiśeṣika philosophers, are the loci of *jāti*. Substances are the loci of substancehood; qualities are the seats of qualityhood and

---

2 *Vaiśeṣikasūtra* 1.2.7 with *Rasāyana* commentary by U.T. Viraraghavacharya, Madras, 1958.

3 *Praśastapādabhāṣya* with *Nyāyakandalī Ṭīkā*, p. 29, ed. Durgadhar Jha, 1963, Varanasi: Varanaseya Sanskrit Visvavidyalaya.

motion individuals are the possessors of motionhood. But, whatever be the locus of any of these universals is also a locus of *sattā*. Every individual substance or quality or motion is cognized as *sat*.

But the Nyāya-Vaiśeṣika position regarding *sattā* has its own problems. Their argument in favour of admitting *sattā* seems to be weak and has to face strong objections. It has been argued against the Nyāya-Vaiśeṣika philosophers that if *sattā* is to be admitted to account for uniform awareness of the form "this is *sat*" concerning a number of different kinds of object, then *sattā* should be admitted not only in substance, quality and motion, but also in universals (*sāmānya*), individual differentiators (*viśeṣa*) and the relation of inherence (*samavāya*), because we have awareness of the form "this is *sat*" with respect to those objects too. If *sattā* is admitted in *sāmānya*, *viśeṣa* and *samavāya*, then *sattā* cannot be a *jāti*, because, according to the Nyāya-Vaiśeṣika philosophers' theory, these three categories of objects cannot be the seat of any *jāti*, due to the presence of some preventive conditions (*jāti-bādhakas*).[4] If, on the other hand, the Nyāya-Vaiśeṣika philosophers deny that the latter three categories possess *sattā jāti*, then they should concede that *sattā* cannot be the cause of awareness of the form "this is *sat*", because, even in the absence of *sattā jāti* in some categories of things, they are recognized as *sat*. The problem can be put in the form of a dilemma: either *sattā* is not a *jāti* or it is not the cause of the awareness of the form "this is *sat*".

The Nyāya-Vaiśeṣika philosophers, however, opine that both the positions can be maintained consistently. They admit *sattā jāti* in *dravya*, *guṇa* and *karma* only, and explain how it is possible to have an awareness of the form "this is *sat*" concerning *sāmānya*, *viśeṣa* and *samavāya* even though none of them is a locus of *sattā jāti*, because to be a locus of any *jāti* is to possess the *jāti* in the relation of inherence; but *sāmānya*, or *viśeṣa*, or *samavāya* does not possess anything by the relation of inherence.

---

[4] Udayanācārya, 1989, *Kiraṇāvalī*, pp. 122 and 161, Calcutta: The Asiatic Society.

We shall refer to two explanations offered by Udayanācārya and Śrīdhara Bhaṭṭa respectively about the awareness of *sattā* in *sāmānya*, *viśeṣa* and *samavāya*. Udayanācārya, in his commentary *Kiraṇāvalī*[5] on Praśastapāda's *Padārthadharmasaṁgraha*, explains that though the entities in question are not loci of *sattā jāti*, they have an indirect relation with *sattā* by virtue of which they are also cognized as *sat*. The indirect relation, in this case, is a relation of co-location (*sāmānādhikaraṇya*) with *sattā* in the proper loci of *sattā*, viz. *dravya*, *guṇa* and *karma*. For example, in *dravya*, a seat of *sattā jāti*, *dravyatva* resides; thus, the universal of *dravatva* has a relation of co-location with *sattā* in *dravya*. In eternal substances, both *sattā jāti* and *viśeṣas* exist; again, *dravya* being a relatum of *samavāya*, *samavāya* exists there in self-link (*svarūpa*) relation. Thus, *viśeṣa* and *samavāya* are also related to *sattā* by the relation of coexistence in the same locus. In the case of other universals, the same relation with *sattā jāti* holds because they exist in *dravya* or *guṇa* or *karma*, each of which is a locus of *sattā jāti*. So, it is possible for *sāmānya*, *viśeṣa* and *samavāya* to be cognized as *sat*.

Śrīdhara Bhaṭṭa, the author of *Nyāyakandalī*,[6] another commentary on *Padārthadharmasaṁgraha*, says that every real entity has a *svarūpa-sattā*, an identity or distinctive nature of its own. *Sāmānya*, *viśeṣa* and *samavāya* also have their *svarūpa-sattā* (distinctive nature). Now, *svarūpa-sattā* is similar to *sattā*, as a result of which we confuse it with *sattā* and attribute *sattā* to the entities which have *svarūpa-sattā*. This is superimposition (*āropa*). So, awareness of *sāmānya*, etc. as *sat* is erroneous. But what Śrīdhara Bhaṭṭa does not mention is the nature of the similarity between *svarūpa-sattā* and *sattā*. We may conjecture that the similarity could consist of their incompatibility with *alīkatva*. A fictitious entity (*alīka*) does not have either *svarūpa-sattā* or *sattā*: both *sattā* and *svarūpa-sattā* can be the property of a real entity (*vastu*) only, so just

[5] Udayanācārya, 1989, *Kiraṇāvalī*, pp. 127-28.

[6] *Nyāyakandalī*, pp. 49-50.

as the possessor of *sattā*, being *vastu*, is opposed to the fictitious, so is an entity with *svarūpa-sattā*. That is why it is possible to confuse *svarūpa-sattā* with *sattā*.

Now, though the Nyāya-Vaiśeṣika philosophers admit that we have an awareness of the form "this is *sat*" concerning *sāmānya*, *viśeṣa* and *samavāya* also, they deny that we have *sat pratyaya* with respect to *ahhāva* (absence). But the way they account for *sat pratyaya* in the case of *sāmānya*, etc. does not exclude the possibility of *sat pratyaya* in the case of *abhāva*. For, an *abhāva* can coexist with *sattā* in some locus, for example, in *dravya* there is *sattā* as well as *guṇatvābhāva*, so an *abhāva* has the indirect relation of co-location with *sattā* just as a *sāmānya* or *viśeṣa* has, and hence there should be *sat-pratyaya* for *abhāva*. To avoid this problem, the Nyāya-Vaiśeṣika philosophers clarify their notion of the relation of co-location with *sattā* by specifying that the co-location must be by the relation of inherence (*samavāya*).[7] That means, if a thing or property exists in the relation of inherence in something where *sattā* inheres, it has the proper co-location with *sattā* and is cognized as *sat*. Since *abhāva* cannot be related to anything in the relation of inherence, it cannot be cognized as *sat*. On the contrary, absence is always cognized as something opposed to *sat*; hence, there is no question of showing the possibility of the awareness of the form "this is *sat*" with respect to *abhāva*. The cases where such awareness arises need to be accounted for.

Against Śrīdhara Bhaṭṭa's account also, it may be argued that *abhāva* being a real entity must have *svarūpa-sattā*, so it is possible to confuse *svarūpa-sattā* with *sattā* and attribute *sattā* to *abhāva*. To this objection, the Vaiśeṣikas' answer would be the same. That is, there is no question of attributing *sattā* on *abhāva* by confusing *svarūpa-sattā* with *sattā* because *abhāva* is always cognized as opposite to *sat*.

Raghunātha Śiromaṇi,[8] a Navya-Naiyāyika, who is famous for

---

[7] *Kiraṇāvalī*, p. 128.

[8] Raghunātha Śiromaṇi, 1976, *Padārthatttvanirūpaṇaṁ*, p. 40, ed. with →

his distinctive views on many issues, does not admit *sattā jāti* for explaining *sat-buddhi.* He says that the cognition of the form "this is *sat*", which we have with respect to all the six positive categories without exception, can be explained in terms of *bhāvatva* (the property of being a positive entity). So, *sattā*, regarded as the cause of *sat-buddhi*, is nothing but *bhāvatva. Bhāvatva*, according to him, can be defined as *abhāvānyatva* (being different from *abhāva*), or it may be regarded as an *akhaṇḍopādhi* which means an unanalysable property.

So far, we have seen that incompatibility between two beliefs: one, that *sattā* is a *jāti* located in *dravya*, *guṇa* and *karma* by which they are cognized alike as *sat* and, the other, that *sāmānya*, *viśeṣa* and *samavāya* are also cognized as *sat* although they cannot be the loci of any *jāti*, have made the Nyāya–Vaiśeṣika position regarding *sat* weaker. We have also seen how the Nyāya–Vaiśeṣika philosophers tried to mend their position.

But, in a recent commentary on the *Vaiśeṣikasūtra*, we find a different solution, or rather, a dissolution of the problem discussed above. In the commentary *Rasāyana*,[9] Vir Raghavacarya, the author, denied that we have *sat-buddhi* with respect to *sāmānya*, *viśeṣa* and *samavāya.* The reason is that an awareness of the same form (*anugata pratīti*) based on which a *jāti* (universal) can be admitted, must be a perceptual awareness, but *viśeṣa* and *samavāya* being imperceptible, it is not possible to have perceptual awareness of the form "this is *sat*" with regard to them. *Sāmānyas* are perceptible in most cases, but they are always perceived as a qualifier (*viśeṣaṇa*) and not as a qualificand (*viśeṣya*). For example, we perceive the universal "cowhood" when we have a perception of the form "this is a cow". In this cognition cowhood figures as the qualifier of an

← elucidation in Bengali by Madhusūdana Bhaṭṭācārya Nyāyācārya, Calcutta: Sanskrit College.

[9] Vir Raghavacarya, 1958, *Rasayana*, a commentary on *Vaiśeṣikasūtra*, p. 45, published from Madras.

individual cow which is referred to as "this". But never do we have a perception where cowhood appears as a qualificand, such as "cowhood is so and so". Same would be the case with *samavāya*, even if it is admitted to be perceptible.[10] *Samavāya* is perceived only as a relation between a qualificand and a qualifier. So, with regard to none of these three categories, viz. *sāmānya*, *viśeṣa* and *samavāya*, we have perceptual cognition of such form as this is *sat*. So, there is no problem in admitting *sattā* as a *jāti* which accounts for our perceptual awareness of the form "this is *sat*" with respect to *dravya*, *guṇa* and *karma* where it is located.

To conclude, we can say that by accepting *sattā* as a *jāti*, the Nyāya–Vaiśeṣika philosophers made it clear that *sattā* is not identical with *vastutva* (being real). If it were so, then nothing other than *dravya*, *guṇa* and *karma* would have been real. But they admit, including *abhāva*, four other categories of reals. It is not the case that to be real is to have *sattā*. But a thing is regarded as real if it is established through some *pramāṇa*. So, both the possessors and non-possessors of *sattā jāti* are real in the same way. In the standard Nyāya–Vaiśeṣika view, *sattā* is not even identical with *bhāvatva*, because it is not present in all the six positive categories (*bhāva padārthas*). *Bhāvatva* is a separate property that does not enjoy the status of *jāti*.

It should, however, be admitted that the reason for there being different notions of *sattā* is an equivocation in the use of the word *sat*. The same word is used to mean different things. Sometimes *sat* means real; sometimes it means the positive entity and sometimes it means the possessor of *sattā jāti*. We may observe that the last use of the word *sat* is rather technical.

---

10 According to the Vaiśeṣika philosophers, *samavāya* is imperceptible, but the Naiyāyikas differ from the Vaiśeṣika on this matter and hold that in a perceptual qualificative cognition where the qualificand and the qualifier are related by the relation of *samavāya*, the relation is also perceived along with the relata.

# 17

# Dṛṣṭisṛṣṭivāda

## The Culmination of Advaita Idealism

The history of Indian philosophy shows the presence of three idealistic trends in the tradition, two in Buddhist philosophies of Vijñānavāda and Śūnyavāda and third in the Advaita Vedānta. Advaita Vedānta upholds idealistic monism; it maintains that *Brahman*, which is of the nature of consciousness, is the only reality. It denies the subject-object duality by denying the independent reality of the world of experience. But Advaita philosophy, which developed from the philosophy of Upaniṣads, has been given different interpretations. There are some extreme and some moderate interpretations. In this chapter, I shall present an extreme idealistic position of Advaita Vedānta known as Dṛṣṭisṛṣṭivāda, that in the first place denies unknown existence of the empirical world and asserts that the world exists only as long as it is experienced.

The moderate version is familiar to most of us. In this interpretation the world of experience is not ultimately real, but neither is it unreal. This world is real for practical purposes. Things of this world are created by God or qualified *Brahman* with the help of *avidyā* or *māyā* and can be known by individual selves by means of *pramāṇas*. This world is removed only when *brahma-jñāna* arises. In this view, three types of being or reality are recognized, i.e. *pāramārthika sattā* (absolute reality), *vyāvahārika sattā* (empirical reality) and *prātibhāsika sattā* (seeming reality). *Brahman* is the absolute reality, *ākāśa* and other *bhūtas* are only empirically real, whereas shell-silver, rope-snake, etc. are seemingly real, i.e. they are there as long as we perceive them. So far as the position regarding the empirical world is concerned, this moderate version seems to maintain Sṛṣṭadṛṣṭivāda or Sṛṣṭidṛṣṭivāda,[1] according to which there is an objectively real empirical world created by God, which individual souls can know.

Dṛṣṭisṛṣṭivāda, which is an extreme version of Advaita idealism, is opposed to Sṛṣṭidṛṣṭivāda (as the very name suggests). To put it briefly, this doctrine denies objective reality or unknown existence of the empirical world; it denies creation in the primary sense of the terms; it holds that *jīva* (individual soul) "creates" the world when he experiences it.

Dṛṣṭisṛṣṭivāda, though developed in the post-Śaṅkara period of Advaita Vedānta, can be said to have a long history in the Indian philosophical tradition. A trend towards this doctrine can be detected in the *Māṇḍūkyakārikā* or *Āgamaśāstra* of Gauḍapāda,[2] who belonged to pre-Śaṅkara period. Another classical work titled *Yogavāsiṣṭha Rāmāyaṇa*[3] advocated a strong idealistic position similar to Dṛṣṭisṛṣṭivāda. We even find the expressions *sṛṣṭidṛṣṭi* and *dṛṣṭisṛṣṭi* in the *Yogavāsiṣṭha.* There is difference of opinion regarding the time of *Yogavāsiṣṭha.* Its authorship has been attributed to Vālmīki. Some hold this to be a work of pre-Śaṅkara and others hold it to be either of Saṅkara's time or of post-Śaṅkara period.

---

1 Appayadīkṣita, 1990, *Siddhāntaleśa Saṁgraha*, p. 346, ed. Bhao Shastry, Varanasi: Chowkhamba Sanskrit Samsthan.

2 Gauḍapāda, 1943, *The Āgamaśāstra of Gauḍapāda*, ed., tr. and annotated by Vidhushekhar Bhattacharya, Calcutta: University of Calcutta.

3 *Yogavāsiṣṭha Rāmāyaṇa of Vālmīki*, ed. and tr. into English by Viharilala Mitra, 1978, Delhi: Bharatiya Publishing House.

According to some scholars, Maṇḍana Miśra, the author of *Brahmasiddhi*, was a precursor of Dṛṣṭisṛṣṭivāda. Maṇḍana and his follower Vācaspati Miśra, the author of *Bhāmatī*, maintained that the *jīva* is the locus of *avidyā* and *jīva* is the creator of the world, which is an appearance only. From this philosophical position, there was a transition to Dṛṣṭisṛṣṭivāda which Prakāśānanda developed in his *Vedānta Siddhānta Muktāvalī*.

There are two versions of Dṛṣṭisṛṣṭivāda, as mentioned by Appaya Dīkṣita in the *Siddhāntaleśa Saṁgraha*:

i. *Dṛṣṭi samasamayā viśvasṛṣṭi*, which means that the creation of the world of experience is simultaneous with its experience; and

ii. *Dṛṣṭireva sṛṣṭi*, which means that the creation of the world is identical with its experience. The latter version was advocated by Prakāśānanda and it seems to be the stronger than the former.

In the first version of Dṛṣṭisṛṣṭivāda, it seems that some distinction is maintained between experience and the world of experience. It asserts that the world is there only when it is experienced. So, the world is concurrent with its experience. But it has not been asserted in this formulation that they are identical. The experiencer, who is a *jīva*, "creates" both the experience and its object. The experience being unreal like a dream, its object, i.e. the world cannot really be created. Nor can the world be there before its experience and it also ceases to exist when its experience ceases.

The second version of the doctrine maintains that the experienced world, which has no existence independent of the experience, is not different from its experience. It is obvious that, according to this version also, there is no unknown existence of the world of experience nor is there a creation of the world. Prakāśānanda has argued extensively in favour his position, i.e. identity between *jñāna* (experience) and *jñeya* (object experienced).[4] He has shown that the distinction between the two can be established by none of the *pramāṇas*. He has also refuted the argument that the very concept of *jñāna* implies that it must have an object which is different from itself. I shall not, however, enter into these arguments here.

Madhusūdana Sarasvatī, in his *Advaitasiddhi*, has elaborated on Dṛṣṭisṛṣṭivāda and proved it to be a tenable position. But neither of the two formulations as mentioned above was endorsed by him. He formulated Dṛṣṭisṛṣṭivāda in a slightly different way.[5] According to him, the intended meaning of Dṛṣṭisṛṣṭivāda is that the world, while being due to some defect (being illusory), has only known existence or, in other words, has no unknown existence. In another formulation given by him, *dṛṣṭisṛṣṭi* means that the world has only known existence while being incapable of being known by others. These formulations, however, imply the first version, i.e. *dṛṣṭi samasamayā sṛṣṭi* (creation simultaneous with experience).

We can therefore say that the minimal thesis of *dṛṣṭisṛṣṭi* is that the world of experience has known existence only. Now, regarding some objects, at least all Advaita philosophers are of the same opinion that they have no existence independent of experience. These are *prātibhāsika* objects like shell-silver, dream-objects and internal states like pleasure and pain. But, the upholders of Dṛṣṭisṛṣṭivāda extend the same status to the entire world of experience, which has been granted the status of *vyāvahārika sattā* by Sṛṣṭadṛṣṭivādins. That means, they obliterate the distinction between dream state and waking state and, therefore, between public and private objects. Even the distinction between empirical truth and error would not be tenable in this view.

---

[4] Prakāśānanda, 1935, *Vedāntasiddhāntamuktāvalī*, ed. Jīvānanda Bhattacharya, pp. 84-103, Calcutta.

[5] *doṣa prayuktatva nibandhanasya jñātaikasattvasya, ajñāta sattvābhāvasya vā । draṣṭrantarāvedyatve sati jñātaikasattvasya vā ॥* – Madhusūdana Sarasvatī, *Advaitasiddhi*, ed. Ananta Krishna Sastri, 1982, Delhi: Parimal Publications.

We may note the following points of Dṛṣṭisṛṣṭivāda:

1. The world has no unknown existence, that means, it is not there to be experienced by *jīva*.
2. The world we experience during our waking state does not differ from the world we experience in dreams. Both worlds are seemingly real (*prātītika*).
3. The world is revealed to us by *sākṣī* without the aid of *pramāṇa* (*kevala sākṣīvedya*), just as a shell-silver, which is considered as an illusory object (*prātibhāsika viṣaya*), is known.
4. The empirical or so-called *vyāvahārika jagat* ceases to exist in the absence of experience; even during *susupti* the world ceases to exist. Therefore, knowledge is not required for its removal.
5. There are no degrees of reality (*sattā traividhya*). There is only one absolute reality, viz. *Brahman*, everything else is unreal (*mīthyā*).
6. The world of experience is not a creation of God.

The last point gives rise to a vital question, i.e. if the world we experience is an imaginary one, then who is its creator? Upholders of Dṛṣṭisṛṣṭivāda maintain that *jīva*, which is consciousness associated with *avidyā* as an adjunct, is the creator of the world, in the sense that it is to him that the world appears. The world is there as long as the individual self experiences it. Now, if there is a plurality of *jīva*, there would be plurality of worlds, each *jīva* experiencing his world created by his own experience. Vācaspati Miśra maintained this position of the plurality of worlds of experience.[6]

Now the advocates of Dṛṣṭisṛṣṭivāda feel that such a position violates the law of parsimony and, so, they hold that there is only one individual self who experiences and thereby creates the world.

---

[6] Madhusūdana Sarasvatī, 1990, *Siddhāntabindu*, a commentary, on *Daśaślokī* of Śaṅkarācārya, ed. Tryambakarāma Śāstrī, pp. 226-30, Varanasi: Chowkhamba Sanskrit Sansthan.

This position is known as Ekajīvavāda.[7] It is difficult to justify this position and hence it has been given various interpretations to render it plausible.

The main argument given in support of this position is that *Brahman* is one and due to one *avidyā*, he appears as *jīva* and undergoes the state of bondage. So, there is no reason to admit the plurality of *jīva*. The problem with this position is that there being plurality of bodily beings, how can the plurality of *jīva* be denied? There are three versions of Ekajīvavāda or one individual soul thesis each of which tries to solve the problem differently.[8] To put it very briefly, the first version, named Ekaśarīra Ekajīvavāda, asserts that only one body is associated with the individual soul (*sajīva śarīra*); other bodies are like dream-bodies lacking relation with the individual soul (*nirjīva*). One obvious objection to this position is how to determine which one of the bodies is related to the individual soul since there is no reason to select any particular body.

According to the second version, there is one chief individual soul (*mukhya jīva*) called Hiraṇyagarbha, who is the reflection of *Brahman*, and other *jīvas* are merely reflections of the *mukhya jīva* like the images or pictures of a person. So, other *jīvas* are only appearances of *jīva* (*jīvābhāsa*) and excepting the body of Hiraṇyagarbha all other bodies are associated with different *jīvābhāsa* (pseudo individual souls). This version is known as Saviśeṣa Aneka Śarīra Ekajīvavāda. Against this version, it has been argued that there is no proof in favour of the position that Hiraṇyagarbha has reflections, so the concept of *amukhya jīva* is unacceptable. Second, there being a different Hiraṇyagarbha in each cycle (*kalpa* of creation), which Hiraṇyagarbha would be regarded as the *mukhya jīva*?

---

7 *sa ca draṣṭaika eva, tannānātve mānābhāvāt* । – Madhusūdana Sarasvatī, *Advaitasiddhi*, p. 539.

8 Madhusūdana Sarasvatī, *Siddhāntabindu*, see *Nārāyaṇī Ṭīkā* on it, p. 234. See also *Siddhāntaleśa Saṁgraha* of Appaya Dīkṣita, pp. 122-26.

The third version is that there is one single individual soul which inhabits all the bodies. This is known as Aviśeṣa Aneka Śarīra Ekajīvavāda. Here, in spite of the apparent differences in respect of bodies, the individual soul is one and the same as limited by one *avidyā*. This position is claimed to be quite plausible. Just as one and the same transmigrating soul is admitted to be attached to different bodies at different births; similarly, the same soul may also be attached to other bodies simultaneously. An analogical case is that of a *yogī* who, by virtue of his Yogic power, can create many bodies (as admitted in scriptures) and being attached to all of them simultaneously can enjoy, suffer the results of his actions and thus exhaust his merits and demerits, which are in fruition (*prārabdha karma*).

Now Ekajīvavāda and Dṛṣṭisṛṣṭivāda are regarded as two sides or aspects of the same philosophical doctrine.[9] It is true that Dṛṣṭisṛṣṭivāda combined with Ekajīvavāda presents an extreme form of subjective idealism.

Dṛṣṭisṛṣṭivāda has a striking similarity with Berkeley's principle *esse est percipi*, i.e. "to be is to be perceived". But Berkeley did not develop it into subjective idealism, rather, he made some concession to epistemological realism by granting some sort of objective reality to the physical world. He admitted that sensible things continue to exist even when they are not being perceived by human beings, because they are constantly being perceived by God, the infinite spirit.

This sort of objective idealism is found in the philosophy of the *Yogavāsiṣṭha*.[10] The author of the *Yogavāsiṣṭha* admits that there is a cosmic world in the form of a system of ideas in the cosmic mind called Brahmā. Before creation, Brahmā imagines the world, and it continues to exist as long as Brahmā lives.

---

9 *mukhyaḥ vedāntasiddhāntaḥ ekajīvavādākhyaḥ, imaṁ eva dṛṣṭi-sṛṣṭivādamācakṣate* । – Madhusūdana Sarasvatī, *Siddhāntabindu*, p. 234

10 *sargādau svapnapuruṣanyāyenādi prajāpatiḥ yathā sphuṭaṁ prakacitaḥ tathādyāpi sthitaḥ sthitiḥ* । – *Yogavāsiṣṭha* III.55.47

So far as Berkeley's view of sensible objects as a collection of ideas existing in the mind of the perceiver is concerned, it resembles Prakāśānanda's position that the objects experienced are identical with experience.

Dr̥ṣṭisr̥ṣṭivāda has a strong similarity with Buddhist doctrine of Vijñānavāda too. The proponents of Vijñānavāda[11] deny the distinction between experience and the object of experience, and the distinction between dreaming and waking state. According to them, the external world has no independent reality. Pure consciousness alone is real, and manifests as both the knower and the known. The external world is as unreal as dream objects, magical objects, mirage and a town in the sky, which are experienced at times. Gauḍapāda uses exactly these analogies in his *Kārikā*:

> *svapnamāye yathā dr̥ṣṭe gandharvanagaram yathā/tathā viśvam idam dr̥ṣṭam vedānteṣu vicakṣanaiḥ* ।

But Vijñānavādins seem to avoid extreme subjectivism by admitting some distinction between purely imaginary called *parikalpita*, like a dream and a mirage and dependent or relative called *paratantra* like tables, chairs and water, that we take to be real.[12] Though both are unreal, the former is purely imaginary or absolutely unreal while the latter is an appearnace which depends on causes and conditions. This distinction seems like the distinction between *prātibhāsika* and *vyāvahārika* as recognized in the moderate version of Advaita idealism, but rejected by Dr̥ṣṭisr̥ṣṭivādins.

---

11 *Laṅkāvatārasūtram*, ed. Sarat Chandra Das and Satish Chandra Vidyabhusana, *sūtras* 1.41 to 1.44; 2.1-2.4, 3.87, Calcutta, 1900.

12 *yena yena vikalpena yad yad vastu vikalpyate* ।
*prakalpita evāsau svabhāvo na sa vidyate* ॥
- Vasubandhu, *Triṁśikāvijñapti-kārikā* 20

*paratantra svabhāvastu vikalpa pratyayodbhavḥ* ।
*niṣpannastasya pūrvena sadā rahitatā tu yā* ॥
- Vasubandhu, *Triṁśikā Kārikā* 21

So we find that Dṛṣṭisṛṣṭivāda is the extreme form of idealism compared to other idealistic doctrines in the Indian tradition. We think that a consistent development of Advaita philosophy leads naturally to this climax. The concept of *adhyāsa* with its two forms, *jñānādhyāsa* and *arthādhyāsa*, as propounced in Advaita Vedānta seems to support the philosophy of *dṛṣṭisṛṣṭi. Adhyāsa* in the sense of *ādhyāsika pratīti* (illusory cognition) and *adhyāsa* in the sense of *adhyasyamāna viṣaya* (illusory object) are interdependent. Illusory cognition means the cognition of an illusory object and by illusory object is meant the object of an illusory cognition. So, none of them can be there without the other; the two must be simultaneous. From this, it follows that illusory objects cannot have unknown existence, i.e. illusory objects cannot be there independently of illusory cognition. Now, this must be true of all cases of illusion or superimposition, be it *ākāśa*, *bhūta*, etc. or shell-silver, rope-snake, etc. So, even *ākāśa*, *bhūta*, etc. cannot have unknown existence. Vidyāraṇya Muni says in the *Vivaraṇaprameya Saṁgraha* that superimposed objects cannot be concealed by ignorance, because when they are being experienced, they cannot be said to be concealed and when they are not being experienced they do not exist at all; superimposed object has existence only as long as it is experienced, just as double moon exist only as long as there is such an illusion.[13] He further argues that if superimposed objects were concealed by ignorance they could never be known, because superimposed objects are not knowable through *pramāṇas* and without the employment of *pramāṇas*, the veil of ignorance cannot be removed, hence they would have remained unknown and unknowable. All these arguments point to the position of *dṛṣṭisṛṣṭi*. After admitting illusory cognition and illusory objects to be simultaneous and each implying the other, it would be very

---

13 *adhyāstasya āvaraṇāyogāt, pratītikāle tāvadāvaraṇa vyāhatam apratītikāle tu svayameva nāsti, dvicandrādivat adhyastasya pratītimātra śarīratvāt* । – Vidyāraṇya Muni, *Vivaraṇaprameya Saṁgraha* with Hindi translation, p. 63. – L.P. Dabral, ed. Śrī Krishna Pant

difficult to prove them to be separate. One may argue that one is the modification of *avidyā* in the form of cognition (*jñānākāra pariṇāma*) and the other is the modification in the form of object (*viṣayākāra pariṇāma*). But, this seems to be only a conceptual or linguistic difference. As Prakāśānanda claimed, there is no conclusive argument to prove that they are distinct. Thus, Dṛṣṭisṛṣṭivāda can be shown to have developed naturally from Advaita philosophy that *Brahman* alone is real and everything else is only an appearance due to *avidyā.*

Perhaps with a view to accommodate common sense, Advaita philosphers like Ācārya Śaṅkara granted the status of *vyāvahārika sattā* (empirical reality) to some objects of the world and admitted that they are there to be experienced by *jīva* till the attainment of *brahma-jñāna.*

But, many Advaita philosophers hold that Dṛṣṭisṛṣṭivāda and Ekajīvavāda present the real position or the highest truth (*mukhya siddhānta*) of Advaita Vedānta, which is comprehensible only to the most competent enquirer (*uttama adhikārī*). For the others, the moderate version known as Sṛṣṭadṛṣṭivāda is intended.

Radhakrishnan, though an advocate of Advaita idealism, was strongly against such subjectivist interpretations of Advaita philosophy as Dṛṣṭisṛṣṭivāda. His interpretation of Advaita philosophy was far more moderate, almost realistic. He argued that according to Ācārya Śaṅkara, the supreme reality of *Brahman* is the basis of the world and what is based on real, though unreal from the transcendental point of view, is not illusory.[14] It is an appearance or phenomenon of the real, which means only that it has no existence apart from *Brahman.* Interpreting Advaita philosophy in this way, Radhakrishnan bestowed some of the reality to the world.

---

14 Radhakrishnan, 1985, *Indian Philosophy*, vol. II, chap. VIII, reprinted, Delhi: Blackie & Son.

# 18

# Emotion and Morality
## A Vaidika Point of View

THE question about the relation between emotion and morality can be formulated as follows: are our emotions conducive to or detrimental to morality? Another question can also be raised: can morality arouse emotions? For emotion, we shall take different affective states of mind like pleasure, pain, fear, shame, compassion and hatred. By morality, we shall mean moral conduct and moral judgement. I shall address these questions from the traditional Indian point of view. The issue, as it is, has not actually been raised or discussed in the Indian philosophical tradition. Still, I believe that from the standpoint of Hindu or Vaidika ethics, an affirmative answer can be given to each of these questions formulated above. It seems to me that in the Indian tradition, the domain of morality and the domain of emotion were not kept separate and unrelated. They would admit that sometimes emotions can facilitate morality; sometimes it can stand in the way of performing a moral duty, and, sometimes the performance of a moral act can also arouse some emotion. We can find examples of their interrelation in Indian literature like the *Mahābhārata* and Purāṇas.

If we consider from a common-sense point of view, it seems quite natural to admit that emotions do have an influence upon our moral life. From our personal experience, we find that sometimes our emotions stand in the way of making the right moral decision.

Sometimes, again, it helps one to make a good moral decision. Many cases of moral conflicts that we face in life are due to certain emotions. There are many such instances. For example, we have seen some passionate patriots sacrifice their life for the freedom of their country. We see malicious persons causing harm to someone intentionally. Sometimes, we find ourselves afraid of speaking the truth. Some persons who do not have enough food to feed themselves are seen to offer their meal to hungry people out of compassion. It is also a fact that a morally good act makes everyone, including the doer, happy. A person can feel remorse in case he fails to do his duty. A morally wrong action, on the other hand, is condemned and makes people angry or sad, and, the wrong doer may also feel remorse for such an act. These instances are there. I think that moral philosophy and psychology, too, cannot deny the relation between emotion and morality.

In the Indian tradition, we find two cases, where emotion has been excluded from the domain of morality: one, in the ideal of *niṣkāma karma* as told in the *Gītā* and, second, in Prābhākara Mīmāṁsaka's interpretation of morality. In those cases emotion has been denied to have any role in leading an agent to perform a moral action. So, emotion has no influence on the performance of action in those cases. Duties are to be performed only for duty's sake. But, I must also mention that in both cases, a feeling of satisfaction is admitted to follow the performance of duty for duty's sake. We shall come to this point later in this chapter.

Let us start with an outline of Vaidika ethics. In Indian terminology, morality is *dharma*; and by *dharma* is meant moral conduct. *Dharma* is discussed in the Śruti, i.e. the Vedas and in Dharmaśāstras, which are based on the Vedas and are called Smr̥ti. These two, viz. Śruti and Smr̥ti, are regarded as two principal sources of the knowledge of *dharma* (moral conduct) as mentioned in *Manu Saṁhitā*, *śloka* 2.9-10. In Dharmaśāstras, we get a code of moral conduct. For every sphere of life these scriptures enjoin what a person should do and what he should not do. Some actions are prescribed and some are prohibited, and the moral law is that the prescribed acts should be performed and prohibited acts should be shunned. The agent will be rewarded with *puṇya* (merits) for performing *vihita karma* (prescribed acts) and performance of *niṣiddha karma* will lead to *pāpa* (demerits).[1]

It may be mentioned in this context that such cases are not uncommon where a person performs a prescribed action not simply because it is enjoined, but his intention is accompanied by emotion as a motive. For example, when a person does an act of charity not merely because it is a prescribed good act, but also with a desire to earn fame, then that action would have a reduced moral value and would earn less merit (*puṇya*). Again, when a person speaks the truth with a motive to cause harm to another person on whom he bears a grudge, then the act seems to have a dual character, it is morally good so far as the injunction is followed, but it is morally wrong so far as it proceeds from the motive of doing harm to a person.

Lists of moral acts or duties that we come across in scriptures include some universal duties, i.e. *sāmānya dharma*, which are to be performed by every person. And, specific duties are there, which are for different specified sections or classes of people. Specific duties also include duties to be performed at different stages of life; as we know, *caturvarṇa* and *caturāśrama* were special characteristics of the Vedic society. Examples of universal duties are speaking the truth, keeping a promise, to shun violence, etc. Some examples of *varṇa dharma* (class-specific duties) are teaching for brāhmaṇas, fighting battles for kṣatriyas, etc. Examples of *āśrama dharma*, i.e. duties specified for different stages of life: studying and practising celibacy for students, having a family and performing several sacrifices, etc. for householders and so on.[2]

---

1 *Praśastapādabhāṣya with Nyāyakandalī Ṭīkā*, by Śrīdhara Bhaṭṭa, 1963, ed. Durgadhar Jha, pp. 660, 677-78, Varanasi: Varanaseya Sanskrit Viswavidyalaya.

2 Ibid., pp. 666-72.

Now some prescribed and prohibited acts are sacrificial rites, and some are non-sacrificial acts. Some sacrificial rites are aimed at achieving other-worldly result like *svarga*; and some are for empirical, i.e. this worldly results like bringing in rain at the time of drought, or, being blessed with a child, etc. From the nature of these duties, it is obvious that the imperatives which enjoin these duties are conditional imperatives. Those duties are to be performed by people who desire to achieve the end mentioned. For example, a childless couple, who want to have a child, will perform a sacrificial rite named Putreṣṭi Yāga. On the contrary, universal duties are unconditional; for example, speaking the truth has not been advised for receiving any specific result.

Thus, in the Vedas and Dharmaśāstras, we get a list of duties. It has also been said in the Dharmaśāstra that a person who performs the duties mentioned in the Śruti and Smṛtiśāstras are praised as righteous or *dhārmika* in this life and will also attain *svarga* in after life (*paraloka*).[3]

Now, the question is: how is a person motivated to perform these duties? The Pūrva-Mīmāṁsā system of philosophy deliberates and elaborates on the *karma-kāṇḍa* of the Vedas, which contains imperatives (*vidhi-vākya*). Both the Bhāṭṭa school and Prābhākara school have their theories of motivation through Vedic imperatives. Other *āstika* systems like the Nyāya–Vaiśeṣika also give an account of the psychological process through which an agent is motivated to perform any voluntary action, be it an ordinary action like cooking or a moral duty prescribed in the Vedas.

As regards any voluntary action performed in daily life, everyone will admit that the will to do such actions is caused by a desire (*icchā*) to fulfil some end, because the action is believed to be a means to that end. The desired end is called *iṣṭa* or *śreya* and the action, which is its means, is known as *iṣṭa sādhana* or *śreya sādhana.* So, a desire for the end leads to a desire for the means,

[3] *Manu Saṁhitā with Ṭīkā* by Kullukabhaṭṭa, chap. 2, *śloka* 9.

i.e. the act. But a will to undertake that action depends on two conditions, viz.:

1. the belief that it is within the power or capacity of the agent to perform that act, and
2. the belief that the act produces the desired good consequence without causing some greater evil.

These are known respectively as *kr̥tisādhyatā-jñāna* and *balabadaniṣṭa ananubandhi iṣṭasādhanatā-jñāna.* Only when these conditions are satisfied, the agent has the will to act. So, a desire for the end, a desire for its means, along with the two belief conditions mentioned above, constitute the psychological process leading to the will to act.[4]

For moral actions as prescribed in the scriptures, the Nyāya-Vaiśeṣika schools admit the same psychological process. The Bhāṭṭa Mīmāṁsā school too agrees on this matter. It admits that there should be the belief that the prescribed act is conducive to one's good since it is prescribed for one in the scripture. One cannot have the will to act unless one believes that the act will lead to his/her desired end (*śreya sādhana* or *iṣṭa sādhana*).

But the Prābhākara school of Mīmāṁsā denies the role of desire in the psychological process motivating an agent to perform a moral action. The concept of duty for duty's sake is true for them. The main cause of the will to do a moral act is the awareness to the effect "This action is prescribed for me by the scripture, so I must do it" or "The imperative instructs me to do this, so I will do it". They call it *kāryatā-jñāna*. The action may result in something good for the agent, but the desire for the good should not be a motive to perform the duty.[5]

---

4 Viśvanātha, *Kārikāvalī-Muktāvalī*, ed. Shri Sankarram Sastri, *kārikā*, 146-48, Delhi, Chowkhamba Sanskrit Pratisthan, 1988.

5 S.K. Maitra, 1963, *The Ethics of the Hindus*, chap. 1, p. 58, Calcutta: University of Calcutta.

The concept of *niṣkāma karma*, as advocated in the *Bhagavadgītā*, is also similar to the concept of duty for duty's sake. A person should do a duty only because it is a duty for him/her, but not for attaining some good desired by him/her; for example, Arjuna as a kṣatriya should fight a battle only because it is his duty/*svadharma* (a duty specific to his class) and not with the desire to conquer a kingdom, though winning the battle would eventually result in winning the kingdom.[6]

So we find that in the moral theory of Prābhākara Mīmāṁsā school and the moral principle recommended in the *Gītā*, desire has no role in morality, not to speak of any other emotion. At this point, we should note that Dharmaśāstra mentions two different paths of action: *pravṛtti mārga* or *pravṛtta karma*, and *nivṛtti mārga* or *nivṛtta karma*. Of these two paths, *nivṛtta mārga* is for only a very few persons who have realized that *mokṣa* (liberation) is the supreme good; it is the only ultimate good and they aspire to attain it. For attaining *mokṣa*, they have to follow *nivṛtti mārga*, which means whatever action they do, they have to do it without any desire (*icchā*) or aversion (*dveṣa*). This is *niṣkāma karma*. Doing duty itself is the end.[7]

*Pravṛtti mārga*, as mentioned in the Śāstras, is for common people, who have not yet realized that *mokṣa* is the supreme good and the only good for them. They aspire for goods in life. For them, ends to be attained in life are confined to *artha*, *kāma* and *dharma*, which are known as *trivarga* (three values) of human life (*puruṣārtha*). Whatever action an ordinary human chooses to do is done with either desire (*rāga*) or aversion (*dveṣa*). So, they follow the path of *pravṛtti*, their actions are *pravṛtta karma*.

It is clear that so far as *pravṛtta karmas* are concerned, desire and aversion have a role in generating the will to perform a duty.

---

6 *Śrīmadbhagavadgītā* with *Gūḍhārthadīpikā-Ṭīkā* by Madhusūdana Sarasvatī, Varanasi: Chowkhamba Sanskrit Series office, 1962.

7 *Manu Saṁhitā*, chap. 12, *śloka* 88.

But, to come to the main issue regarding a relation between emotion and morality, and to make an assertion about such a relation, we shall have to search for cases where some other emotion plays a role either in facilitating or in hindering moral actions. Let us start with some such cases found in the stories of *Mahābhārata* and Purāṇas.

Take first the case of Arjuna's refusal to fight after he arrived at the battlefield of Kurukṣetra. This event led Śrī-Kṛṣṇa to advise him on morality and action, and on the nature of the self, which constituted a part of the content of the *Bhagavadgītā*. We know that Arjuna, a member of the Pāṇḍava group, had decided to take part in the war with Kauravas and their allies. But when he reached the warfield, he wanted to back out, and he told this to Śrī-Kṛṣṇa. The reason for his change of mind was his love for his kin and the fear that he would have to kill them in war. He was so overwhelmed by these emotions that he wanted to withdraw the moral decision to fight, which he had taken earlier. So, we find that here is a case where an emotion stands in the way of performing a moral duty. As a kṣatriya, Arjuna's moral duty was to fight, but being moved by the emotion of love and fear, he refused to do his duty.

The second case is the case of Pāṇḍava mother Kuntī's act of hiding the truth that Karṇa was her son, whom she had forsaken immediately after his birth. Why did she do this? It is because she wanted to save herself from the shame of being an unwed mother. There were occasions when she should have told the truth, but she did not. So here also, an emotion prevented her from doing a moral duty.

The third case is the case of Droṇa and Ekalavya. As we know Droṇa was the teacher of the art of archery to the sons of royal family, i.e. Pāṇḍava and Kaurava princes, and Ekalavya was an outcast boy. Ekalavya mastered in the art of archery, though he was not instructed by the teacher Droṇa, he revered him as his idol and teacher. When Droṇa came to know about the amazing expertise of Ekalavya in archery, he asked Ekalavya to cut off the thumb of his right hand and to offer it as the honorarium (*guru-dakṣiṇā*) to Droṇa, whom, he considered as his teacher of archery. Losing the right thumb Ekalavya did not remain as skillful in archery as before. Droṇa did this deliberately out of his love for and favour towards Arjuna whom he wanted to see as the best performer in archery. So, here is a case where an emotion influenced a person to do an immoral act. To punish someone without any fault or to harm someone for someone else's benefit is not a morally right act; it is a case of unjustified violence.

The last case is from a Purāṇa story. A king named Uśīnara was a kind-hearted, righteous king. Once a pigeon being attacked by a hawk took shelter on the king's lap. The hawk demanded that the pigeon be given to him as it was his food. The king said that since the pigeon came to him for protection, he could not hand it over to the hawk; instead he was ready to give whatever the hawk demands in lieu of the pigeon's life. And on the hawk's demand, the king agreed to give his flesh amounting to the weight of the pigeon, and finally ended up giving away the flesh of his entire body. From this story, it seems that it is not merely the sense of duty to protect a bird who took shelter under him, but the king's compassion for the bird inspired him to that act of charity. So, here, an emotion is conducive to a moral act.

Now, we find that in the above-mentioned instances, emotions are seen to influence moral decisions favourably or unfavourably. What happens there is that some emotion acts as an inhibiter (*partibandhaka*) and some as an *uttejaka*[8] (stimulus) with respect to

---

[8] Bhattacarya Sukhamay, 1983, *Purvamīmāṁsā-darśana* (in Bengali), pp. 126-31, Rajya Pustak Parshad.

The concepts of *pratibandhaka* and *uttejaka* have been used by Indian philosophers in several contexts. A *pratibandhaka* is a hindering condition that prevents a cause from producing the effect. It may be a substance or attribute or action hindering the production of an effect; or it may be a cognition that prevents the occurrence of another cognition. In any case, a condition that stands in the way of the occurrence of something is called *pratibandhaka*. *Uttejaka*, →

the will (*pravṛtti*) towards the moral act, which is enjoined (*vihita*) or prohibited (*niṣiddha*). Now we are to see how emotions act on our will in accordance with the Vaidika moral theory. For this, we have to refer to the psychological process through which the will to perform a particular duty is generated. As already said, this process includes a belief that the act concerned produces some good consequence without causing some greater evil consequence (*balabadāniṣṭānanubandhitve sati iṣṭasādhanam*). This belief, if somehow withheld, there cannot be the will to do that act. And this belief can be interfered with if the second part of the belief, i.e. the act does not cause greater evil, is exposed to doubt. We see that certain emotions can cause this doubt and, as a result, a necessary causal condition for will is not fulfilled. Thus, the will is hindered. In some other cases, we find that some emotions accompanying the belief that the act is conducive to a greater good make the belief stronger and thus stimulate the will to do the duty.

In Arjuna's case, being overwhelmed by love for the kin and the fear of losing them in war, he started believing that his fighting the battle will cause a greater harm than good. So, the required belief that fighting will lead to good consequences without causing greater evil is hindered. Therefore, Arjuna did not have the will to fight though he knew that fighting was a prescribed duty for him.

In the case of Kuntī's hiding of the truth about Karṇa's birth, it is her fear of being disgraced for being an unwed mother of Karṇa led her to believe that the consequence of speaking the truth in this case will cause greater evil to her. This stopped her from telling the truth, which is a universal duty.

Droṇa's resorting to the cruel act of asking Ekalavya to chop off his right thumb was due to his love for and favour to his celebrated

---

← on the other hand, is a stimulating condition which helps a cause overcome the negative influence of the *pratibandhaka*. It is a reinforcing condition that renders the *pratibandhaka* ineffective and facilitates the causation of an effect.

disciple Arjuna. Here, this love led him to believe that his act was not an evil and perhaps made him oblivious to the remote consequence of incurring *pāpa*. He did not have the will to refrain from that cruel act, which is a prohibited one.

Again, when King Uśīnara wanted to save a pigeon's life at the cost of his own life, he had, besides his sense of duty as a protector, great compassion for the helpless bird. This compassion made him believe that his action would lead to the greater good than the evil consequence. He had the will to do that painful act of giving away the flesh from his own body.

I claim that these explanations conform to the Indian moral theory. To justify my claim, I would bring the Indian philosophers' view on some of the Vedic sentences known as Arthavāda. These sentences are contained in that part of the Vedas, which deals with *karma*, i.e. action. In that part, along with *vidhi-vākyas* (imperative sentences), there are some sentences that either praise some prescriptive actions or condemn some prohibited actions; these are called Arthavāda *vākya*. These Arthavādas are related to the imperatives, both positive (*vidhi*) and negative (*niṣedha*). Their function is to reinforce the power of imperatives to motivate the agent to do the act, so they are regarded *uttejaka/uttambhaka* (reinforcing factors) of *vidhi*. For the strongly-willed people who have great reverence for the Vedas, Arthavāda *vākyas* in addition to *vidhi* are not needed to motivate them. But for ordinary people, this is needed, because, due to some reasons or considerations, they may not have the will to do the enjoined act; it is then, the Arthavādas, through the praise or condemnation of the consequence of the act facilitate the *vidhi* to cause the will to do the prescribed act or the will to refrain from doing the prohibited act. Thus, the Arthavāda supports the belief that the enjoined act has as a consequence the greater good, or, the prohibited act causes greater evil and thus strengthens the will to act.[9]

---

[9] *Nyāyadarśana sūtra* 2.1.64.

A further point to note is that mythical stories or stories of Purāṇas, the *Rāmāyaṇa* and *Mahābhārata* have been regarded as Arthavāda by the Mīmāṁsaka philosophers. So, I think the explanation I have given above as to how emotions can influence morality conforms to the Indian theory of morality.

One may ask how is Arthavāda relevant to emotions? To this, I would like to say that Arthavāda *vākyas* can be shown to have a relation with emotion. Through praise or condemnation of certain prescribed or prohibited acts, an appeal is actually made to emotions like aspiration or craving (*abhilāṣa/spr̥hā/lobha*) or fear. For example, there is an imperative that says that one who is desirous of wealth should perform a particular sacrifice (*yajña*) to gain favour of Vāyu-*devatā*. And Arthavāda says that Vāyu is the most agile God (*kṣipra*), which by implication says that the specified sacrifice will yield a quick result. This praise of the act appeals to the agent's aspiration. In another prohibitory imperative, it is said that in a particular sacrifice called Varhi Yāga silver should not be offered to the priest and the related Arthavāda is that silver (*rajata*) is created from Rudra's tears, which implies that giving silver will cause some sad incident in the agents life. Here, fear is aroused.

One last question regarding the relation between emotion and morality needs to be answered now. For the question: can morality arouse any emotion in the agent who performs a moral duty? the answer would again be positive. The Indian philosophers admit that after performing a moral duty successfully, the doer feels satisfaction which is a state of pleasure (*sukha*). On the other hand, after doing an immoral or wrong action, many conscientious persons feel remorse (*anuśocanā* or *anutāpa*), which is a feeling of pain.[10] The satisfaction of fulfilling a moral duty successfully has been admitted by Indian philosophers even in the case of *niṣkāma karma*. They admit that for an agent, who is doing a duty for duty's sake, though there is no desire for pleasure, he can still experience

---

10 *Manu Saṁhitā*, chap. 11, *ślokas* 228, 234.

a pleasure for being able to perform the duty and may also get happiness as a consequence of the act though not desired by him. This would be true even for the philosophers of the Prābhākara Mīmāṁsā school, who hold that doing duty is always without a motive for the good consequence. In their view, the desire for the good consequence is not a factor in the psychological process leading to the will to do the duty. But still, the action by its nature would produce the good consequence, and the agent will achieve it.[11]

[11] Chattopadhyay, Bankim Chandra, 1976, *Śrīmadbhagavadgītā*, in *Bankim Rachanāvali* (Bengali), vol. 2, p. 742, Calcutta: Sahitya Samsad.

# Glossary of Sanskrit Words

*abhāva*: absence, negation

*abhyāsadaśāpanna*: familiar situation

*adhikārī*: competent enquirer

*adhyāsa*: superimposition

*āgantuka*: adventitious/contingent

*agnihotra*: name of a sacrificial rite

*ahaṁ*: I

*ākāra*: form

*ākāśa*: an unitary substance that fills the space

*akhaṇḍa dharma*: simple, unanalysable property

*alaukika*: non-physical

*āṁśika*: partial, in part

*anabhyāsadaśāpanna*: unfamiliar situation

*anavadhāraṇā*: uncertain cognition

*anavasthā*: infinite regress

*aneka-vṛtti*: present in many

*aniṣṭa*: evil

*anitya*: non-eternal, perishable

*aṇu parimāṇa*: infinitesimal size/smallest size

*anubhava*: experience/non-recollective awareness

*anugata*: common

*anumāna*: inference

*anupalabdhi*: non-perception

*anuvyavasāya*: after perception, perception of a cognition

*anvaya vyāpti*: pervasion by presence, positive form of pervasion

*anvīkṣā*: examination of a position with the help of arguments based on proofs

*apara*: lesser, less extensive

*apramā*: non-veridical cognition

*āpta*: authoritative person

*arthādhyāsa*: superimposition of objects

*arthāpatti*: presumption

*arthavāda*: Vedic sentences praising or condemning some actions

*asamavāyī kāraṇa*: a cause which functions through its relation of inherence with the substrate of the effect

*asandigdha*: indubitable

*atideśa vākya*: a statement of similarity

*atīndriya*: imperceptible

*ativyāpti*: over coverage

*ātma-jñāna*: knowledge of the self

*ātman*: the soul/the self

*avadhāraṇā*: cognition with certainty

*avaśyavedya*: to be known as a matter of rule

*avayava*: parts

*avidyā*: ignorance

*avyabhicāritva*: non-discrepancy

*avyavahitatva*: being immediate precedent/being unobstructed

*ayathārtha*: false

*ayogya vākya*: semantically incompetent sentence

*bahirindriya*: external sense organ

*bhautika*: product of elements

*bhāvatva*: being a positive entity

*bhrama*: illusory cognition

*bhūta*: physical elements

*caitanya*: consciousness

*cākṣuṣa*: visual

*caturāśrama*: four stations in life in the Vedic society

*caturvarṇa*: four classes of people in the Vedic society

*dharma*: property/merit/duty

*dharmī*: owner/locus/subject

*dhvaṁsābhāva*: annihilative absence

*dik*: direction

*dravya*: substance

*dṛṣṭānta*: instance

*duḥkha*: pain, suffering

*dveṣa*: aversion

*dvyaṇuka*: dyad

*gavaya*: the name of an animal, bison

*guṇa*: quality/attribute/merit

*hetu*: inferential mark/probans

*hetvābhāsa*: defective or invalid argument

*icchā*: desire

*idantā*: thisness

*indriya*: sense organ

*iṣṭa*: good

*Īśvara*: God

*janaka*: cause, producer

*janya*: caused/effect

*jāti*: universal property

*jātibādhaka*: conditions preventing admission of universal

*jijñāsā*: desire to know

*jīva/jīvātmā*: individual self

*jīvana*: life

*jñāna-ajanya*: not caused by cognition

*jñānādhyāsa*: superimposition of cognition

*jñāna-janya*: caused by cognition

*jñāna-lakṣaṇā sannikarṣa*: a cognition functioning as a non-physical relation between object and the sense organ

*jñātā*: knower/cognizer

*jñātatā*: knowness

*kāla*: time

*kāraṇa*: cause

*karaṇa*: instrumental cause

*karma*: action, motion

*koṭi*: alternative predicates

*kṛṣṇasāra*: pupil of the eye

*kṣaṇa*: moment

*laukika*: empirical

*loka-vyavahāra*: ordinary linguistic usage

*madhyama parimāṇa*: medium size

*madhyastha*: mediator

*mahat parimāṇa*: infinitely large size

*manas*: mind, internal sense organ

*mānasa pratyakṣa*: mental/internal perception

*mokṣa*: liberation

*mūrcchā*: swoon, faint

*navya*: new/modern/later

*nidrā nāḍī*: organ for sleep

*nimitta kāraṇa*: efficient cause

*nirvikalpaka pratyakṣa*: indeterminate perception

*niścaya*: certainty of cognition

*niṣkāma karma*: actions done without desire as a motive

*niṣkampa pravṛtti*: unwavering will

*nitya*: eternal, ever-existing

*nivṛtti mārga*: way of renunciation, acting without desire

*pada*: word

*padārtha*: categories of reals

*pakṣa*: subject of inference

*pāpa*: demerits/evil unseen results of actions

*parā*: supreme, highest, most extensive

*parāmarśa*: immediate antecedent cause of inferential cognition

*pāramārthika*: ultimate, transcendental

*parataḥ prakāśa*: revealed by some other cognition

*parataḥprāmāṇya*: extrinsic veridicality

*pariṇāma*: transformation, modification

*parokṣa*: mediate

*prācīna*: old/earlier

*prakāra*: qualifier of the subject/predicate

*pramā*: veridical (true) cognition

*pramāṇa*: means of veridical cognition

*prāmāṇya*: validity, veridicality

*prāmāṇya jñapti*: knowledge of veridicality

*pramuṣṭaviṣayā*: partly forgotten object

*pratibandhaka*: hindering condition

*prātibhāsika*: illusory, apparent

*pratīti*: awareness

*pratiyogī*: counterpositive, adjunct

*pratyabhijñā*: recognitive awareness

*pratyakṣa-jñāna*: perceptual cognition

*pravṛtti mārga*: way of acting with desire

*pravṛtti nimitta*: reason for application of a word

*prayatna*: volition/will

*prayojya*: effect of a remote cause

*puṇya*: merits/good unseen results of actions

*pūrvāṅga*: preconditions

*pūrvānubhūta*: previously experienced

*śābda-jñāna*: verbal cognition/cognition by testimony

*śābda-pramāṇa*: verbal testimony

*sādhya*: inferable entity, probandum

*sādṛśya*: similarity

*sākṣāt-jñāna*: immediate cognition

*sākṣāttva*: immediacy

*śakti*: power of meaning

*samāna dharma*: general characteristics, common property

*sāmānya*: universal

*sāmānya guṇa*: generic qualities

*samavāya*: relation of inherence

*samavāyī kāraṇa*: the substrate of the effect

*sambhāvanā*: cognition of probability

*saṁjñā-saṁjñī sambandha*: name-thing relation

*saṁśaya*: doubt, doubtful cognition

*saṁskāra*: impression/disposition

*saṁskārajanakam*: causing impressions

*saphala pravṛtti*: successful volition

*sarvajña*: omniscient

*satpratipakṣa*: name of a defective/invalid argument

*sattā*: existentness

*sāvayava*: substance with component parts

*savīkalpaka pratyakṣa*: determinate perception

*smṛti*: memory/remembrance

*śreya*: good, desirable

*śreya sādhana*: means leading to good

*sukha*: pleasure/happiness

*suṣupti*: dreamless sleep

*svābhābika*: essential, natural

*svadharma*: duties for different classes of people in the Vedic society

*svapna*: dream

*svaprakāśa*: self-revealing

*svarga*: heaven/other-worldly pleasure

*svataḥ prāmāṇya*: intrinsic veridicality

*tajjātiya*: belonging to be same kind

*tarka*: indirect argument

*tattā*: thatness

*tejas*: fire

*tvak*: skin, tactile sense organ

*udbhūta rūpa*: manifest colour

*udbodhaka*: reviving factor

*upādhi*: compound property

*upamiti*: cognition by comparison

*upekṣanīya*: ignorable, trivial

*utpatti*: origin, production

*uttejaka*: reinforcing condition

*vākya*: sentence

*vastutva*: reality

*vibhu*: all-pervasive, present everywhere

*vicāra*: philosophical debate

*vidhi vākya*: imperative sentences/injunctions

*vimarṣa*: doubt

*vināśī*: destructible, perishable

*vipratipatti vākya*: contradictory statement

*virodha*: opposition

*viśeṣa*: individual differentiator

*viśeṣa dharma*: special characteristics

*viśeṣa guṇa*: specific qualities

*viśeṣya*: subject

*visiṣṭabuddhi*: qualificative cognition

*vyāpaka*: pervader

*vyāpti-jñāna*: cognition of pervasion

*vyāpya*: pervaded

*vyāpyatva*: being pervaded

*vyatireka vyāpti*: negative form of pervasion

*vyāvahārika*: empirical, worldly

*vyavahitadhī*: mediate cognition

*vyavasāyātmaka*: of the nature of certainty

*vyāvṛtti*: differentiation

*yajña/yāga*: sacrificial rites

*yathānubhava*: exact copy of previous experience

*yathārtha*: true

*yogya anupalabdhi*: appropriate non-perception

*yogyatā*: semantic competency

*yugapad*: simultaneous

# Bibliography

Annaṁbhaṭṭa, 1963, *Tarkasaṁgraha*, ed. Athalye, Bodus and Pusalkar, Bombay Sanskrit Series, no. LV.

Annaṁbhaṭṭa, 1969, *Tarkasaṁgrahaḥ with Dīpikā*, with nine commentaries, ed. Shri Satkariram Bangiya, Varanasi: Chowkhamba Sanskrit Series Office.

Appayadīkṣita, 1990, *Siddhāntaleśa Saṁgraha*, Varanasi: Chowkhamba Sanskrit Sansthan.

Banerjee, K.K., 1988, *Language, Knowledge and Ontology*, New Delhi: Indian Council of Philosophical Research, and Riddhi India, Calcutta.

Bhaṭṭa, Nāgeśa, 1989, *Vaiyākaranasiddhānta Laghumañjūṣā*, Varanasi: Chowkhamba Sanskrit Series Office.

Bhattacharya, Gopinath (edited with English translation and elucidation), 1976, Annaṁbhaṭṭa's *Tarkasaṁgrahadīpikā*, Calcutta: Progressive Publishers.

Bhattacharya, Haridas (ed.), 2001, *The Cultural Heritage of India*, vol. III, Calcutta: The Ramakrishna Mission Institute of Culture.

Bhattacharya, Sukhamay, 1983, *Pūrvamīmāṁsā Darśana* (in Bengali), Calcutta: Rajya Pustak Parishad.

Bhattacharya Shastri, Dinesh Chandra, 1972, *Prācina Bhāratīya Manovidyā*, Calcutta: Nagendra Prajnamandir.

Bilimoria, Purushottama (ed.), 2006, *Contemporary Philosophy and J.L. Shaw*, Kolkata: Punthi Pustak.

Chattopadhyay, Bankim Chandra, 1976, "Śrīmadbhagavadgītā", in *Bankim Rachanavali* (Bengali) vol. 2, Sahitya Samsad.

Citsukhācārya, 1985, *Tattvapradīpikā*, ed. Swami Yogindrananda, Varanasi: Saddarshan Prakashan.

Dharmakīrti, 1968, *Pramāṇavārttika*, ed. Dwarika Das Sastri, Varanasi: Bauddha Bharati.

Dharmarājādhvarīndra, 1960, *Vedāntaparibhāṣā*, ed. Panchanana Sastri, Calcutta: Sanskrit Pustak Bhandar.

Divatia, Shuchita C., 1994, *Idealistic Thought in Indian Philosophy*, New Delhi: D.K. Printworld.

Gadādhara, 1970, *Gādādharī*, A Commentary on *Dīdhīti*, ed. Vindhyeswari Prasad Dvivedi et al., Varanasi: Chowkhamba Sanskrit Series Office.

Gaṅgeśa, 1970, *Tattvacintāmaṇi*, Anumāna Khaṇḍa *with Dīdhīti and Gādādharī*, ed. Vindhyesvari Prasad Dvivedi, Varanasi: Chowkhamba Sanskrit Series Office.

——, 1974, *Tattvacintāmaṇi*, Pratyakṣa Khaṇḍa, ed. Kamakhyanath Tarkavagish, Delhi: Motilal Banarsidass.

Gauḍapāda, 1943, *The Āgamaśāstra of Gauḍapāda*, ed., tr. and annot. Vidhushekhar Bhattacharya, Calcutta: University of Calcutta.

Gautama, 1985, *Nyāyadarśanam*, ed. Tārānātha Nyāyatarkatīrtha and Amarendramohan Tarkatirtha, New Delhi: Munshiram Manoharlal.

Jagadīśa, 1958, *Jāgadīśī*, a commentary on *Tattvacintāmaṇi*, ed. Swami Ramaprasannacharya, Varanasi: Chowkhamba Sanskrit Series Office.

——, 1980, *Śabdaśaktiprakāśikā*, ed. Madhusūdana Nyaycharya, Calcutta: Sanskrit College Research Series.

Jayantabhaṭṭa, 1982, *Nyāyamañjarī*, ed. Gourinath Sastri, Varanasi: Sampurnānanda Sanskrit Visvavidyālaya.

Kaṇāda, 1969, *Vaiśeṣikasūtra*, with Saṅkara Miśra's commentary *Upaskāra*, ed. Nārāyaṇa Miśra, see Saṅkara Miśra: Varanasi: Chowkhamba Sanskrit Series Office.

Kapila Muni, 1954, *Sāṁkhyadarśanam*, with explanation in Bengali by Kalivara Vedantavagish, ed. Durgacharan Sankhya Vedantatirtha, Calcutta: Central Book Agency.

Keśava Miśra, 1968, *Tarkabhāṣā* with Hindi commentary by Badrinath Shukla, Varanasi: Motilal Banarsidass.

Krishna, Daya and K.L. Sharma (eds), 1991, *The Philosophy of J.N. Mohanty*, New Delhi: Indian Council of Philosophical Research and Munshiram Manoharlal.

Kuppuswami Sastri, S.P., 1932, *A Primer of Indian Logic*, Madras: P. Varadachary & Co.

*Laṅkāvatārasūtram*, ed. Sarat Chandra Das and Satish Chandra Vidyabhusan, 1900, Calcutta: Buddhist Text Society.

Maitra, S.K., 1963, *The Ethics of the Hindus*, Calcutta: University of Calcutta.

*Manu Saṁhitā* with *Ṭīkā* by Kullūkabhaṭṭa, ed. with Bengali translation by Manabendu Bandyopadhyay, 2002, Kolkata: Sanskrita Pustak Bhandhar.

Matilal, B.K., 1985, *Logic, Language and Reality*, Delhi: Motilal Banarsidass.

——, 1986, *Perception: An Essay on Classical Indian Theories of Knowledge*, Oxford: Oxford University Press.

Miśra, Padmanābha, 1983, *Setu Ṭīkā* on *Praśastapādabhāṣyam*, ed. with *Setu, Sūkti* and *Vyomavatī Ṭīkā* by Gopinath Kaviraj and Dhundhiraj Shastri, Varanasi: Chowkhamba Sanskrit Granthamala.

Miśra, Pārthasārathi, 1978, *Nyāyaratnākara Vyākhyā* on Kumārila Bhaṭṭa's *Ślokavārttikam*, ed. Swami Dwarikadas Shastri, Varanasi: Tara Publications.

——, 2008, *Śāstradīpikā (Tarkapāda)*, ed. Vijay Sharma, Varanasi: Chowkhamba Surabharati Prakashan.

Miśra, Saṅkara, 1969, *Upaskāra* or *Vaiśeṣika Sūtropaskāraḥ*, ed. Nārāyaṇa Miśra, Varanasi: Chowkhamba Sanskrit Series Office.

——, 1917, *Kaṇādarahasyam*, in *Praśastapāda-Bhāṣya-Ṭīkā Saṁgraha*, ed. Vindhyeswari Prasad Dvivedi, Benares: Chowkhamba Sanskrit Series Office.

Mukhopadhyay, P.K., 1982, "The Theory of Universals" in *Logical Form, Predication and Ontology* (Jadavpur Studies in Philosophy, vol. IV), ed. P.K. Sen, Delhi: Macmillan India.

Nāgeśa Bhaṭṭa, 1989, *Vaiyākaraṇa Siddhānta Laghumañjuṣā*, part I, ed. Pandit Madhava Shastri Bhandari and Pandit Narahari Shastri Pendsey, Varanasi: Chowkhamba Sanskrit Series Office.

Nārāyaṇa, 1933, *Mānameyodayaḥ*, ed. C. Kunhan Raja and S.S. Suryanarayana Sastri, Madras: Theosophical Publishing House.

Narayana Goswami, 2003, *Adhyāpanā Ṭīkā* (in Bengali) on *Tarkasaṁgraha-Dīpikā*, Calcutta: Sanskrit Pustak Bhandar.

Nrisimha Shastri, 1988, *Prabhāṭīkā* on Viśvanātha's *Kārikāvalī-Muktāvalī*, ed. Shri Sankarram Sastri, Delhi, Chowkhamba Sanskrit Pratisthan.

Paṭṭābhiram Śāstrī, 1988, *Mañjuṣā Ṭīkā* in Viśvanātha's *Kārikāvalī-Muktāvalī*, ed. Shri Sankarram Sastri, Delhi: Chowkhamba Sanskrit Pratisthan.

Prakāśānanda, 1935, *Vedāntasiddhāntamuktāvalī*, ed. Jivananda Bhattacharya, Calcutta: Shri Ashubodh Vidyabhushana and Shri Nityabodh Vidyaratna.

Radhakrishnan, S., 1985, *Indian Philosophy*, repr. Delhi: Blackie & Son Publishers.

Rucidatta, 1989, *Kiraṇāvalī Prakāśa-Vivṛti*, in Udayana's *Kiraṇāvalī*, ed. Śiva Chandra Sarvabhauma, Calcutta: The Asiatic Society.

Sadānanda, 1981, *Advaita Brahmasiddhi*, ed. Pandit Vamana Shastri, Delhi: Parimal Publications.

——, 1979, *Vedāntasāra* with *Vidvatmanorañjanī Ṭīkā* with Explanation in Hindi by Badrinath Sukla, Varanasi: Motilal Banarsidass.

Saha, Sukharanjan, 2003, *Eistemology in Pracina and Navya Nyaya*, Kolkata: Jadavpur University.

Śālikanātha Miśra, 1961, *Prakaraṇapañcikā*, ed. Pundit A. Subrahmanya Shastri, Benaras: Banaras Hindu University.

Sarasvatī, Madhusūdana, 1982, *Advaitasiddhi*, ed. Ananta Krishna Sastri, Delhi: Parimal Publications.

——, 1990, *Siddhāntabindu*, A Commentary on *Daśaślokī* of Śaṅkarācārya, ed. Tryambakarama Sastri, Varanasi: Chowkhamba Sanskrit Sansthan.

Sastri P.S., 1975, *Indian Idealism*, Delhi: Bharatiya Vidya Prakashan.

Sastri, Panchanana, 1963, *Muktāvalīsaṁgraha* on *Muktāvalī Ṭīkā* by Viśvanātha, in *Bhāṣāparicchedaḥ*, Bengali edition, Kolkata: Sanskrit Pustak Bhandar.

Śiromaṇi, Raghunātha, 1985, *Dīdhīti*, in Gaṅgeśa's *Tattvacintāmaṇi*, Anumānakhaṇḍa, ed. Tārānātha Nyāyatarkatīrtha and Amarendramohan Tarkatirtha, New Delhi: Munshiram Manoharlal.

——, 1976, *Padārthatattvanirūpaṇam*, ed. with Bengali translation and elaboration by Madhusūdana Nyayacharya, Calcutta: Sanskrit College.

Śrīdhara Bhaṭṭa, 1963, *Nyāyakandalī*, A Commentary on *Praśastapādabhāṣya*, ed. Durgadhar Jha, Varanasi: Varanaseya Sanskrit Viswavidyalaya.

Śrīharṣa, 1979, *Khaṇḍanakhaṇḍakhādya*, ed. Swami Yogindrananda, Varanasi: Saddarshana Prakashan Pratisthan.

*Śrīmadbhagavadgīta* with *Gūḍhārthadīpikā Ṭīkā* by Madhusūdana Sarasvati, 1962, Varanasi: Chowkhamba Sanskrit Series Office.

Udayanācārya, 1911, *Tātparyapariśuddhi*, in *Saṭīkanyāya-vārttika-tātparya-pariśuddhi*, ed. Śiva Chandra Sarvabhauma, Calcutta: Asiatic Society.

——, 1957, *Nyāyakusumāñjali*, ed. Padmaprasad Upadhyay and Dhundhiraja Sastri, Varanasi: Chowkhamba Sanskrit Series Office.

——, 1989, *Kiraṇāvalī*, with *Prakāśaṭīkā* by Vardhamana Upadhyaya, and *Prakāśavivṛtti* by Ruchidatta, Calcutta: Asiatic Society.

Uddyotakara, *Nyāyavārttika* in *Nyāyadarśanam*, see Gautama.

Vācaspati Miśra, 1982, *Sāṅkhyatattvakaumudī*, ed. Shri Narayan Chandra Goswami, with Bengali translation, Calcutta: Sanskrit Pustak Bhandar.

——, 1985, *Tātparyaṭīkā* in Gautama's *Nyāyadarśanam*, ed. Tārānātha Nyāyatarkatīrtha and Amarendramohan Tarkatirtha (see also, Gautama), New Delhi: Munshiram Manoharlal.

Vardhamānopādhyāya, 1911, *Nyāya-nibandhaprakāśa*, A Commentary on Udayana's *Tātparyapariśuddhi*, Calcutta: Asiatic Society.

Vardhamahopadhyaya, 1989, *Kiraṇāvalī-Prakāśaḥ*, in *Kiraṇāvalī*, ed. Śiva Chandra Sarvabhouma, Calcutta: The Asiatic Society.

Vasubandhu, 2015, *Triṁśikā Kārikā* in *Vijñaptimātratā-siddhi*, ed. with translation by Mahesh Tiwari, Varanasi: Chowkhamba Vidya Bhavan.

Vātsyāyana, *Bhaṣya* on *Nyāyasūtra* in *Nyāyadarśanam*, ed. Tārānātha Nyāyatarkatīrtha and Amarendramohan Tarkatirtha, New Delhi: Munshiram Manoharlal, 1985.

Vidyāraṇya Muni, 1996, *Vivaraṇa Prameya Saṁgrahaḥ*, ed. Shri Chandiprasad Shukla Shastri and Shri Shrikrishnapanta Shastri, Kashi: Achyuta Granthamala Karyalaya.

Vīrarāghavācārya, T., 1958, *Rasāyana*, a commentary on *Vaiśeṣikasūtra*, Madras: V.S. Venkata Raghavacharya and others.

Viśvanātha, 1988, *Kārikāvalī-Muktāvalī*, ed. Shri Sankarram Sastri, Delhi: Chowkhamba Sanskrit Pratisthan.

Vyomśivācarya, 1983, *Vyomavatī Ṭīkā* on *Praśastapādabhāṣya*, ed. Gaurinath Sastri, Varanasi: Sampurnānanda Sanskrit Vishvavidyalaya.

*Yogavāsiṣṭha Rāmāyaṇa* of *Vālmīki*, ed. and tr. into English by Viharilala Mitra, 1978, Delhi: Bharatiya Publishing House.

# Index